FRAMED FOR
POSTERITY

AMERICAN POLITICAL THOUGHT

EDITED BY
WILSON CAREY McWILLIAMS & LANCE BANNING

FRAMED FOR POSTERITY
THE ENDURING PHILOSOPHY OF THE CONSTITUTION

RALPH KETCHAM

UNIVERSITY PRESS OF KANSAS

© 1993 by the University Press of Kansas
All rights reserved

Published by the University Press of Kansas (Lawrence, Kansas 66049), which was organized by the Kansas Board of Regents and is operated and funded by Emporia State University, Fort Hays State University, Kansas State University, Pittsburg State University, the University of Kansas, and Wichita State University

Library of Congress Cataloging-in-Publication Data

Ketcham, Ralph, 1927–
    Framed for posterity : the enduring philosophy of the Constitution
  / Ralph Ketcham.
        p. cm. — (American political thought)
    Includes bibliographical references and index.
    ISBN 0–7006–0591–6 (alk. paper)
    1. Political science—United States—History—18th century.
  2. United States—Constitutional history. I. Title. II. Series.
  JA84.U5K47 1993
  342.73'029—dc20
  [347.30229]   92-43247

Printed in the United States of America

10 9 8 7 6 5 4 3 2 1

DEDICATION

Like thousands of others,
to my Syracuse University teachers:

NELSON BLAKE

STUART BROWN

MARGUERITE FISHER

PARKE HOTCHKISS

DONALD MEIKLEJOHN

DAVID OWEN

EDWARD PALMER

MICHAEL SAWYER

T. V. SMITH

In setting up an enduring framework of government [the framers] undertook to carry out for the indefinite future and in all the vicissitudes of the changing affairs of men, those fundamental purposes which the instrument itself discloses.

—*Justice Harlan F. Stone, 1941*

CONTENTS

PART III. THE BILL OF RIGHTS

PART IV. THE CONSTITUTION
IN THE TWENTY-FIRST CENTURY

PREFACE

In the wake of the "bicentennial season" (1987–1991), I need to say what this book is and what it is not. Where does it fit among the hundreds (perhaps thousands) of works generated by that commemoration? It is not a systematic history of the origins, drafting, and ratification of the Constitution and the Bill of Rights. It does not attempt an analytical explanation of the "philosophy" of either document, or of either the *Federalist Papers* or of the antifederalist opposition. It is not a case-oriented study of the constitutional and legal meaning and development of the Bill of Rights. Fine studies abound on those subjects, some of long standing, some stimulated by the bicentennial celebrations. Rather, in seeking to understand the Constitution and the Bill of Rights, I pay particular attention to the world of political ideas in which the documents were drafted, debated, and ratified. If we can comprehend, fully and richly, the kinds of political *questions* that concerned the founding generation—for example, what is human nature, what is justice, and what is the purpose of government?—and the answers they were inclined to come to (not always agreed on, of course), then we can better understand the documents they put forth. The language of political discussion, the often unstated assumptions about politics, and the commonly understood historical and philosophical allusions of the late eighteenth century are all part of the climate of political ideas that nourished the Constitution and the Bill of Rights.

In a way, then, this book contributes to the debate over "original intent," though it rejects both the literal "originalist" interpretation, and the "growing Constitution" argument that downplays recourse to the original meaning of the Constitution (see chapter 14). Instead, I look for the original intent in a more general and, I hope, more fundamental way: By knowing something of the world of political thought within which the framers lived, we can better understand the nature and meaning of the documents they produced. The original intent can be best apprehended not by a narrow, exegetical approach to the documents themselves, but rather by understanding the broader meanings, intentions, and purposes of all the different people who can be regarded as "framers." Thus we can discern general principles—republicanism, liberty, the public good, and federalism—that reveal their "intent" in the deepest and most lasting sense. We can note the context, connotations, and significance of these principles in the minds of those who originally spoke and wrote of them. These general principles, moreover, were thought to have enduring validity. The need currently, then, is not so much to discern literal "original intent" or to promulgate new guidelines to replace outmoded aspects of the Constitution as to understand how the *general, enduring* principles can still provide crucial meaning and direction in admittedly vastly changed conditions and circumstances—as the framers and ratifiers well knew would be the case.

To see the Constitution and the Bill of Rights in such broad terms requires as a foundation a knowledge of what the framers took to be the nature both of political life itself and of *constitutional* government. In general, they (including both opponents and advocates of the Constitution of 1787) gave a large, Aristotelian meaning to the scope of the political, and they took seriously the idea of a "higher law" and its embodiment in the Constitution and the Bill of Rights. These dispositions are themselves an essential part of the understanding of the documents.

My intent, then, is not to explain in detail the history and original meaning of particular clauses of the Constitution in ways that would be applicable to specific cases arising under them (for example, "regulate Commerce . . . among the several states," or "keep and bear arms"). I try instead to explore more fully the meaning of not only the clauses of the documents themselves, but also the connotations of the words used, the reasons behind both accepted and rejected propositions, the thinking entailed in arguments for or against particular clauses, and the assumptions undergirding both questions raised and answers given. Only this full context of political thinking can reveal the general principles that the founders intended to be the enduring meaning of the documents that are still the basis of the American polity.

My best respondents and critics for this work have been the students, under-graduate and graduate, who over the years have talked with me in class and seminar and written papers about the Constitution and the Bill of Rights. Special thanks are due to Peter Gaudioso, Danielle Van Dalen, Jeffrey Stag-nitti, Faye Kelle, Douglas Challenger, Robert Udick, Tom Pugh, Steve Ross, Ma Lan, Cori Zoli, Bruce Yenawine, Karen Freed, Lisa Stockman, Elisa Koff, Ross D'Emanuele, Martha Lee, William Griffith, and Robert Kravchuk. Among the many scholars who have commented on parts of the manuscript to my particular benefit have been a former teacher, Donald Meiklejohn, and a former student, Paul Finkelman. Many others, including Robert McClure, David Epstein, Manfred Stanley, Donald Lutz, Peter Onuf, John Stagg, Lance Banning, Saul Cornell, Paul Rahe, Alan Gibson, Jack Rakove, Joseph Julian, Marie Provine, Roger Sharp, and William Wiecek have in person or in their writings been important informants, stimulators, and critics. Jeanne Erwin and Margaret Smith performed with skill and good nature the considerable task of converting the manuscript from my nearly inscrutable scrawl to typescript and to word processor.

Many friends and teachers have spurred the work along by affording me opportunities to talk about the Constitution and the Bill of Rights: Cora Wayne Wright of Wesleyan College, Brian Barry of Rochester Institute of Technology, Josephine Pacheco of George Mason University, Johanna Kardux of the University of Leiden (Netherlands), Yang Sheng-Mao of Nankai University (PRC), Liu Zuochang of Shandong Teachers' University (PRC), Sasa-ki Hajimu of Tohoku University (Japan), Herman Wellenreuther of Göttingen University (Germany), Martin Fausold and Allan Shank of SUNY Geneseo, James Carroll of Project Legal at Syracuse University, Suzanne Morse of the Kettering Foundation, Rhoda Miller and Stuart Gerry Brown of the University of Hawaii, Ted Estess of the University of Houston, Taylor Littleton of Au-burn University, and Michael Mezey of DePaul University. Special thanks are due to the Bellagio (Italy) Center of the Rockefeller Foundation for providing a perfect atmosphere for study and writing during the summer of 1989. Most particularly, the faculty and chairs of the political science, history, and public affairs departments, the deans of the Maxwell School, and the graduate school and office of academic affairs, all of Syracuse University, have provided gen-erous support, encouragement, research leave, and funding without which this project could not even have been undertaken, much less completed. Most deeply and gratefully, I thank my wife, Julia, and now-grown children, Ben and Laura Lee, for being, as always, skilled, thoughtful, and good-natured sustainers, commentators, critics, and editors.

Ralph Ketcham
The Maxwell School
Syracuse University

PART I

WHAT IS A CONSTITUTION?

1

THE QUESTION OF
ORIGINAL INTENT

In defending the "activist" orientation of the Supreme Court, Justice William Brennan observed in 1985 that "the precise rules by which we have protected fundamental human dignity have been transformed over time in response to both transformations of social conditions and evolution of our concepts of human dignity." Although Brennan spoke as well of "overarching principles" implanted in the Constitution, and of its "placing certain values beyond the power of any legislature," he generally emphasized the need for the Constitution to "evolve" and for contemporary interpretation, mindful of "the complexity of modern society," to eschew "the anachronistic views of long-gone generations." He thus argued not only that changing circumstances required "adaptability . . . to cope with current problems and current needs," but also that basic concepts unknown or at least unarticulated two hundred years ago, and thus unstated in the Constitution, might now need recognition as part of our fundamental law.[1] Brennan believed, that is, that "fundamentals" and "basic concepts" themselves ("eternal verities"?) in fact evolved from age to age. The Constitution was hence a document of changing rather than fixed meaning.

In a different view, which also rejects the idea of fixed values and unchanging principles, Judge Robert Bork has argued that judges should not impose their own moral absolutes on society by invalidating laws with which they disagree. Although Bork insists that judges discern and adhere to the original intent of the Constitution (and thus might, and should, strike down statutes violating it), he takes a limited view of this original intent. It consists only in what is clearly and literally stated in the Constitution (including amendments) and what can be shown explicitly to have been in the minds and intentions of the drafters and ratifiers. Subsequent judges are not to depart from that text and that exegesis, especially not to infer new concepts not stated specifically in the Constitution or to impose their moral judgments on legislators or on the society they represent. This view makes the Constitution itself a fixed standard, of course, but Bork sees this as simply an agreed-upon legal commitment rather than as immutable principle. Thus Bork rejects both the recently articulated right of privacy in Supreme Court decisions and its recently discovered right to abortion. Such moral injunctions by judges are unwarranted, he argues, because there is no "single correct moral theory [that], in today's circumstances, all people of good will and moderate intelligence must accept." Judges have no grounds, then, for imposing their own moral views on legislation or on society—much less finding those views, at a late date, to be sanctioned by the Constitution. "There is going to be no moral philosophy," Bork concludes, "that can begin to justify courts in overriding democratic choices where the Constitution does not speak."[2] Since there are no agreed-on moral principles in contemporary society, and since the Constitution does not speak clearly on them, it is up to state and national legislatures, in their respective spheres, to set social policy. Judges are not authorized, Bork insists, in a democratic society, to set their moral views above those of the people and their representatives.

Both Brennan and Bork, of course, reflect a version of what Alasdair MacIntyre has observed is a basic dilemma in the modern world: "In a society where there is no longer a shared conception of the community's good as specified by the good for man, there can no longer . . . be any very substantial concept of what it is to contribute more or less to the achievement of that good."[3] If that is the case, on what grounds can a judge, or any public official for that matter, declare a law passed by a legislature, or a moral imperative held by some group, to be invalid? If no substantial, generally accepted community or national good exists, then it is hard to say what is fundamental or basic. Under such circumstances we are likely, with Justice Brennan, to think of fundamentals as evolving, or with Judge Bork to think there is "no moral philosophy that can . . . justify courts in overriding democratic choices." Brennan is inclined to give the Supreme Court a large role in discerning and applying a public morality for the modern age, while Bork wants generally to leave that to elected representatives in legislatures. Although Brennan does believe that the Supreme Court ought to uphold general conceptions of human dignity and Bork has his own personal moral imperatives, and both grant the Constitution a certain sanctity as paramount law (though they differ on what it is), neither seems to believe that the Constitution, in some lastingly valid way, is a higher law that embodies "a shared conception of the community's good." But it is some such idea of higher law, shared axioms about the good life for the political community, that the founding generation, federalists and antifederalists, Hamiltonians and Jeffersonians alike, took for granted as basic to their idea of what a constitution was and thus was an essential part of their intent. Understanding the philosophy of the Constitution of the United States must begin with what it means to have such a document undergirding a polity, which in turn helps us see its place in contemporary American public life.

2
THE CONSTITUTION
AS HIGHER LAW

The idea of higher law, and of a constitution as an embodiment of it, was in 1787 basic to the political culture of the new United States. In 1775 John Adams had asserted that the principles of the American Revolution, ever valid, were "the principles of Aristotle and Plato, of Livy and Cicero, of Sydney, Harrington and Locke—the principles of nature and eternal reason." Writing at about the same time, Alexander Hamilton saw "the clear voice of natural justice" and "the fundamental principles of the English constitution" as the grounds of the American Revolution. Eight years later Thomas Jefferson declared that the 1776 constitution of Virginia derived from "the freest principles of the English Constitution" and from "natural rights and natural reason."[1]

Emphasizing another tradition, the Reverend Elisha Williams of Connecticut in 1744 said that "the members of a civil state do retain their natural Liberty or Right of judging for themselves in Matters of Religion. . . . Everyone is under an indispensable obligation to search the Scripture for himself . . . and to make the best use of it he can for his own Information in the Will of GOD, the Nature and Duties of Christianity. . . . Man by his Constitution, as he is a reasonable Being capable of the Knowledge of his MAKER, is a moral and accountable being." The duties of Christians, and the Holy Scriptures, were themselves part of the natural law.[2] Thomas Paine, as always, put the matter simply in *Common Sense* in 1776, calling for independence: "Tis repugnant to reason, to the universal order of things, . . . to suppose that this continent can long remain subject to an external power." In America, Paine declared, "THE LAW IS KING" and was from above, in accord with "the Divine Law, the Word of God."[3] Thus, the very impulse to the American

6

Revolution itself was rife with ideas of higher law and its embodiment, more or less, in a written constitution. Those who formed governments in the newly independent states and who sought as well a confederation of the states always assumed they had to begin with a constitution that would provide fundamental law. Furthermore, as the constant reference to "nature" and to "natural right and natural reason" and the easy fusing of natural law and God's law made clear, the idea of a constitution was tied intimately to the notion of higher law.

Although the word *constitution*, meaning "the system or body of fundamental principles according to which a nation, state, or body politic is constituted and governed," had an ancient usage, being applied, for example, retrospectively to "the Constitution of Nehemiah" and "a collection of ecclesiastical regulations purposing to have been made by the Apostles," it came into wider use in seventeenth- and eighteenth-century England. In a famous definition of 1750, Bolingbroke said a constitution was "that Assemblage of Laws, Institutions and Customs, derived from certain fixed Principles of Reason, that compose the general System, according to which the Community hath agreed to be governed."[4] In English North America, settlers either brought with them "founding documents," adopted them upon arrival, or soon sought them from authorities "at home" (as colonists referred to England before 1776). The Pilgrims, for example, realizing in 1620 that they were in an unknown place on the Atlantic coast and not wanting to be without government, adopted the simple, one-page document known as the Mayflower Compact. They agreed to "covenant and combine ourselves together into a civil body politick . . . and to enact, constitute, and frame such just and equal laws, ordinances, acts, constitutions, and offices . . . as shall be thought most . . . convenient for the general good of the colonie."[5]

Ten years later, when a much larger group of English Puritans came to Massachusetts Bay, they brought with them a Royal Charter granted in 1629. This charter provided for government of the affairs of the Massachusetts Bay Company in North America by a governor, his assistants, and a General Court chosen by its stockholders, called "freemen." When John Winthrop and others transferred the company and its charter to Boston in 1630, it in effect became the constitution of the colony and the revered basis for self-government there, rather than control from London. The enactment of the so-called Body of Liberties in 1641, codifying certain principles of English common law as well as adopting parts of the Mosaic code, further strengthened the idea of a written, constitutional foundation for government. By adopting the Fundamental Orders as a constitution of Connecticut in 1639 (which lasted in some form for nearly two hundred years), and then by agreeing to a charter by the New England Confederation in 1643, the colonists strengthened the idea of written and ratified constitutions. Later, crucial arguments over the Charter of Massachusetts, resulting in the granting of a new Royal Charter in 1691, and the continuation of governments in Connecticut and Rhode Island that provided for elected rather than royally appointed governors firmly established concepts of higher law and of government under written constitutions in New England.[6]

In Virginia, founded in 1607, the use of a joint-stock company charter as a government, the frequent revision of that charter, the provision within the charter for an elected government in the colony in 1619, and then the dispute with James I that led to the appointment of a royal governor in 1624 all focused attention on written frames of government. Just establishing a colony, that is, required rules that became one way or another a kind of constitution, or law above law, that guided the government.

Perhaps the most significant constitution adoption occurred in Pennsylvania. In 1681 Charles II had granted a Royal Charter to William Penn, who thus became proprietor of a large tract of land, called Pennsylvania by the king, that Penn intended to become a Quaker colony. Although Penn as proprietor retained the power of governorship, he provided a Great Law of Pennsylvania (1682), establishing a legislature in the colony to be elected by the "freemen" (taxpayers and property owners) and given wide powers of government. The general confirmation of this constitution and the addition of bill of rights provisions in the Charter of Privileges of 1701 made Pennsylvania a model of constitutional government during the eighteenth century.

At the same time the colonists listened to an intense debate in England (Great Britain after the union of 1707) over its constitution. The great "settlements" that attended the Glorious Revolution (1688), the oath of the king to "govern . . . according to the statutes of Parliament agreed on and the laws and customs of the same," the Bill of Rights, and the Toleration Act all emphasized the idea of a fixed if unwritten constitution to which all branches of government would conform. This constitution defined the "rights of Englishmen" that were at the center of discussions of liberty in the English-speaking world in the eighteenth century.

The debate leading up to the American Revolution was in one sense simply an extension of this constitutional preoccupation. As colonials read the flood of English tracts on this subject, they applied its principles to their situation, which they increasingly saw in universal or natural terms, rather than merely English ones. John Dickinson, for example, wrote in 1766 that the concrete specifications of British law were also "created in us by the decrees of Providence, which establish the laws of our nature. They are born with us; exist with us. . . . They are founded on the immutable maxims of reason and justice." John Adams observed that these rights were part of "a frame, a scheme, a system, a combination of powers for a certain end, namely—the good of the whole community."[7] Thomas Paine included in the second edition of *Common Sense* James Thompson's summarizing couplet:

> Man knows no master save creating Heaven,
> or those whom choice and common good ordain.

Thus, by 1776 the British colonists in North America had a wide experience in constitutional government, a good grounding in the specifically British debate over it, and a tendency to project the debate in terms of universal, natural law.

Between 1776 and 1787 all thirteen states either altered or drafted at least one constitution. The new nation as a whole experienced ad hoc government under the Continental Congress and then drafted and adopted (1781) the Articles of Confederation. The assumptions throughout were that a written form of higher law was the foundation of just government, that such a form could define and protect natural rights, and that the people were the essential ratifiers of such fundamental law. When Jefferson calculated that the thirteen states had had 143 (13 times 11) years of experience in republican government by 1787, he meant particularly that they had made many trials at formulating and using constitutions.

This 150-year experience came more and more to embody, in thinking on both sides of the Atlantic, the Lockean idea of a people contracting to form a government of their own choosing, for their safety, convenience, and happiness. In Locke's words:

> Men being, as has been said, by nature all free, equal, and independent, no one can be put out of this estate, and subjected to the political power of another, without his own consent, which is done by agreeing with other men to join and unite into a community for their comfortable, safe, and peaceable living one amongst another, in a secure enjoyment of their properties, and a greater security against any that are not of it. This any number of men may do, because it injures not the freedom of the rest; they are left as they were in the liberty of the state of nature. When any

number of men have so consented to make one community of government, they are thereby presently incorporated, and make one body politic, wherein the majority have a right to act and conclude the rest.[8]

Hence, by 1787 Americans were confirmed "constitutionalists." They believed that government must accord with basic principles, "natural right and
natural reason," higher law, and that a document of fundamentals, a constitution, was the just, proper, and authoritative embodiment of them. When the
Federal (Constitutional) Convention gathered in Philadelphia in the summer
of 1787, then, everyone—the delegates, the people of the country, and indeed
the whole world—knew what they were doing: they were engaging in the
natural right of proposing a framework for self-government (this was so even
though the formal charge to the convention was only to revise the Articles of
Confederation). The deliberate ratification by the people of the states was
further in accord with the Lockean paradigm. Then, with the formal inaugu-
ration of government under the duly ratified document in March–April 1789,
the Constitution as paramount law was in place. This solemn process,
enacted self-consciously and with repeated assertion of its establishment of
a "supreme Law of the Land," represented the deep and universal acceptance
of the idea of constitutionalism itself as the core of the philosophy of the
Constitution.

3
CONSTITUTIONALISM
IN THE UNITED STATES

The doctrine of constitutionalism received explicit enunciation in the early actions of the U.S. Supreme Court. In Chief Justice John Marshall's most important decision interpreting the new federal frame of government (1819), he declared, against those who belittled the document, that "it is a constitution we are expounding." What distinction, or point, was he trying to make? He insisted that there was a qualitative difference between laws made by Congress or the state legislatures and the Constitution itself. As he had explained sixteen years earlier in declaring a law passed by Congress unconstitutional, "all those who have framed written constitutions contemplate them as forming the fundamental and paramount law of the nation, and consequently, the theory of every such government must be, that an act of the legislature, repugnant to the constitution is void. This theory is essentially attached to a written constitution, and is, consequently, to be considered . . . as one of the fundamental principles of our society. . . . The constitution is . . . superior, paramount law, unchangeable by ordinary means."[1]

A constitution, then, is not ordinary law, but rather an embodiment of fundamental principles, higher law, law above law, propositions regarded both as enduring and as controlling of actions taken by agencies of government themselves created and empowered by the constitution. At least that was the clear, nearly unanimous understanding of those who drafted and advocated the Constitution of 1787 and the Bill of Rights—and, for that matter, those who opposed them as well. All were aware that they were talking about a basic act of political community. They were validating, solemnly and deliberately, the enduring principles according to which they intended to conduct the public business. The Supreme Court soon underscored the point. Justice Joseph Story declared in 1816 that the people "in framing this great charter of our liberties [i.e., the Constitution] . . . did not . . . provide for minute specifications . . . [or] provide merely for the exigencies of a few years, but [intended it] to endure through a long lapse of ages." A few years later Marshall asserted that in a constitution "designed to approach immortality as nearly as human institutions can approach it, . . . only the great outlines should be marked, [and] important objects designated," while "minor ingredients" and the "prolixity of a political code" should be left to succeeding generations.[2]

Embedded in this sense of permanence, though, is a philosophy and cosmology that more basically than anything else separates eighteenth-century thinking from that of our own day: Franklin, Washington, Madison, and the other framers believed in some version of the natural law theory holding that there were universal, enduringly true precepts, discernible through reason. These were the only just guides in personal and public life—what Jefferson in 1776 had called "inalienable rights" and which Sir Edward Coke termed "the first principles of civil society . . . written with the finger of God in the heart of man."[3] Eighteenth-century thinking regarded these principles as fixed, absolute, permanent, God-given, universal—all words generally repudiated by the evolutionary, pragmatic, positivist, relativist, or deconstructionist modes of thought dominant in the twentieth century. Modern thought, for the most part, simply rejects that enduring, universal principles exist. All ideas or principles are said to be relative, or evolving, or changing, or culturally conditioned, or situational, or mere reflections of social forces or masks disguising them. But just as widely, eighteenth-century thought familiar to the American founders accepted universal principles implanted in nature, discernible by reason, and/or articulated as God's law—all versions of higher law by which mere human or mundane laws and deeds were to be judged.

To begin to understand the philosophy of the Constitution, then, we need first to see how seriously the framers took the idea of higher law—and keep in mind how very distant this seriousness is from our equally common rejection of the idea of fixed or universal principles, at least both in general parlance and in now long-dominant varieties of academic philosophy or discourse. As one scholar has put it recently, "openness—and the relativism that makes it the only plausible stance in the face of the various claims to truth and the various ways of life and kinds of human beings—is the great insight of our times. Any college teacher can test this pervasiveness by asking any class of entering students whether they think truth is relative—virtually all will say yes—and be quite sure no other answer is either possible or acceptable."[4] To see this point is to understand how hard it is now for us to read our foundational documents with anything like the eyes of their promulgators. Jefferson gave profound, substantial meaning to the phrases "the Laws of Nature," "self-evident truths," and "inalienable rights." In weaving them into an argument for independence, he fashioned what he later called "the common sense" of the time on the subject of government, that is, the agreed on basic principles. If common sense in the 1990s just as readily does *not* give much force or meaning to those phrases, then we have a measure of the difference between our climate of opinion and that of the American founders. It is simply impossible to understand the Constitution without acknowledging this basic difference in modes of thought.

In fact, because some idea of higher law was so taken for granted in the eighteenth century, it is not even necessary to sort out very carefully the varieties of thought it encompassed. Many people still regarded higher law as God's law, revealed in the Scriptures and understood and absorbed in the beliefs and practices of organized religion. This view received emphatic endorsement in the founding era from those who took seriously the Puritan tradition of measuring *all* human affairs by God's law, a test that Charles I had failed, and, according to Patrick Henry's defiant warning, George III was about to do as well, to his peril. People with this outlook would be as inclined to accept the idea of a properly sanctioned higher law as they would the need to rebel against a violator of such law. On the other hand, those who had absorbed more secular versions of higher law, usually called natural law in the eighteenth century, from Locke, Sidney, Burlamaqui, Voltaire, Vattel, and others, were equally prepared to implant enduring principles in a higher, constitutional framework (see chapter 4). The often complementary understanding of these perspectives was captured in John Wise's approving appeal to Plutarch's saying that "to follow God and obey Reason is the same thing."[5]

The idea of higher law still retains some currency even in the twentieth century, though, especially in our thinking about the Constitution. In 1910 the Supreme Court declared it to be "peculiarly true of constitutions" that they embodied enduring principles "capable of wider application than the mischief which gave them birth." Eighteen years later Justice Louis Brandeis insisted that clauses in the Bill of Rights "guaranteeing to the individual protection against specific abuses of power, must have a . . . capacity of adaption to a changing world" and apply to circumstances "of which the [founding] fathers could not have dreamed." In the famous World War II flag salute cases (see chapter 11), Justice Robert Jackson declared that "one's right to life, liberty and property, to free speech, a free press, freedom of worship and assembly, and other fundamental rights may not be submitted to vote; they depend on the outcome of no elections."[6] Justice Jackson asserted, as John Marshall had before him, that the Constitution was "higher law," which state legislatures, as well as Congress, however much they embodied the majority will of the people, had no rightful power to violate. No matter how "the times changed" or how new, situational ethics altered guideposts or how agencies of government might claim authority to "adjust" the Constitution to new circumstances, some "legal principles" remained, subject to no votes or majority rule or political manipulations.

Despite the generally relativist, antiuniversalist climate of modern opinion, nearly all students will agree with at least the substance of Jackson's opinion: surely children should not be compelled to salute the flag if that act violated their religious belief. Society, most modern students believe, should be open to and accepting of all religious (and nonreligious) persuasions. Students even go along with Jackson's argument that there are "fixed principles" that "depend on the outcome of no election" that the Court should uphold—even against the law of a democratically elected legislature seeking the laudable goal of fostering wartime patriotism. These same students, when they consider the case, generally agree that Franklin Roosevelt should not have attempted to "pack the Court" in 1937, despite the Court's invalidation of New Deal legislation passed overwhelmingly by Congress and widely supported in the nation. They somehow believe the Supreme Court and its power to invalidate unconstitutional laws are essential parts of our system of government and thus ought not to be tampered with, even when they seem to resist change or the popular will.[7] The arguments of both Justice Brennan and Judge Bork reflect much of the evolutionary, pluralistic thought of the modern era, yet both also see a place for the Constitution as "law above law."

The opinion of Justices Jackson and Brennan and of Judge Bork in fact reveal a tension in American government as old as the Declaration of Independence. They accept in various ways that there are "self-evident truths" and "inalienable rights" that in the nature of things cannot in justice be contravened—even by democratically elected legislatures. Yet the next clause of the Declaration asserts that "governments . . . derive their just powers from the consent of the governed." That is, laws passed by the consent of the people, by representative legislatures, acquired in that process a justification: they were valid (acceptable) simply because they were so promulgated. The prob-

lem arises precisely because such legislatures can and with troublesome fre-
quency *do* pass laws contravening the fixed principles, the higher law. This
tension has been present in American government from congressional passage
of the Alien and Sedition Acts (1798) to state statutes requiring racial segre-
gation and the teaching of "creation biology" and will remain as long as
American political thinking validates both propositions—as it will while the
Constitution itself remains in effect.

Thus, an effort to understand the Constitution must begin with a recognition
of its assumption that a higher law undergirds the polity. Yet, the need to
sustain fixed principles in American public life exists along with a recognition
that government must respond to the often changing needs of the people as
reflected in the laws passed by their representatives. It was probably the intent
of the framers that this tension exist, though they hoped, as we sometimes still
do, that public wisdom and responsibility would mature in a way causing it to
be more and more in accord with the higher law. Jefferson stated the ideal in
1790: "It now rests with [the United States] . . . to show by example the suf-
ficiency of human reason for the care of human affairs and that the majority,
the natural law of every society, is the only sure guardian of the rights of
man."[8] American political and constitutional history, moreover, has been interesting and at least potentially instructive precisely because of the attempt to
retain both of these attractive but not always compatible propositions.

PART II

THE ENDURING PRINCIPLES
OF THE CONSTITUTION

4

THE ENLIGHTENMENT

To a remarkable degree, the Constitution of the United States and its Bill of Rights rest on the intellectual movement in the Western world known as the Enlightenment, or Age of Reason. Undergirding all the particular clauses, empowerments, and limitations is the Age of Reason assumption that they represent enduring, natural law conformable to reason, human and divine (see chapter 2). For the most part, those who drafted, ratified, opposed, and explained the Constitution and the Bill of Rights understood what they were doing in terms of their Enlightenment milieu. This was their worldview, the perspective and philosophic orientation within which they lived. To understand the Constitution and Bill of Rights, then, we must know something of what that worldview was.

Following the French philosophe and Anglophile Voltaire, Thomas Jefferson regarded Francis Bacon, Isaac Newton, and John Locke as his "trinity of immortals." It was their thought (with important help from Descartes, Galileo, a notable group of Dutch scientists, and others), empirical, reasonable, scientific, and mundane, that transformed the European intellectual universe in the seventeenth century, laying the foundation for the world of ideas known as the Enlightenment. Its essence was an attitude toward humankind and the world, past, present, and future. As the Marquis de Condorcet (1743–1794), writing in the last year of his life, expressed it, in the Enlightenment:

scholarship, which seemed doomed by its respect for the past and its deference towards authority always to lend its support to harmful superstitions, has nevertheless contributed to their eradication, for it was able to borrow the torch of a sounder criticism from philosophy and the sciences. It already knew how to weight up authorities and compare them; it now learned how to bring every authority before the bar of Reason. It had already discounted prodigies, fantastic anecdotes, facts contrary to all probability; but after attacking the evidence on which such absurdities relied, it now learned that all extraordinary facts must always be rejected, however impressive the evidence in their favor, unless this can truly turn the scale against the weight of their physical or moral probability. Thus all the intellectual activities of man, however different they may be in their aims, their methods, or the qualities of mind they exact, have combined to further the progress of human reason. Indeed the whole system of human labor is like a well-made machine, whose several parts have been systematically distinguished but none the less, being intimately bound together, form a single whole, and work towards a single end. . . .

The discovery of the correct method of procedure in the sciences, the growth of scientific theories, their application to every part of the natural world, to the subject of every human need, the lines of communication established between one science and another, the great number of men who cultivate the sciences, and most important of all, the spread of printing, together all these advances ensure that no science will ever fall below the point it has reached. The principles of philosophy, the slogans of liberty, the recognition of the true rights of man and his real interests, have spread through far too great a number of enlightened men, to fear that they will ever be allowed to relapse into oblivion . . . .

Will men approach a condition in which everyone will have the knowledge necessary to conduct himself in the ordinary affairs of life according to the light of his own reason, to preserve his mind free from prejudice, to understand his rights and to exercise them in accordance with his conscience and his creed; in which everyone will become able, through the development of his faculties, to find the means of providing for his needs; and in which at last misery and folly will be the exception, and no longer the habitual lot of a section of society?[1]

Although Condorcet thus expresses the general spirit of the Enlightenment and properly captures its essential meaning among its American devotees in the eighteenth century, the Enlightenment was by no means clear and simple either in its timing in history or in its philosophic content. In general, the Enlightenment drew its strength from the repudiation of what it regarded as the millennium of superstition, other-worldliness, mysticism, and dogma known as the Middle, or Dark, Ages, when Christianity reigned in Europe, as doctrine, as institution, and as ritual. Before the Dark Ages there had been the vibrant, mundane, and intellectually critical classical world of Greece and Rome, and after it the Renaissance ("rebirth") of learning and the growth of scientific knowledge in the era of Galileo, Huygens, and Harvey. The Enlightenment, then, sought to overcome the superstitious Dark Ages by flooding it, reasonably and systematically, with the "light" of the classical writers and of modern science.

Although the Enlightenment, like the Renaissance, exalted an individualism and a universalism that owed much to Christianity, its more direct attention was turned toward the culture of Greece and Rome. Virtually all the great thinkers of the Enlightenment were learned in the ancient languages (some even continued to write in Latin) and adopted some of the worldview of their classical texts. Although simple exposure to non-Christian thought and culture produced a substantial enlargement of perspective, the critical and probing nature of many of the rediscovered ancient texts also provoked burst after burst of intellectual energy. This vigor provided impetus to more human understanding in the creative new directions heralded by Condorcet, but it stirred as well a deep reverence for the whole of classical civilization. As renaissance stimulated progress, then, it also restored to Europeans the heritage of Greece and Rome.

In England, as the "modern" thought of Bacon, Descartes, and others propelled the scientific revolution of the seventeenth century and led to the founding of the Royal Society (1662) and other scholarly institutions, the "ancient" wisdom of Greece and Rome was reevoked so powerfully that English letters entered a neoclassical age. In aesthetics, rhetoric, morality, and politics especially, ancient wisdom and classical models became the vogue. Ciceronian rhetoric, Stoic moderation and self-control, Epicurean love of life, Plutarchian moral leadership, Homeric patriotism, Aristotelian emphasis on political obligation, and Socratic love of public discourse became the models for students and for a wide variety of aspiring writers and leaders. Since this classical emphasis came early in life as students learned Greek and Latin and was regarded as well as a means of broadening and enlightening Christianity itself, it was there as a foundation for the novel and exciting ideas of modernity. Jefferson, for one, came to his reverence for Bacon, Newton, and Locke only after he had been stirred by Cicero's republican patriotism, enriched by Epicurean morality, and impressed with Aristotle's sense of the importance of the political in human life. The Enlightenment thus was, at least in its earlier phases, profoundly neoclassical.

The more innovative aspects of the Enlightenment, however, flowed from its enthusiasm for science. Following the new inductive approach (the scientific method) explained by Bacon and Descartes, scientists in the seventeenth century paid careful attention to the collection of facts about everything in the natural universe, sought to induce from them hypotheses and laws to explain all phenomena, tested these hypotheses in careful experiments, and presumed they could thus understand and explain the entire physical universe. "The true and lawful goal of the sciences," Bacon wrote in 1605, "is none other than this: that human life be endowed with new discoveries and powers." Descartes made the same confident, forward-looking point in 1637 when he scorned "the syllogisms . . . of the Schools" as capable only of "explaining to others things that are [already] known," while the inductive method was effective in "learning what is new." This method, he declared, was a "more powerful instrument of knowledge than any other that has been bequeathed to us by human agency" and would, if properly applied, enable men to "render [themselves] the masters and possessors of nature" (*Discourse on Method*).

Thus the Enlightenment meant not only a revival of ancient learning and wisdom, but also, and perhaps more significantly, a resolute search for new facts and new principles that would propel the rational progress of humankind to previously unknown heights. European settlers in North America not only took this outlook with them to the New World—indeed such an outlook furnished an important part of the impetus and confidence to seek and settle what were to them new worlds—but once there they found an environment unsuited to rigid orthodoxies but welcoming to the new, the untried, and the unformed. In Boston, Philadelphia, and Williamsburg, the Enlightenment impulse to pursue and exploit the new and the unknown was an integral part of North American colonization.

The most important and lasting impact of the Enlightenment in North America, however, came through its influence on political thinking and government in the new United States. The appeal in the Declaration of Independence to "the Law of Nature and of Nature's God," the assertion in the preamble of the Constitution that justice, domestic tranquility, the common defense, the general welfare, and the blessings of liberty were the proper purposes of government, and the preference in the *Federalist Papers* for "reflection and choice" over "accident and force" as the foundation of political society all reveal devotion to the Enlightenment creed of reason. Although these ideas also drew on classical and Judeo-Christian patterns of thought much older than the Enlightenment, that era so heightened such thinking that it gave systematic and lasting expression to a theory of government resting on reason.

As the struggle between mother country and colonies intensified in the 1770s, for example, the issue increasingly became whether the very idea of colonies—one part of the world ruled by another—was not itself a violation of the law of nature and, therefore, of reason. In reason and nature, could an island rule a continent? Could a legislature (or, eventually, a king) in London be expected to rule provinces 3,500 miles away with an understanding of their common good? In 1772 Samuel Adams proclaimed colonial protests of British acts were justified by "the Rights of the colonists as Subjects" of the British Crown and by "the Rights of the Colonists as Christians," but preeminently he claimed justification under the "Natural Rights of the Colonists as Men, [including] . . . First, a Right to *Life*; Secondly to *Liberty*; [and] Thirdly, to *Property*." Continuing his paraphrase of John Locke, Adams insisted that "all positive and civil laws, should conform as far as possible, to the Law of natural reason and equity." In a categorical statement of Enlightenment faith, Adams concluded that "the natural liberty of man is to be free of any superior power on earth, and not to be under the will or legislative authority of man; but only to have the law of nature for his rule."[2] John Adams, Alexander Hamilton, James Wilson, Thomas Jefferson, and other spokesmen for American rights wrote pamphlets making largely similar arguments based on the Enlightenment worldview. Thomas Paine applied the idea directly to government: "Establish the rights of man, enthrone equality; let there be no privileges, no distinction of birth; make safe the liberty of industry and of trade, the equal distribution of family inheritance, publicity of administration, freedom of press; and all these things established, you will be assured of good laws."[3]

The American Revolution and the new governments it spawned in fact became symbols throughout the world for a freer and better life. A French historian wrote poetically in 1789 of North America that "this vast continent that the seas surround will soon change Europe and the world. There arise for us, in the fields of America, new interests and a new system of politics." A Russian poet earned the ire of Catherine the Great and exile in Siberia for writing about America, "to you my inflamed soul aspires, to you, renowned land, . . . your example has revealed the goal." A British vessel, stopping at the Comoro Islands in the Mozambique Channel in 1784, even found the people in revolt against their Arab masters saying "America is free. Could we not be?"[4]

The greatest influence, though, of the Enlightenment ideals of the American Revolution and in the Declaration of Independence came in their projection into the government of the new United States. Alexander Hamilton expressed the basic hope in the first *Federalist Paper*: "it seems to have been reserved to the people of this country, by their conduct and example, to decide the important question, whether societies of men are really capable or not of establishing good government from reflection and choice, or whether they are forever destined to depend for their political constitutions on accident and force." The Declaration of 1776, defended in the revolutionary war, would achieve its fulfillment, Hamilton hoped, in a political system, rationally agreed upon by the people, that embodied the Enlightenment ideals of rule by consent and of natural rights, altogether resulting, finally in human history, in good government. Hamilton and other American revolutionists understood, too, the importance of enlightened thinking by those who took part, leaders and citizens, in this government. Following Diderot's definition of a *philosophe*, the need was "to act out of a feeling for Order and Reason, . . . suffused with concern for the good of civil society."[5]

The formation of government under the Constitution, then, was in a way a climax of the Enlightenment. It seemed to prove to the rest of the world that in that most fateful arrangement of human society, government itself, ideals of freedom and choice could be put into practice. It showed that popular sovereignty, a social contract, responsible citizenship, religious liberty, freedom of expression, balance of powers, human rights, and other rational ideals could be written into constitutions and could, as R. R. Palmer has observed, "be made the actual fabric of public life among real people, in this world now"[6]— as Condorcet had hoped in 1794. George Washington, writing in 1783 as he turned his attention from war to statecraft, expressed the enlightened mood of the new nation: "The foundation of our Empire was not laid in the gloomy age of Ignorance and Superstition, but at an Epoch when the rights of mankind were better understood and more clearly defined, than at any former period; the researches of the human mind, after social happiness, have been carried to a great extent, the Treasures of knowledge, acquired by the labors of Philosophers, Sages, and Legislators . . . are laid open for our use, and the collected wisdom may be happily applied in the Establishment of our forms of Government."[7]

There were, of course, many other influences beyond Enlightenment thought on the founding documents of the United States. Native American concepts of justice and federated government, especially the Iroquois Confederacy centered in the Onondaga longhouse, were well known to Benjamin Franklin and other framers and had some influence (though not a very direct one) on the formation of the Constitution. Madison and others at the Constitutional Convention knew of and learned lessons from the histories of "Ancient and Modern Confederacies," especially the still existing Dutch and Swiss federations. Judeo-Christian ideas from Biblical critiques of monarchies to statements of moral law such as the Ten Commandments, the Sermon on the Mount, and the Pauline Epistles also were important, though mostly unarticulated, foundations. Puritan concepts (themselves largely derived from the Bible) of covenant, calling, personal responsibility, and active, moral leadership were also widely significant, as were Great Awakening ideas of universal salvation and lay participation in church as well as state government. But the dominant, fresh, and creative intellectual energy behind the Constitution and the Bill of Rights was that of the eighteenth-century Enlightenment. John Adams called it, of all the ages of man, "the most honorable to human nature, . . . [where] knowledge and Virtues were increased and diffused, Arts, Sciences useful to men, ameliorating their condition, were improved, more than in any former equal period." Jefferson agreed with these "eulogies," adding that "to the great honor of science and the arts, their natural effect is by illuminating public opinion, to erect it into a censor, before which the most exalted tremble for their future, as well as present fame."[8] This outlook pervaded the basic principles of the Constitution and the Bill of Rights.

5

REPUBLICANISM

If we ask what, substantially, was the framers' intent in drafting the Constitution, we can see four basic principles, or higher laws, each as rich and complex in meaning in the 1990s as in the founding decades. These principles, stated abstractly and by themselves—republicanism, liberty, the public good, and federalism—might seem at first glance so broad and vague as to be meaningless. Yet, taken seriously and invested with profound, substantial meaning (as they were in 1787–1791), they convey what the framers intended to be permanent and everlasting, the underlying philosophy, of the Constitution and the Bill of Rights. They were the words intoned repeatedly in the legislatures and newspapers of the day, and they were the touchstones by which all the devices of government— modes of election, powers of Congress, jurisdiction of courts, and so on—were to be tested. To grasp the deepest, most important intent of the framers, then, as Brennan, Bork, and others still seek to do, and to discern the constitutional principles that might still guide the public life of the nation during its third century, an understanding of those four concepts is useful.

Republicanism, perhaps, is the concept whose eighteenth-century connotations are the most difficult today to recapture. To clarify a common confusion, the word, ideologically, has no particular connection with the modern political party of the same name. Its continued use simply suggests that the idea of republicanism lingers in the nation's collective memory enough to be thought useful politically. Nor does its eighteenth-century meaning have much to do with the current argument that this nation was intended to be a republic rather than a democracy. It is true that the framers (including the antifederalists) usually scorned the word *democracy* because it had Aristotelian connotations

26

of mob rule and also meant direct government by citizens. They instead used the word *republic* to convey their positive aspirations. They did not, however, intend for "republican" to mean something less democratic than the modern meaning of that word. To argue that the framers intended a republic rather than a democracy, to establish that they did not believe in democratic government as it exists now in the United States, misses the point. The sorts of representative governments existing today in genuinely democratic countries around the world are generally within what the framers thought of as republican. Those countries are generally *not*, though, what the framers thought of as democracies, because they used that word as Aristotle did to connote direct rule by the people, demagogy, turbulence, and majority tyranny. The positive connotations of the word *democracy* triumphed in Anglo-America only in the eras of Robert Peel and Andrew Jackson. Before that in both countries the word was usually pejorative. In general, then, what we mean today by *democratic* the framers intended with the word *republican*.

To the framers, to be a republic meant to be a self-governing community where representatives of the people made laws for the good of the nation as a whole. The essence, as Locke (the great fountain of republican ideology for the framers) put it, was that "every Man, by consenting with others to make one Body Politick under one Government, puts himself under an obligation to everyone in that Society, to submit to the Determination of the Majority."[1]

One gets a ready sense of both the centrality and urgency of this ideal in revolutionary America by looking at the first six complaints against George III in the Declaration of Independence. All protest his crimes against self-government: He and his appointed governors had refused to approve (and thus make effective) laws colonial legislatures had passed "wholesome and necessary for the public good"; he had refused to grant powers of self-government to some "large districts of people"; and he had dissolved, summoned "unusual, uncomfortable sessions of," and suspended elections to colonial legislatures. The effect was to deny the colonies the self-government they had more or less put into practice by 1776. This denial took from the colonists the only true security for all their other rights: the right to govern themselves; that is, republicanism.

The hostility of the colonists toward their king, though, which only developed late in the prerevolutionary struggle, gave an emphasis different from customary British claims for government by consent. Within the British polity, as Locke himself had argued, the existence of a constitutional monarch (after 1688) and a still-important House of Lords did not violate the idea of government by consent as long as an elected House of Commons with special powers over taxation and the spending of public money existed. But in America, the term *republic*, requiring popular rather than hereditary government, could, after the Declaration of Independence (from George III), have its full, consistent meaning: a polity resting entirely on the people, without a monarch.

The new American states, freed from allegiance to the British king, promptly set about to establish their own republics; that is, some form of self-government embodying elected legislative, executive, and, in some cases, even judicial officers. The United States as a whole moved toward the adoption of a confederacy, or league of governments, that would also conform to the republican principle of decision making according to the vote of elected delegates. Although spirited argument abounded over the form of self-government in the various states, there was no dispute about the basic republican principle. In both the coming of the American Revolution and in the establishment of new constitutions after 1776 the undergirding proposition was always republican: government according to the consent of the governed. As John Adams put it a few weeks before the Declaration of Independence: "No colony, which shall assume a Government under the People, will give it up. . . . An whole Government of our own choice, managed by Persons whom We love, revere, and can confide in, has charms for which Men will fight."[2]

At every step of the federal drafting and ratification process in 1787–1788, those involved had as their basic resource the self-government experiences of the states between 1776 and 1787. This knowledge was especially important in trying out the various devices that would give practical effect to the ideal: How large should election districts be? Would some form of referendum or recall be useful? Was a unicameral or a bicameral legislature best? Perhaps most basic, could the quality of legislation, its justness and long-term wisdom, be somehow improved over the often poor record of other republics?

In Pennsylvania, for example, the crosscurrents of pre-revolutionary politics left control in 1776 in the hands of those with few ties to the somewhat oligarchic colonial government. Thus, the drafters of the new state (or "commonwealth" as it called itself) constitution undertook to establish a thoroughgoing republicanism. In the excited atmosphere of the summer of 1776 one pamphleteer ("Demophilus," appropriately) urged intimacy between rulers and the ruled, while another declared that "a government made for the common good should be framed by men who can have no interest besides the common interest of mankind."[3] In order to assure that rulers had the common good at heart, the constitution began by asserting that "all power being originally inherent in, and consequently derived from the people; therefore all officers of the government, whether legislative or executive, are trustees and servants, and at all times accountable to them." Full law-making power was given to a unicameral legislature "of persons most noted for wisdom and virtue" to be elected annually by "all free men having a sufficient common interest with, and attachment to the community" (in effect, all male taxpayers and their sons over twenty-one years of age—a broad franchise for the time). All elections were to be "by ballot, free and voluntary," and electors and candidates who gave or received "meat, drink, monies, or otherwise" for votes would be disqualified. Legislators could serve only four years of any seven, and to ensure fair representation "and make the voice of the majority of the people the law of the land," a septennial census was to be the basis of frequent reapportionment. The debates in the legislature were to be open to the public, its proceedings to be published weekly, and all bills were to "be printed for the consideration of the people." To prevent "hasty determinations," passage by two annual assemblies would be necessary for final enactment of laws.

In further efforts to ensure self-government, an executive council with carefully limited powers was to be elected partly by the people and partly by the legislature. Finally, every seven years the people would elect a twenty-four member Council of Censors, to "enquire whether the constitution had been preserved inviolate in every part; and whether the legislative and executive branches of the government had performed their duty as guardians of the people."[4] Although this provision (and indeed the whole 1776 Constitution, which was in effect for only fourteen years) was never really tested, its intent was clear: to ensure in yet another way that the government would be faithful to the people, an instrument of their welfare.

Furthermore, though there were some "checks and balances" in the Pennsylvania Constitution, the emphasis was more on clear and direct control by the people through elections. Another Pennsylvanian made the point explicitly in 1787 in upholding this direct electoral emphasis as preferable to many parts of the new federal Constitution: "If, imitating the Constitution of Pennsylvania, you vest all legislative power in one body of men . . . elected for a short period, . . . excluded by rotation from permanency, and guarded from precipitancy and surprise by laws imposed on its proceedings, you will create the most perfect responsibility, for then, whenever the people feel a grievance they cannot mistake the authors, and will apply the remedy with certainty and effect, discarding them at the next election."[5] Although the federal Constitution of 1787 is not much like the 1776 Pennsylvania Constitution, it nonetheless sought to embody the same republican principle: All power came ultimately from the people, and the soul of good government was a reliance on their "honesty, common sense, and a plain understanding," which, "when unbiased by sinister motives, [was] fully equal to the task."[6]

The experience of the states between 1776 and 1787, and the theoretical reactions of thoughtful people to it, raised serious question, though, about the validity of the republican principle. In a searching paper on the "Vices of the Political System of the United States," written in April 1787, James Madison focused on the "Injustice of the laws of the States." This phenomenon, evident Madison thought in virtually all the states under their new republican consti- tutions, "brings into question the fundamental principle of republican Govern- ment, that the majority who rule in such Governments, are the safest Guardians both of public Good and of private rights." This state of affairs challenged, he observed, the "Republican Theory [that] Right and power being vested in the majority, are . . . synonymous." If this was a dubious assumption, as the per- formance of the self-governing states seemed to make obvious, then the prob- lem was much more complex than, for example, the Pennsylvania idealism of 1776 seemed to contemplate.

The causes of the "injustice of the laws of the States," Madison thought, could be either in the representatives who made the laws or in the people who elected them. Representatives often sought office to satisfy personal ambition or to pursue some selfish interest. Although such unfaithful legislators might be voted out of office, Madison noted that "the same art and industry which succeeded in the first [election, might] again prevail on the unwary to mis- place their confidence." Furthermore, even an honest and public-spirited leg- islator might become the dupe of a demagogic leader whose "sophistical arguments varnished with the glowing colors of popular eloquence" might arouse passions or mask selfish intentions.

Even more "fatal" to republican theory, the people themselves might be choosing and acting from selfish or short-sighted motives. Madison thought that the reasons sometimes cited to validate popular judgment, that the people would see "their own good as involved in the general and permanent good of the Community," that they would act wisely in order to uphold the "character" of the nation abroad, or that religious motivations would "restrain injustice," were inadequate. Hence the most profound flaw in the republican principle was the strong possibility that the people themselves, far from being free from the "base designs" of tyrants and oligarchies, might also have corrupting motivations.

Madison's response to the problem, though, far from being one of despair or rejection of republicanism, was to seek restraining or mitigating factors. He thought that a refining of popular sentiments through sometimes layered or indirect processes of elections (the electoral college, for example) might "extract from the mass of the society the purest and noblest characters which it contains."[7] More fundamentally, he thought both formal checks and balances to "oblige the government to control itself" and the informal check on unjust measures inherent in a large country where the "multiplicity of factions" would restrain each other would be a "republican remedy for the diseases most incident to republican government."[8] That is, the principle of majority rule could be preserved while its tendency toward unjust results could at least be meliorated. Thus, though the revolutionary era was replete with sober words that have led some to suppose many of the founders were antidemocratic, the dominant impulse was similar to Madison's: to recognize, realistically, the weaknesses in human nature that made self-government problematic, but then to go ahead and seek remedies, republican remedies, that would diminish the bad results. The era hence may be understood not so much as antidemocratic but as cautiously, wisely democratic in its search for effective solutions to real problems. To have ignored such problems, as, for example, the Pennsylvania Constitution seemed to do, would have been not zealously democratic, but merely foolishly democratic.

Edmund Pendleton—the learned judge, elder statesman, supporter of the Constitution at the Virginia ratifying convention, and a correspondent of Madison's—expressed the essential problem as it appeared to many of the framers.

> My reading and Observations on the History of mankind long ago fixed me in an opinion that a limited Monarchy was in general a Government best calculated to produce the happiness of Societies, as their peace and security depended upon Fixed Laws, and not on the one hand on the mere will of a despot, or on the other on the decision of a multitude, oft directed by the harangue of a designing popular orator, to serve his own, and not the public purpose. . . . Yet, reflecting on the . . . [American] Revolution, . . . he would be a Madman indeed who would think of any other than a republican form of Government [for the United States.]"[9]

Like Madison, Pendleton sought, within the republican (nonmonarchical) form, to retain the benefits of constitutional rule ("depending on fixed laws") geared to "the public purpose," while avoiding popular, demagogue-driven excesses.

The Constitution of 1787, then, rests on either an explicit insistence on the republican principle or an even more fundamental tacit assumption of it. All the states, for example, are guaranteed "a republican form of government." This clause meant that there could be no military or other arbitrary takeover of any state, nor could new states be admitted with other than self-governing constitutions. All the "parts" of the nation would have to be faithful to the basic principle—and since the states had an important agency in the general government, the permeation of republicanism was presumed to be comprehensive and permanent. Although some state governments have not always seemed very republican in practice, the form has remained and in time has restored democracy. The importance of the clause has not been its frequent use (in fact little case law rests on it) but its clear rejection in advance of state departures from the norm of self-government.

The substance of this guaranteed republicanism is rather simple, and it received nearly universal acceptance in 1787. It meant most basically government by consent, without aristocracy, privilege, or opportunity for arbitrary interference by a monarch, military junta, or other source of power not drawn from the people. The essential mechanism needed to give effect to this idea was a representative system: elections by qualified people who gave evidence of having "a stake in the community" and of being likely to take part in government in accord with the meaning of the word *res publica*, of or as part of the public, or commonwealth. Although this might, and has, justified restrictions on participation, debates at the Constitutional Convention reveal clearly that the framers intended the new Constitution to display no "tincture of illiberality," to use Madison's phrase, on questions of full representation of the people, suffrage, and citizenship. George Mason had, in the very first debate on representation, insisted that the Congress "ought to know and sympathize with every part of the community, . . . ought to attend to the rights of every class of the people." James Wilson followed by arguing that, since he hoped the "federal pyramid" would rise to include many powers of government, he "wished to give it as broad a basis as possible." Only then could it possess the necessary "confidence of the people." Madison added his opinion that "the great fabric to be raised would be more stable and durable, if it should rest on the solid foundation of the people themselves."[10]

Later in the convention, the framers discussed, and then rejected, a motion to restrict voting in federal elections to freeholders. Mason argued that "every man having evidence of attachment to and permanent common interest with the Society ought to share in all its rights and privileges." Since many people without wealth or land could have such attachment, Mason rejected the freehold criteria. Benjamin Franklin suggested that soldiers who had fought in the Revolution, however poor, had given weighty evidence of their attachment to the country and that immigrants who chose to come to the United States to enjoy its laws and opportunities were also likely to become responsible citizens. After observing that there was no correlation between virtue and wealth, Franklin insisted that the main point was to do nothing "that tended to debase the spirit of the common people." Everything in a republic depended on their "virtue and public spirit." Hence they should be treated well and allowed to take part in voting and other aspects of public life. The very act, then, of expanding suffrage and participation was essential to the idea of republicanism and its effective establishment in a nation. Madison concluded the debate by pointing out that the freehold restriction violated "the fundamental principle that men can not be justly bound by laws in making which they have no part."[11]

These lines of thought, not unanimous but generally controlling at the convention, led it to keep "illiberal" restrictions on suffrage and naturalized citizenship out of the Constitution, thus leaving such matters to state or federal legislation. The presumption (not always justified) was that "liberality" would gradually gain sway in such bodies. Liberal political thought of the day required that suffrage qualifications be determined at the local level. The suffrage was gradually enlarging in the states in 1787, so the new Constitution simply required that this expansion apply in federal elections. (Article I, Section 2: electors for the House of Representatives "shall have the same qualifications requisite for electors of the most numerous branch of the state legislature.") Thus, though the ideas of the Fifteenth, Nineteenth, Twenty-fourth, and Twenty-sixth amendments were not even faintly on the agenda in 1787, the thinking, the intent, of Wilson, Mason, Madison, Franklin, and others pointed unmistakably toward the eventual end of racial, gender, poll tax, and over-age-eighteen restrictions on voting. But in 1787 such matters were left to the states, both under the principle of federalism and because it was clear there were no nationally acceptable rules for franchise restriction. Since neither the convention, the states, nor the people had any such ideas in mind, of course the convention failed to adopt or even discuss the terms of the later amendments. There is, nonetheless, no explicit hostility toward them in the document of 1787. Rather, they are in some sense foreshadowed both in the debates of the convention and in the clauses of the document itself.

Extensions toward the principle of "one-person, one-vote," which became the basis of the landmark *Baker* v. *Carr* decision on fair apportionment in state legislatures (1962), are thus clearly within the intent of the framers, even though in creating the U.S. Senate they explicitly sanctioned one substantial departure from that principle. But even that sanction was accepted by many delegates only as a political expediency and was resisted strenuously by defenders of "the republican principle." To Madison that principle required "that the representatives ought . . . to bear a proportion to the votes which their constituents, if convened, would respectively have." James Wilson insisted that since "all men wherever placed have equal rights and are equally entitled to confidence, . . . the majority of people wherever found ought in all questions to govern the minority." Thus, from the beginning, many of the framers saw malproportioned legislatures as "pernicious, . . . bad principle," contradictory to the basic republican idea of majority rule.[12] Although the argument for "one-person, one-vote" as articulated in *Baker* v. *Carr* and other modern cases was not yet ready for enactment in 1787 and depends technically on the Fourteenth Amendment not adopted until 1868, its basic principle was both known to and widely accepted by the framers. One feels certain that, as grotesque examples of antiquated and deliberately unjust apportionment in state legislatures accumulated, they would have favored federal pushes in line with their cherished "republican principle."

Edmund Pendleton identified a further key aspect of republican representation when he warned Madison during the ratification contest of the danger that "designing men . . . in opposition to Government" might "impose" on the good judgment of the people. Since under the Constitution elected representatives, not the people directly, made public decisions, "they should use all their circumspection and judgment, preferring abilities and Integrity in whomsoever they find them and in them place their confidence, as they submit their lives, liberty, and property to their disposal." Then Pendleton urged, as he accepted for himself as a delegate to the Virginia ratifying convention, that representatives come to "deliberative Assemblies with a mind open to Conviction, resolved to hear all that can be said, and decide as . . . Judgment shall direct . . . to the general Good."[13] Notice the words Pendleton emphasized— judgment, integrity, deliberative assemblies, conviction, and general good— all qualities he considered essential to the process of representative self-government. Representation had not only to be full and equal ("access" in modern terminology), but it also required thoughtful, conscientious, well-informed judgment by both the people in choosing representatives and by the representatives in making public decisions.

Another essential feature of republicanism was the insistence that government be by law. In considering the rights of the British colonies in 1764, James Otis had asserted that legitimate authority must "govern by stated laws," a limitation imposed not only by the British constitution but also by "God and nature."[14] That is, taxes, conscription, regulations, and any other public acts were valid only when passed by a legislature in which the people being taxed, conscripted, and regulated were represented. This mechanism ensured that the people would not be controlled by what they had not consented to and required that all officers be themselves bound by published law. The Constitution requires the president, and through his full responsibility for the executive department, all his subordinate appointees to faithfully execute the laws and "preserve, protect, and defend the Constitution." Covert actions not authorized by law, informal (that is, irresponsible) exercise of power by some of the president's staff, evasions of the intent of the law, and secrecies masked by exaggerated national security claims all violate the republican insistence on government by law. The Constitution is not, however, hostile to the idea of an active, initiating executive pursuing the public good—both Roosevelts come to mind—as long as the president and all subordinate officers are responsible to the public and obey both the letter and the spirit of the laws. Although the framers could not have anticipated the technological possibilities of modern exercises of illegitimate power, there can be little doubt about their clear intent to proscribe the style and substance of Watergate, Irangate, and all other gates to irresponsibility and violation of the principle of consent.

The central role of the courts, and the nearly universal opinion in 1787 that a national judiciary would be a necessary part of any new constitution, further emphasized both the rule of law and the idea of a higher law. From the first explanations of the Supreme Court in 1787–1788, and especially from the landmark decisions of Chief Justice John Marshall (1801–1835)—who had been a member of the Virginia ratifying convention of 1788 where he heard Madison, Patrick Henry, George Mason, and others debate the meaning of the Constitution—the judiciary was viewed as especially important to the evolving idea of American republicanism. First, the Supreme Court would be *the* place where the Constitution as supreme, higher law would be both interpreted and upheld. Second, the Court would insist that the rule of law be paramount and that other agencies—both other branches of the federal government and the parts of state government falling under the provisions of national law— conform to the Constitution. In this conception, the federal judiciary, though appointed for long, indefinite terms remote from direct political recall, was itself sanctioned by the people to be their particular guardian of *their* Constitution. Although this concept might seem to limit the law-making responsibilities of legislative bodies, in fact, it helped ensure that the laws were authoritatively understood by the people and officials alike, thus validating and dignifying them as public acts.

A final mark of the republican foundation of the Constitution is the provision that "new states may be admitted by Congress into this Union." These new states would themselves have to have "republican governments" (as the Constitution requires), and they would be fully equal to existing states. Thus the groundwork was laid for what Jefferson often termed "an empire of liberty," deliberately inverting, as Tacitus, Sir Francis Bacon, and Bolingbroke had done before him, the usual idea that empires consisted of conquered people ruled by a tyrannical emperor. Under the American republican Constitution, however, "empire" could apply *only* to free, equal, and self-governing extensions. As John Quincy Adams put it in 1821 on the forty-fifth anniversary of independence, when as secretary of state he watched sympathetically but anxiously the revolt of Spain's American colonies, the United States "would be the well-wisher of freedom and independence" everywhere in the world, "but she goes abroad not in search of monsters to destroy. She would commend the general cause by . . . her voice and . . . her example, but she should not attempt to become the dictatress of the world. She would [thus] no longer be the ruler of her own Spirit."[15] By applying the principle of the Declaration of Independence and the Constitution to the nation's expansion, Adams and Jefferson proposed to "convert dangerous enemies into valuable friends" and to contain in the United States "such an extent of territory under a free and moderate government as [the world] has never yet seen."[16] Although the United States has not always abided promptly by the "empire of liberty" idea, it has, in conformity to the republican principle, always regarded either statehood or independence as the only proper status, ultimately, for lands under American jurisdiction.

Thus, the first principle of the Constitution is the practice of self-government, government by consent, republicanism. To the framers, neither the Declaration of Independence nor the Constitution made any sense without that idea. There simply was no way the American polity could be other than republican and still exist under the Constitution. Furthermore, the framers regarded republicanism as an evolving concept. They thought of the new United States as in the vanguard of republican government, an ideal then imperfectly understood and practiced. They supposed, therefore, that it could be improved and that the future might reveal refinements they had not anticipated. Thus, their intent is surely on the side of such latter-day extensions as widened suffrage, more direct participation in elections, and more equitable election districts. The Constitution, that is, was intended for a nation on the forefront of the idea and practice of self-government in the world.

6

LIBERTY

The second basic idea underlying the U.S. Constitution, the most popular, ringing word of the day, was *liberty*. It decorated the banners of surging crowds in American streets before independence, it dominated the mastheads of revolutionary newspapers, and it served as the peroration of countless speeches in public square and legislative assembly. Everywhere liberty poles, liberty presses, and liberty boys contributed to "the contagion of liberty" that Bernard Bailyn explains is the heart of American revolutionary ideology.[1] When Patrick Henry proclaimed "give me liberty or give me death," he but summarized the commonplace centrality given to the word in the rhetoric of the revolutionary and early national eras. The last and culminating purpose stated in the preamble of the Constitution is that it "secure the blessings of liberty to ourselves and our posterity," an unequivocal statement of the most explicit purpose of the Constitution.

Since the appeal to liberty in the Western world, and especially in England in the seventeenth and eighteenth centuries, was to oppose the intrusions and oppression of kings and tyrants, it had in some ways strongly negative connotations. Liberty was defined as a series of limitations on the power of monarchical government; things it was no longer to do, thus protecting the rights and freedom of the people. Beginning with Magna Charta (1215) and culminating in the debates of the Puritan era (1640s) and the Declaration of Rights of the Glorious Revolution (1689), Englishmen defined their rights and liberties against the monarch: freedom of speech, press, petition, assembly, and religion; trial by jury, habeas corpus, freedom from unlawful search and seizure, and so on. Referred to endlessly during the Revolution on both sides of the

Atlantic as "the rights of Englishmen" as well as natural rights and prefixed in some form to most of the state constitutions adopted in 1776 and after, such liberties, expressed as restraints on rulers, were the very purpose of the Revolution.

Article I, Section 9 lists many "freedoms from government": habeas corpus cannot be denied and bills of attainder, ex post facto laws, and the granting of titles of nobility are all forbidden. The liberty of the people required that government *not* do those things. Although the Convention of 1787 felt further explicit statements of rights were unnecessary because they were already implicit in a carefully limited frame of government and because state bills of rights were thought a sufficient protection, public opinion called out for a federal bill of rights. Both advocates and opponents of the Constitution agreed to add one as soon as possible under the new government. "A bill of rights is what the people are entitled to against every government on earth," Jefferson declared, in urging addition of one to the new constitution.[2] The particular thrust of his statement, of course, in the long English tradition of bills of rights against those who wield power, was that the people might even need such protection against nonmonarchical, republican governments.

The final ratification of the Bill of Rights in 1791 is properly seen, then, not as an addition changing the intent or substance of the document of 1787, but rather as the explicit confirmation of the views of the framers (and ratifiers) on the subject of individual liberties. The absence of a bill of rights in the 1787 Constitution is not evidence of hostility by the convention to the substance of such a bill but reveals instead a tactical judgment Madison and other members were willing to amend when Jefferson and others made persuasive counterarguments (see chapter 10).

These rather formal protections of liberty, however, were only the most visible part of the enlarging theory and practice of individual opportunity and lack of restraint on personal freedom in the new nation. Open access to new lands, the repeated experience on the frontier of establishing often minimal government from a "state of nature," the individual aspirations of multitudes of immigrants, and the vigorous, laissez-faire ethos of the burgeoning American economy all heightened the sanctification of individual liberty and the often consequent denigration of the role of government. Indeed, nineteenth-century America seemed to be the glorious fulfillment of what people and society might become when loosely governed.

This circumstance would generally have delighted the framers. It is impossible to read their words and understand their thinking without seeing the centrality of this concern—and no contemporary understanding of the Constitution can be on target unless it shares this clear desire that the nations's laws and institutions push human freedom to the limit circumstances allow. We should not, for example, ascribe to the framers narrow interpretations of personal freedoms against wiretapping, electronic surveillance, and data-bank use, or argue that their views are irrelevant because they didn't possess the technology. With resounding force and crystal clarity they sought repeatedly, according to the circumstances and standards of their time, to enlarge human liberty. That intent is still implicit in the Constitution today (see chapter 13).

More complex, and more difficult to translate into the ethos and language of our day, is the equally important idea implanted in the Constitution of "positive liberty," or the liberty of the citizens of a self-governing society to participate and act for the public good and to use their government to seek, in Aristotle's words, "not merely life alone, but the good life." Sustained in the civic republican tradition revived in Renaissance Italy and articulated vigorously by neo-classical English theorists, this positive idea of freedom remained at hand when the American framers had to build, rather than pull down, government. The essence was the Greek notion that to be fully human, to be truly a citizen of a polity, one had to take part—by deliberating, voting, holding office, and so on—responsibly and honestly in pursuing the public good. Without this active participation and ability to in some degree subordinate private to public perspective, one wasn't really free. Rather, one was in the bondage of self-love, narrow-mindedness, and social indifference. Furthermore, one was leaving to others the determination of public policy or, by selfish participation, corrupting the polity's public life. One thus deprived one's self of the genuine liberty and enhancement of life that comes from living and taking part in a well-governed state. (Chapters 7 and 12 more fully explain the constitutional principle of good government.)

This larger understanding of liberty was, despite the long English emphasis on "liberty from," always an important part of American revolutionary ideology. In Virginia, for example, the effort to draft a declaration of rights and a constitution suitable for an independent commonwealth revealed strong concern for both liberty from the oppression of government and liberty for the people to conduct the affairs of the new state toward the public good. The convention in May–June 1776, which instructed Virginia delegates to the Continental Congress to take the lead in declaring "the United Colonies free and independent states," also adopted a constitution suited to the new condition of independence. To this was prefaced a Declaration of Rights, printed in draft form in Virginia, then reprinted in newspapers all over the country, and, soon thereafter, all over the world. It was also largely copied and included in declarations of rights by many other of the newly independent states, thus becoming the best-known, most detailed, quasiofficial statement of the ideals, or goals, of the American Revolution.

The form of this famous declaration is revealing. In its preamble and first clause it asserted that "certain inherent rights" including "life and liberty, with the means of acquiring and possessing property, and pursuing and obtaining happiness and safety, [were] . . . the basis and foundation of government." The next six clauses began the definition of freedom by affirming the nature and principles of meaningful self-government; that is, the foundational liberty of the people to control their own affairs and thus move toward happiness and safety. "Since all power is vested in, and consequently derived from the People," it declared, all officials were "at all times amenable to them." Such government had as its only purpose "the common benefit, protection, and security of the people, nation or community," and if found "inadequate or contrary to these purposes, a majority of the community hath a right to reform, alter, or abolish it." Within such a government, devoted to the public good, privileges, payment, and offices, due only to those who performed "public services," could not be hereditary. In order that executive and legislative officials "may be restrained from oppression," they were "at fixed periods to be reduced to a private station, . . . and the vacancies to be supplied by certain, frequent, and regular elections." Next, those elections were to be free and open to all "having sufficient evidence of permanent common interest with, and attachment to the community," thus assuring that no one would be taxed without their consent, "nor bound by any law to which they have not . . . assented, for the public good." Finally, "any authority" was forbidden to suspend laws or their execution "without consent of the Representatives of the people." Only after thus establishing the foundational liberties to take part in and exercise control over the government were the familiar personal rights of the people, to trial by jury, freedom from unlawful search and seizure, freedom of the press, liberty of conscience, and so on, affirmed.[3] (Indeed, even such personal liberties as trial by jury and freedom of expression were also understood as essential to the political freedom of participation.) In this declaration of rights, the liberty to take part and to have government serve the public good were thus at least as much emphasized as were liberties from government interference.

Although in the frame of the federal Constitution the active freedoms to take part in government are implicit and embedded in the body of the document, and the rights against government ("Congress shall make no law . . . ") are appended, stated explicitly, and thus more clearly highlighted, the understanding of the word "liberty" in 1787 nonetheless *began* with emphasis on freedom to take part in and control *all* acts of government (see chapter 15 on this point). This right would assure both that personal liberty would be protected (would the people willingly violate their own rights?) and that the people would be able to act as a political community to seek the public good as they saw fit. In fact, in concern for the proper fulfillment of this freedom even amid its recitation of personal liberty the Virginia Convention declared that only "a firm adherence to justice, moderation, temperance, frugality, and virtue" in the people could assure "free Government [and] the blessings of liberty." This Aristotelian proposition, then, in a sense surrounded the statements of personal rights, furnishing the only context in which they could be assured.

Although this conception of active citizenship (referred to in the eighteenth century as the right of "the freeman") is not spelled out explicitly in the Constitution, the document in many respects assumes or envisions it, and the framers themselves overwhelmingly accepted such a conception. At the Constitutional Convention concerns about the qualifications for citizenship (the freedom to take part in government) arose often. The delegates realized that "the people," like other "bad" rulers, could as citizens act foolishly, selfishly, or brutally in exercising their powers. In opposing direct election of the executive, for example, George Mason "conceived it would be as unnatural to refer the choice of a proper character for Chief Magistrate to the people, as it would to refer a trial of colours to a blind man."[4] Mason thought the people probably lacked the wisdom and public mindedness to choose a good president (a concern, of course, not unknown to modern democratic states). The question then becomes either how to find a more preferable mode of selection likely to produce better leadership, or how to enlighten the people so that they themselves would choose "a proper character" to be president. The device of the electoral college was the convention's attempt to solve the problem by responding to the first question, but its meaninglessness throughout our history leaves the problem of how to develop in the people the character and understanding needed to properly exercise their active freedom as participants in government.

Benjamin Franklin revealed the only faithfully republican direction to take in improving the quality of participation when he spoke to the convention on suffrage restriction and on immigration policy. He opposed any property or wealth limitation on the right to vote. "Some of the greatest rogues he was ever acquainted with," Franklin observed, "were the richest rogues." Furthermore, "the possession of property," far from making people less greedy, he thought, "increased the desire for more property."[5] Hence, the ancient system of limiting suffrage to landowners or taxpayers was flawed because it failed to discriminate properly: it enfranchised some selfish voters and disenfranchised others who might have possessed the vital moral qualifications. As Franklin had pointed out in probing the meaning of republicanism, revolutionary soldiers and others who had acted patriotically during the war for independence and immigrants who *chose* to come to the New World to enjoy its freedom and opportunity were likely to be loyal and responsible citizens. Notice that Franklin's grounds for citizen qualification are entirely moral, having to do with attitudes and intentions, without race, gender, or wealth bias. Thus, though neither he nor his convention colleagues were prepared to make such liberalizations explicit, their *reasoning* required it, and the language put in the Constitution did not impede its realization as sentiment in the country changed. (The language of the Fifteenth, Nineteenth, Twenty-fourth, and Twenty-sixth amendments is directed most importantly against *state* restrictions on suffrage.)

Franklin was simply thinking through what was required for people to be politically free, that is, to exercise wisely, virtuously, and effectively their "office of citizen." He clearly thought this freedom required that there be qualifications, but these were moral qualities, not wealth or class or race or gender. To be truly free, to be an active, effective participant in the public life of the nation, it was necessary to possess in some degree certain qualities: wisdom, good judgment, a sense of justice, and, most important, what Franklin called "public spirit"—the capacity to in some measure look at public problems and opportunities from an enlarged point of view attentive to the good of the country as a whole. To live up to this standard meant, particularly, achieving the opposite of the broad, eighteenth-century meaning of the word "corruption." To be corrupt was to act selfishly, or partially, or in a way hostile to or neglectful of the "permanent and aggregate interests of the community."[6] Thomas Jefferson, for example, thus spent a lifetime seeking to forestall corruption in a self-governing polity by improving people's occupations, by promoting public education, and by invigorating local government in order that all the people might eventually be qualified, as "freemen," to fulfill the obligations and possess the rights of citizenship.

Liberty, then, as used in the Constitution, surely meant the broad and growing freedom of individuals from the tyrannies and restraints of government, and the general enlargement of individual opportunity in the nation—the usual connotations of the word today. But it also meant the freedom to *take part*, thus enabling *citizens* to fulfill their own natures as political beings, to avoid the dependence (lack of freedom) that goes with living under edicts or laws made by others, and to contribute constructively to the civilizing, enhancing, prospering, humanizing, and beautifying potential of the nation as a whole. Although the framers were attracted by the benefits of limited government, of an "open" society, and of lack of restraint on individuals (the burgeoning "liberal tradition"), they were also still deeply attracted to the ancient idea of the substantial freedom achieved only by citizens participating in government. The U.S. Constitution, then, gains some of its effectiveness and creative ambiguity because the framers were, so to speak, of two minds: they were *both* modern, liberal advocates of freedom *from* government and devotees of the classical ideal of public-spirited citizens participating freely and responsibly in their own government.

Although the modern mind accepts readily the notion of individual liberty imposing limits on the power of government, it less easily appreciates the enhancing, enabling, even ennobling freedom to act constructively that goes with the responsible exercise of governmental power. Just as much as Article I, Section 9 (and the Bill of Rights) protects liberty by restricting government, Article I, Section 8 fulfills liberty by authorizing the exercise of power on behalf of the public good: collecting taxes for defense and welfare, regulating commerce, coining money, providing postal service, protecting patents and copyrights, organizing the armed forces, and establishing a seat of government are all enterprises that, if conducted wisely and responsibly, protect and enrich the lives of the people and thus make them more free. Likewise the executive power to execute the laws, appoint officials, and command the armed forces, and the judicial power to settle disputes, to enforce equality before the law, and to uphold the Constitution contribute enormously, again when wisely and responsibly exercised, to the nation's well-being—and to the practical liberty of the people. Who is less free than someone too terrified to walk the streets at night, or too poor to maintain good health, or too ignorant to gain employment or understand the world environment?

Publius had warned in his opening *Federalist Paper* that "a dangerous ambition more often lurks behind the specious mask of zeal for the rights of the people than under the forbidding appearance of zeal for the firmness and efficiency of government." Although by no means neglectful of the rights of the people understood as limitations on government, Publius was at least as concerned with enabling the exercise of positive freedom to seek the public good. Thus he asserted that "the great body" of the people in the country were determined to balance "the inviolable attention due to liberty" from excessive power with the freedom to use power for their own benefit. He further declared energy in government "essential to the steady administration of the laws . . . and to the security of liberty against the enterprises and assaults of ambition, of faction and of anarchy."[7] (In chapters 10–12 these restraints as expressed in the Bill of Rights, and their place in American constitutional thought are explained.) In fact, the whole spirit of Publius, as he extolls the more energetic quality of the new Constitution to correct the ineffective Articles of Confederation, is to fulfill the promise of the American Revolution that the people of the former colonies be free to govern themselves.

7
THE PUBLIC GOOD

When Thomas Jefferson had occasion, in the last year of his life, to list "the elementary books of public right" that undergirded the thinking of the revolutionary and founding generation, he mentioned particularly Aristotle, Cicero, John Locke, and Algernon Sidney.[1] (Recall that John Adams's list in 1775 was the same, but added Plato, Livy, and Harrington; see chapter 2.) Locke and Sidney make Jefferson's list as the revered spokesmen for the concepts of limited government, majority rule, and protection of the natural rights of individuals that were the compelling, fresh ideals of the Enlightenment (chapter 4). They stated the propositions about freedom and equality, natural law and limited government that filled the revolutionary newspapers and were in 1787–1788 gospel to federalists and antifederalists alike. Taken by themselves, however, they reflect a largely negative view of government: they sought to define what governments (almost all tyrannical in the eighteenth century) should *not* do in order that (individual) natural rights not be infringed upon. But as we have seen, the idea of liberty for the founders also included a positive concept of participation in government that as well fulfilled the republican ideal of self-government. It is the joining of these two concepts under the goal of achieving the public good that Jefferson had in mind in placing Aristotle and Cicero among the "elementary" thinkers, an essential complement, in his mind, to the Locke-Sidney emphasis on limitation and natural rights.

Jefferson, like Madison, John Adams, Hamilton, and others of the founding generation, learned from Aristotle (directly or indirectly) how important government was in human affairs, what good government consisted of, and why a concern for the public good was of crucial significance. In accepting Aristotle's dictum that "man is a political animal," Jefferson, Madison, and others agreed that an essential part of human fulfillment was the right and responsibility to take part in public affairs, to participate in government, to serve in "the office of citizen." Without such participation an element of human potential remained unrealized, and the public was denied the important contribution responsible citizens make to the deliberative consideration of the shared business of their political community.

In profound tension with the Lockean emphasis on limited government, Americans of the founding era, schooled in classical language and lore, also accepted Aristotle's argument that "a state exists for the sake of the good life, and not for the sake of life only. . . . Political society exists for the sake of noble actions, and not of mere companionship."[2] Protecting national security, preventing injustice, promoting trade, and enhancing convenience were important functions of government, but they did not exhaust the possibilities for moving toward "the good life" of the political community as a whole. That is, government was much more than a "necessary evil" that made the state *necessary*. It was also an agency for promoting the public good in a way that made the *state* necessary. Although Publius often argued the "necessary" part of this argument, he also repeatedly recurred to the "state" part. In *Federalist* No. 1 he pointed out the possibility of "establishing good government from reflection and choice." In No. 10 he sought to neutralize faction in order to uphold "the permanent and aggregate interests of the community." In No. 37 he urged stability to secure "the effects of good government." In No. 57 he desired representatives possessing "most wisdom to discern, and most virtue to pursue, the common good of the society." In No. 70 he insisted that "energy in the executive is a leading character in the definition of good government," and in No. 78 he argued that the Constitution was "fundamental law" to be upheld against "ill humors" that might sometimes arise in society. There is simply no way to understand these phrases about government apart from an active intent to pursue the public good.

John Adams, another founder who signed the Declaration of Independence, who admired the Constitution and had a major role in establishing government under it, had implanted explicit conceptions in the Massachusetts Constitution of 1780 of how state governments might seek the public good. In presenting the draft constitution to the people for their ratification, the Massachusetts convention declared that as "representatives of a wise, understanding and free people," the delegates to the Constitutional Convention had sought to answer "the great inquiry . . . wherein the common interest consists." Reacting against both general weakness of government in some of the other state constitutions and a tendency to concentrate power in the lower house of the legislature, the Massachusetts convention sought empowerment of government, lest the state "sink into anarchy," and a better balance among its branches. The convention provided for annual, popular elections of the governor and of both houses of the legislature and gave the governor as well as both houses veto power over legislation, "to the end that it may be a government of laws and not of men." Faithful to the goals of government by consent and of protection of the liberties of the people, Adams and his colleagues nonetheless, using as they put it, "the highest skill in political architecture," sought to frame a constitution capable as well of fulfilling "the common interest."

Adams also was determined that the state's government nourish and promote "the good life" in Massachusetts. To that end the constitution authorized public support of teachers of "piety, religion, and morality" because "the honor and happiness of a people depend upon morality." Although the constitution also proclaimed that "the free exercise of *the rights of conscience*" prohibited state interference with any form of public worship, the delegates were unwilling to abandon what had long been regarded as essential links between virtue, religion, and state support. To the heirs of John Winthrop's Puritan "city upon a hill," where the magistrates had full responsibility for maintaining a pious and upright commonwealth, it was entirely natural to continue the empowerment of government to seek the public good. It was only necessary, responding to the Enlightenment ideals of the American Revolution, to put the lofty goals in more secular terms. The Massachusetts Constitution of 1780 thus set forth three broad duties for legislators and magistrates: "To cherish the interests of literature and the sciences, and all seminaries of them, public schools and grammar schools in the towns: to encourage private societies and public institutions, rewards and immunities for the promotion of agriculture, arts, sciences, commerce, trades, manufactures, and a natural history of the country; to countenance and inculcate the principles of humanity and general benevolence, public and private charity, industry and frugality, honesty and punctuality in their dealings; sincerity, good humor, and all social affections, and generous sentiments, among the people."[3]

Although the intention to inculcate good character and, especially, the conventional assumption that state-supported religion was necessary to achieve a proper public morality sound strange and even intrusive and intolerant to modern ears, they nonetheless reveal the common conviction in the founding era that government had a broad power and responsibility to pursue the public good. Even the thinking behind the growing movement to separate church and state generally insisted on the importance of sustaining religious and moral influence in government—even if the institutional forms were to be changed. Following a line of thought deriving from Roger Williams and others, a principal purpose of freeing religion from state control was to make it more genuinely influential in society. If people were willingfully faithful and freely committed to high moral standards, the argument went, then those principles would rest on firm ground and thus be more effectively projected into public life—by active citizens in a self-governing polity.

James Madison, for example, accepted this argument in 1819, declaring that in Virginia "there has been an increase of religious instruction since the Revolution." The old churches built under the colonial establishment of religion, he said, were "in many instances gone to ruin . . . and the flocks deserted to other worships." On the other hand, under Virginia's famous Statute for Religious Freedom, churches of all sorts flourished. "On a general comparison of the present and former times," Madison reported, "the balance is certainly and vastly on the side of the present, as to the number of religious teachers, the zeal which activates them, the purity of their lives, and the attendance of the people of their instruction." The time-honored opinions "that Civil Government could not stand without the prop of a Religious establishment and that the Christian religion itself would perish if not supported by a legal provision for its clergy" had both been proven false. Under disestablishment, civil government was firm and stable, and "the number, the industry, and the morality of the [clergy] and the devotion of the people have been manifestly increased."[4]

Madison's point was not that government had no interest in or responsibility for public morality, but rather that morality in the polity was best enhanced by leaving religious worship and instruction to unestablished churches that nourished and depended upon the freely given devotion and commitment of their adherents. Alexis de Tocqueville saw the same phenomenon fifteen years later when he reported approvingly that, contrary to conventional European dogma, religious disestablishment in the United States left it with greater religious vitality, higher moral standards, and more influence of religious and moral principles of public life than any country in the world (see chapter 12).

The opinion of Madison and other founders on public education carries a similar assumption of the concern for the public good implicit in the Constitution. Although the federal government is given no power over education, the debates of 1787–1788 repeatedly acknowledged that the new Constitution would work well only if there were well-informed and public-spirited citizens. Delegates complained that the people lacked "information and are constantly liable to be misled" and that they were thus ill qualified to elect a wise and able president. Others pointed out that everything depended on "the virtue and public spirit of our common people" and that the welcoming of "meritorious strangers" to the United States would benefit the country.[5] The argument did not then proceed to explicit suggestions for federal support of education, but it was clear both that the delegates believed an educated citizenry was essential to the effective operation of the Constitution and that they expected the states to act to achieve that end. Jefferson and Madison had in fact recently urged (so far without success) that Virginia pass a "bill for general education" so that the people "would be qualified to understand their rights, to maintain them, and to exercise with intelligence their parts in self-government."[6] Some New England states already had rudimentary systems of public education.

Benjamin Rush had written in 1786, in a document well known to many members of the Constitutional Convention, that "the business of education has acquired a new complexion by the independence of our country. The form of government we have assumed has created a new class of duties to every American." Nine years later President Washington proposed that citizens should be prepared for these duties by a "plan of universal education . . . to be adopted in the United States."[7] Neither Rush nor Washington thought the federal government should be entirely responsible for this public (i.e., for public purposes) education, though Washington and each of his five immediate successors as president did propose a federally supported national university in the capital district to be the "capstone" for such education.

Madison summarized the philosophic connection between self-government and public education when in 1822 he endorsed a Kentucky plan "for a general system of Education." "A popular Government, without popular information, or the means of acquiring it, is but a Prologue to a Farce or a Tragedy; or perhaps both. Knowledge will forever govern ignorance: And a people who mean to be their own Governors, must arm themselves with the power which knowledge gives." "Learned Institutions," Madison continued, "ought to be favorite objects with every free people." Then both citizens and legislators would be more inclined to frame wise, consistent, and stable laws sustaining a "just and equal spirit in which the great social purposes are to be answered." Reflecting on the nature of the Union, Madison noted that "a salutary emulation" among the states could give Kentucky "the merit of diffusing the light and advantages of Public Instruction" to other states. Thinking more broadly of the impact of public education, Madison hoped that students by studying geography would become acquainted with "the characters and customs which distinguish . . . foreign countries, . . . weaken local prejudices, and enlarge the sphere of benevolent feelings." By thus fostering public education Madison hoped, finally, that "the cause of free Government" would prove itself "as favorable to the intellectual and moral improvement of Man as to his individual and social rights."[8] Although Madison was speaking of a state rather than a national system of public schools, it is clear that he considered such education to be integral both to the wise operation of the Constitution within the United States and to the spread of free government around the world.

The point is not, of course, that the U.S. Constitution gives direct power to the federal government over religion and education or that it even implies or envisions doing so. Indeed, in the case of religion such power is forbidden explicitly, and education, except for the possibility of a national university in a federally controlled capital district, is left in state and private hands. What is certain, however, is that as part of the Constitution's intent to nourish the nation's public good, it seeks to leave scope for religious and educational institutions. For religion, this meant leaving churches free so that they might elicit genuine, heartfelt commitment among their members, and through the public efforts of the faithful furnish moral guidance to the body politic. The framers and ratifiers of the Constitution thus supposed they were acting on behalf of the public good by sustaining the religious and moral vitality implicit in freedom of conscience. The Supreme Court recognized this sympathetic relationship as late as 1970 in asserting that throughout its history American government had displayed a "benevolent neutrality toward churches and religious exercise generally" (see chapter 12). Churches and other charitable institutions could be encouraged because they enhanced "cultural and moral improvement and the doing of good works . . . in the community."[9] One should remember, too, that the First Amendment, by providing that "Congress shall make no law respecting the establishment of religion," protected religious establishments in New England and hence, to some, represented another kind of sympathetic relationship (see chapter 10).

For education, the Constitution just as clearly intended that state and private agencies undertake the vital nourishment to good self-government, often with substantial, constitutionally validated federal support. From the provision in the Northwest Ordinance (passed in 1787 by a Congress many of whose members were also delegates to the Constitutional Convention) reserving one lot in each township "for the maintenance of public schools," through the Morill Act

(1862) providing federal land grants to higher education, to the "grant-in-aid" programs of the twentieth century, the federal government has undergirded educational efforts because, it was believed, good government required well-educated citizens and other public officeholders, as well as skilled practitioners in every walk of life. Furthermore, they supposed that the diversity of effort, and the spirit of "salutary emulation" among the states as encouraged by the principle of federalism, would yield a system of public education better able to nourish good government in the public interest than a more rigid and bureaucratic national system.

In a way, then, pursuing the public good was an important principle of the Constitution even when it prohibited certain powers to the federal government, or when it simply left them to the states. This is another manifestation of the effort in the Constitution to combine the best of the Aristotelian and Lockean approaches to government. The sense of limitation, of seeing constitutional government as a barrier to unwise and illegitimate actions, is palpable in both the document itself and in the arguments over its drafting and ratification. A buoyant bias in favor of allowing as much scope as possible to individual energy and initiative is also evident. Yet, these Lockean emphases are always viewed as parts, perhaps even subordinate parts, of a subsuming social context in which government is a vital component—"man is a political animal." The ideas that government is no more than a necessary evil, that we must think politically of man versus the state, and that a dogmatic diminishment of government is always desirable are simply absent from the political discussions of the founding era. Rather, with Aristotle, the assumption was that the state had wide responsibility and potential (for good or evil) and that part of "establishing good government from reflection and choice" is deciding not only what powers government shall or shall not exercise, but also what levels of government, national, state, and local, shall exercise them.

Throughout, the question of the role of the state is an open one: could this or that purpose or function be usefully and justly accomplished by the collective force of the community (government)? If the answer is "yes" then the next question for "reflection and choice" is what form and empowerment of government will most likely achieve the desired end? Only if the answer is "no" (as, for example, in the matter of enlivening conscience) does the founder's understanding of government require constitutional proscriptions. In matters where the answer is uncertain, or at least uncertain as to the level of government best suited for a particular purpose, the Constitution is deliberately vague, intending to leave the issue up to subsequent legislative action at either the state or federal level. For example, the Constitution declares federal law, treaties, and constitution "supreme," but leaves the states all "powers not delegated to the United States by the Constitution." Thus federal and state legislatures and courts, responding to an active citizenry, have weighty and ongoing political obligations—as both Aristotle and Locke taught.

One gets a vivid sense of the overall importance and general purposes of government in the founding era from the preamble of the Constitution. Although, as the courts have always held, the preamble confers no specific powers and thus cannot be appealed to in defining those of the federal government, it is a guide to the larger purposes to be achieved in exercising the legislative, executive, and judicial authority defined in the body of the Constitution. The process of government, detailed in the body of the Constitution, is merely instrumental to the purposes enunciated in the preamble. The six substantial phrases in the preamble—"form a more perfect Union, establish Justice, insure domestic Tranquility, provide for the common defence, promote the general Welfare, and secure the Blessings of Liberty"—reveal both a sense of public good aspired to and the dangers to be avoided.

What, for example, was intended by the words "more perfect Union"? The phrase has to do not only with the structure and processes of government, the formal union, but more profoundly with the *quality* of the bonds. Were suspicion, insecurity, and alienation common in the attitudes of and relationships among the people and parts of the union? Or, on the other hand, were trust, goodwill, and common purpose characteristic of the bonds? The point is something like what Jonathan Edwards had in mind in declaring that "union is one of the most amiable things that pertains to human society: yea, it is one of the most beautiful and happy things on earth, which indeed makes earth most like heaven." Although Edwards had religious bonds in mind, he also declared "civil union, or harmonious agreement among men in the management of their secular concerns ... amiable" as well. [10] "A more perfect Union," then, would offer the sort of bonds of friendship and common concern for the public good that Aristotle had declared to be the vital dynamic of citizens working together. This is another way of saying that proper *public* education in the deliberative ways of responsible citizenship is a key part of forming "a more perfect Union."

Although the Constitution of 1787 embodied a better process of government and was, thus, mechanically a more perfect union than the Articles of Confederation, it also sought qualitative improvement—could the union be "amiable" and "harmonious," for example? If one understands the full, rich sense implicit in the idea of "a more perfect Union," then, it is clear that the original intent of the Constitution had in view complex nourishments by a variety of federal, state, and private agencies of the nation's capacity to work harmoniously at its public business. Again, the details were left for a self-governing people to settle in their legislative assemblies.

The Constitution also aspired to an idea of justice above its cynical definition as "the interest of the stronger." It aspired to fairness, equity, compassion, and "minding one's own business" diligently and responsibly, rather than corruption, inequity, arbitrary privilege, and greed. Although the details of the idea, in the 1790s as in the 1990s, might be contestable, this perennial problem of precise definition in fact highlights a large agreed-upon core: some practices are clearly corrupt and unfair, while others are not. Common sense affirms the idea of the general distinction even if the exact point of separation is not always clear. Like the founders, we can readily affirm today the relative justice or lack of it, and the aspects of life where it exists to a greater or lesser degree, in various polities. In the eighteenth century were land tenure policies more just in New England or in France? In the twentieth century has the treatment of accused persons been more equitable in Great Britain or in Chile? Were the needs of hungry people in the eighteenth century dealt with more justly in Holland or in Russia? Or in modern times in the People's Republic of China or in Ethiopia? Were elections more corrupt in the Britain of Lord North or in the Pennsylvania of Benjamin Franklin? In Canada or in Mexico in the 1980s? Surely there are universal standards of justice that help define the public good. And in seeking to "establish Justice" in the United States, the drafters of the Constitution intended that our public affairs be han-dled fairly, equitably, and compassionately, in accord with those standards—however far actual practice has been from that ideal in 1787 or at any time since.

The meaning of the phrase "domestic Tranquility" is also clear. A society possessing it, the founders understood, would be orderly, obedient to law, safe, peaceful, and characterized by a certain quietude and unaggressiveness. It would not be chaotic, lawless, and violent, its people filled with fear and discord and hostility. A government, then, pursuing the public good, would accentuate the first qualities and diminish the latter. The inclusion of both justice and tranquility as part of the public good, furthermore, helps diminish possible shortcomings of each standing alone. Tranquility attuned to justice is more likely to avoid the delusion of mere quiescence (the "order" of the prison), and justice tempered by a tranquil spirit is less likely to be hard-eyed and strident. These combined results, as apparent to the founders as to us, were part of their larger "reflection and choice" in establishing the new Constitution.

To "provide for the common defence," especially in a dangerous world of sovereign (and anarchic) nations, is also an undeniable part of the public good. The devastations of invasion, war, conquest, and colonialism—the effects often of inadequate common defense—are obvious, as are the benefits of a society's control over its own destiny. Although warding off conquest may be beyond the power (temporarily at least) of *any* government of a given polity (one thinks of India in 1759, Poland in 1939, or Hungary in 1956), this in no way denies the palpable difference between the conquered and the unconquered state (as the same illustrations again attest). That is, a government that possesses the wisdom, diplomatic skill, military effectiveness, internal vigor, and willing support of the people (what Jefferson meant in 1801 when he declared that the United States had "the strongest government on earth") necessary to assure national integrity is surely better than one that leaves the nation vulnerable to violent and predatory neighbors. This was part of the public good sought in the Constitution of 1787, as *Federalist Papers* Nos. 2–5 argue specifically.

Promoting the general welfare is perhaps the broadest, most positive aspect of the public good asserted in the Constitution—but, since it leads to less agreement on specifics, it is also the most controversial. It has, throughout American history, provoked disputes over funding the public debt, tariff policy, sale of public lands, control of "trusts," sale of alcoholic beverages, achieving full employment, and, more recently over the welfare system, allocation of resources, industrial policy, and so on. These were and are not matters on which a free and diverse people are likely to reach easy policy agreement. Indeed, some are so problematic that many observers (including some of the founding generation) argue that government ought to reduce its initiatives and responsibilities regarding "the general Welfare." Such diminishment may in fact, at times, be the best way to "promote the general Welfare," but Madison, for example, would have seen this as a reflective choice of government itself, not a dogma. General guidelines, though, that distinguish better from worse are discernible. Surely prosperity and beauty in a society are better than stagnation, poverty, and ugliness. With thoughtful, well-informed, and public-spirited attention, it was the "original intent" that by using governments under the Constitution (local, state, and national) society might move toward the better of those directions.

The two great interpreters of the Constitution and formulators of the nation's purpose during its early years, Alexander Hamilton and Thomas Jefferson, reveal how much ideas of the general welfare can differ, but they also demonstrate both that the Constitution intended active pursuit of the general welfare and that many and varied actions are possible within its clauses. Hamilton's plans for the new nation, proposed by the executive branch to the legislature as the Constitution provided, amounted to a comprehensive, government-guided effort to promote the general welfare. Funding the public debt (incurred by the nation in winning its independence) was a plan to at once put government finances in order, provide for the expansion of credit and enterprise, and promote honest exchange both inside the country and with foreign nations. Hamilton proposed the national bank and defended its constitutionality, both as a means to control credit and money in the country and to make clear the broad powers of the federal government. Finally, the Report on Manufactures was nothing less than an industrial policy to guide the nation's economic expansion. Hamilton thought both that the Constitution conferred implicitly on the federal government the powers necessary to enhance the general welfare and that it was primarily the responsibility of the executive branch to initiate and promote the requisite plans. The Constitution, Hamilton asserted, "ought to be construed liberally in advancement of the public good. This rule does not depend on the particular form of government, . . . but on the nature and objects of government itself, . . . [in order that] national exigencies . . . be provided for, national inconveniences obviated, [and] national prosperity promoted."[11] Although Hamilton was a zealous friend of capitalism and free enterprise, he always assumed they were to be subsumed, guided by the government as part of its larger responsibility to "promote the general Welfare."

Jefferson did not disagree generally with this sense of wide governmental responsibility, but rather he had substantially different ideas of what the general welfare consisted of and what government (at various levels) ought to do, or not do, about it—as the Constitution intended would be the case in the free politics of the new nation. He believed as much as Hamilton that the *intention to seek* the general welfare by at least some citizens and other officials would improve the *quality* of public-policy decisions. As Hamilton himself noted, when they both served in Washington's first cabinet Jefferson "was generally for a large construction of the Executive authority."[12] As secretary of state he helped design the new "federal city," devised plans for weights, measures, and coinage, proposed a systematic trade policy to combat British commercial restrictions, and in many ways helped organize the power of the federal government to promote the general welfare. Earlier he had proposed "republican-izing" laws in Virginia to establish a public school system, gradually abolish slavery, revise the penal code, and change land tenure, while in the Continental Congress he had urged establishing a library of Congress and had helped write the ordinance for government of the Northwest Territories—all proposals for the active pursuit by government of the general welfare. Later, as president, he established a military academy, proposed that Congress found a national university, and envisioned a system of "public education, roads, rivers, canals, and such other objects of public improvement" as might be authorized under existing powers of Congress or by constitutional amendment.[13]

These proposals arose as Jefferson saw that federal government receipts from imposts (taxes on imports) and land sales seemed, in peacetime, likely to exceed expenditures. What would be more patriotic, more useful to the general welfare, the president proposed, than that "public efforts may be directed honestly to the public good?" Jefferson in executive office thus accepted broad responsibility for pursuing the general welfare—and differed from Hamilton mainly about how different levels and branches of government could best serve that end. Jefferson asserted that he was for a federal "government rigorously frugal and simple, [and] . . . not for transferring all the powers of the States to the General government, and all those of that government to the executive branch." He also declared, though, that he intended to preserve "the general government in its whole constitutional vigor" and that the republican governments provided for under the Constitution would be "the strongest government on earth" because of the willing support and participation of all citizens.[14] Thus, Hamilton and Jefferson each took seriously the injunction in the preamble to promote the general welfare, through the active guidance of the federal government (Hamilton's preference) or through emphasis on the essential instrumentality of state and local government (Jefferson's preference).

In using phrases like "public good" and "general welfare," as the founders did all the time, they had in mind something much more commonly understood and agreed upon than is usual in the late twentieth century, where the concepts are often either scorned entirely as having no objective meaning or defined simply as the outcome of "conflict-of-interest" politics and the legislative process in a free and democratic polity. Committed generally to concepts of natural law and to religious or philosophic traditions that argued for objective, even universal understandings of moral and political principles, the framers and ratifiers of the Constitution would have supposed that those principles were the foundations of the public good (see chapter 2). The idea was not that such concepts would produce agreement on all questions of public policy; in a free and diverse society of course there would be disagreement. Rather, these principles, generally thought of as natural law, would both provide guidance on particular policy questions and in the long run lead toward "harmonizing sentiments" (Jefferson's phrase)[15] in the nation as a whole.

The point is clearer in the universally understood meaning of the term viewed as the opposite of the public good: corruption. It meant much more than giving or taking bribes or the taint of other forms of dishonest exchange or exercise of power by public officials. The term *corruption* carried the full classical connotation of the displacement of the public good by private interest. The distinction was essentially a moral one defined by the intent either to seek the public good, which made one a good ruler or good citizen, or to seek private or special interests, which was corrupt. Lord Bolingbroke, whose writings on politics and morality were widely known in eighteenth-century America, asked "what expectation can be entertained of raising a disinterested public spirit among men who have no other principle than that of private interest, who are individuals rather than fellow citizens, who prey on one another, and are, in a state of civil society, much like to Hobbes's men in his supposed state of nature?" This private orientation, Bolingbroke insisted, destroyed "that public morality which distinguishes a good from a bad citizen."[16] Supreme Court Justice James Wilson made the same point in the United States three years after he had played a leading role in drafting the Constitution: "By the will and by the interest of the community, every private will and every private interest must be bound and overruled."[17]

Bolingbroke and Wilson were not denying, or even particularly condemning greedy, factional, and self-interested motivations—those qualities were indelible parts of human nature and could provide useful entrepreneurial energies in society at large. What they condemned, and found poisonous to the general welfare, was the converting of "a factious habit and a factious notion . . . into a notion of policy and honor."[18] That is, the basic corruption of a polity came not only from the widespread presence of self-interested motivations in rulers or citizens (troublesome enough but not entirely eradicable), but more seriously from the *celebration* of those traits understood as the clever balancing and manipulation of a wide variety of special interests (called factions in the eighteenth century) as useful to government. This combined acceptance and celebration of the energies of self-interest in government, then, was the essence of corruption because it negated emphasis on public spirit, the only perspective that could result in the promotion of the general welfare.

Madison made the point explicitly in *Federalist* No. 10. Factions, understood as any number of citizens "united and activated by some common impulse of passion, or of interest, adverse to the rights of other citizens, or to the permanent and aggregate interests of the community," were "sown in the nature of man . . . and [were] everywhere brought into different degrees of activity . . . in civil society." In a large country, however, they could be expected to counteract each other, thus preventing the realization of the corrupt or tyrannical intentions of any one or conniving group of factions. Furthermore, a large, democratic nation was the best possible "republican remedy for the diseases most incident to republican governments" because it included the largest number of factions and most thoroughly dispersed the power of their influence on government. Madison intended, though, in this "remedy" not that public policy be simply the resultant of these competing and countervailing fractions, but rather that they be *neutralized*, rendered of no effect, in order that deliberative attention be given to "the permanent and aggregate interests of the community," that is, the public good—the phrase appears nine times in *Federalist* No. 10.

The essence of this public-spiritedness, then, was in the first instance an interest in the public, a willingness to take the polity seriously and to adopt a perspective that attempted to see its needs and concerns, what was good for the whole, as identifiable and perhaps distinct from private interests. In a self-governing society this meant that all the citizens, as the ultimate rulers, had a responsibility to seek this perspective and carry it, as much as possible, into discussions of public affairs, into the voting place, into any formal public office they might hold, and into any other informal civic activities in which they might engage. The founders knew, as we do, that human beings are not likely to entirely achieve such a public perspective and that individuals in a free society have a right to advocate their private needs in public arenas. But these limitations and private intentions are ancient facts of life, tendencies to be curbed, Madison and his colleagues thought, rather than qualities to be encouraged. In this way, the classical ideal of the benefits derived from a society guided by a wise and good leader might be in some degree achievable in a democratic society.

Finally, the preamble of the Constitution enjoins that the union "secure the Blessings of liberty"—a charge to be subsequently clarified by the addition of a bill of rights. The freedoms and rights thus set forth—freedom of religion, speech, and press, freedom from unreasonable search and seizure, the right of habeas corpus, the prohibition on ex post facto laws and bills of attainder, the right to trial by jury, and so on—define the more formal "Blessings of Liberty." These liberties, though, no matter how morally obligatory or theoretically "unalienable," are made real in any society only when accepted and given effect by government. When courts and their officers prevent invasions of religious liberty, when government disciplines itself in assuring the rights of the accused, and when the enforcement of law makes our streets safe, then, and only then, are we really free to worship as we please, to prevent our unlawful imprisonment, to walk the streets at will, and so on. As Joseph Galloway warned Americans in 1775, to be free meant not "protection from foreign powers only, but also against the private injustice of individuals, the arbitrary and lawless power of the state, and of every subordinate authority" (see chapter 12). Only, too, in a government-sustained free society can creativity, enterprise, pluralism, and diversity truly flourish. Government cannot itself accomplish those things, but its proper conduct and encouragement can make them more possible. Conversely, bad governments can impose repression, brutality, and conformity: that is, they can deny liberty in a way that denies its manifest blessings to the people. Again, the supremely important core of the idea of liberty is both clear in its meaning and profoundly dependent on the kind of government any society has. The press gangs, the storm troopers, the secret police, the lynch mobs, and the concentration camps of history leave little doubt about what the blessings of liberty are—or about the critical impact good or bad government can have on our lives.

By encapsulating these components of the public good, then, the preamble of the Constitution makes clear the assumption of the framers that one could, in broad terms, define a "good society." With this understanding in mind, it becomes possible, and even obligatory, to set forth some general responsibilities of government. These responsibilities, furthermore, instead of being the charge of a benevolent despot or mandarin official, were, under the republican principle, thrust upon the people themselves. It was this inclusion of the active effort and power of the people in the affairs of a government entrusted with broad responsibility for pursuing the public good that attuned the Constitution most fundamentally to the aspirations of the American Revolution.

8

FEDERALISM

The final enduring principle of the Constitution, federalism, is a unique understanding and arrangement of governing powers arising both as a response to the particular geography and history of the new nation and as an effort to give practical effect to the ideas of republicanism, liberty, and the public good. The essence of federalism is the preservation of both the state and national governments in their important and proper powers. As Jefferson defined it in his first inaugural address, it meant "the support of the state governments in all their rights, as the most competent administrations for our domestic concerns and the safest bulwarks against anti-republican tendencies; [and] the preservation of the general government in its whole constitutional vigor, as the sheet anchor of our peace at home and safety abroad."[1]

The size of the new United States, and the isolated nature of the former colonies, often more connected each with Britain than with each other, had prevented the establishment of anything like a unitary state on the French, Chinese, or even British models. In fact, the first "union," established ad hoc, 1774–1781, and then given formal expression in the Articles of Confederation, was really a league of states where "delegates," representing governments (not the people), assembled to conduct common business—the usual meaning of both "confederation" and "federation" in the eighteenth century. This origin and experience attached the people firmly to their state governments and helped them develop habits of local government understood as vital to republicanism and liberty. The states were important existing realities, useful agencies both to enhance self-government and to protect the liberties, negative and positive, of the people. Hence, any general government was bound to respect and ensure the existence of the states.

With its emphasis on division of power between the state and national governments, moreover, the idea of federalism was an important part of the larger, and growing, ideology of balance, or separation of powers, seen as essential to liberty. Resting on a wide range of seventeenth- and eighteenth-century historical and philosophical writing culminating in Montesquieu's *Spirit of the Laws* (1748), liberty had come increasingly to be seen to result from a balance of power or forces that prevented any one from being dominant; that is, tyrannical. Although the idea of balance, check, or separation of powers came in many varieties and guises, from emphasis on empowering the different orders in a still-feudal society to a more modern attention to the different branches or functions of government, the underlying idea was always the same: only power could check power. In Voltaire's epigram (1733) celebrated on both sides of the Atlantic, "liberty was born in England of the quarrels between tyrants."[2]

In this understanding, English constitutional history was viewed as the slow evolution of limits on the power of the crown. From Magna Charta (1215) on, and especially in the Glorious Revolution of 1689, the growth of liberty in England was seen as proportional to the steadily more effective counterbalancing of the once-absolute power of the Plantagenets, Tudors, and Stuarts. After 1689, when the Crown in England agreed to rule according to laws made by Parliament, in both Great Britain and her North American colonies, writers linked the maintenance of liberty with the perpetuation of the balance between king, lords, and commons. The general acceptance of this settlement in eighteenth-century Great Britain led James Otis of Massachusetts to declare in 1764 that Britain's was "the best national civil constitution in the world. . . . See here the grandeur of the British Constitution! See the wisdom of our ancestors! The *supreme* legislative, and the supreme *executive*, are a perpetual check and balance to each other." Foreign observers, most notably Voltaire and Montesquieu, had also endorsed this view of British government.

Although Otis emphasized, as did most eighteenth-century writers, the checks between the branches of government, he went on to praise as the particular bulwark of colonial liberty the power of their "subordinate legislatures" to share tax and other law-making authority with "the grand legislature of the nation." If these dual balances were sustained, Otis thought, it "would firmly unite all parts of the British empire, in the greatest peace and prosperity; and render it invulnerable and perpetual."[3] This emphasis, linking balanced power with liberty and prosperity and distinguishing Britain from the "absolute tyrants" of Asia and Africa and the "arbitrary authority" of France and Prussia,[4] was a constant theme in the prerevolutionary debates and left devotion to devices for the balancing of powers firmly planted in American political thought.

John Adams did more than any other American revolutionary to underscore ideas of balance and separation of powers in American constitutional thought and practice. Thomas Paine's famous pamphlet *Common Sense* provoked Adams to clarify his thoughts on the importance of counterpoising powers. Paine had condemned British government as "so exceedingly complex" that it confused the people about "the head from which their suffering springs." Instead, following the principle that "the more simple anything is, the less liable it is to be disordered, and the easier repaired when disordered," Paine proposed equitably apportioned, annually elected, unicameral legislatures to govern both the colonies individually and the union as a whole. He asserted that a constitutional convention, having settled on such simple, equitable frames of government, would then merely have to "draw the line of business and jurisdiction between them" to provide "a mode of government that contained the greatest sum of individual happiness, with the least national expense." Paine's almost offhand mention of drawing "the line of business and jurisdiction" between the state and national governments overlooked, of course, the long, intense, and complex debate on precisely that point in the prerevolutionary dispute over the respective powers of the colonial legislatures and of the Parliament in London.[5]

When John Adams read *Common Sense* in February 1776 he praised its fervent call for independence for the colonies, but otherwise had serious reservations. Paine's "Notions, and Plans for Continental Government," Adams thought, showed Paine "has a better Hand at pulling down than building." He had "very inadequate Ideas of what is proper and necessary to be done, in order to form Constitutions for single Colonies, as well as a great Model of Union for the whole." Late in life Adams called Paine's constitutional proposals "*a Star of Disaster*," a "System of Anarchy" that was so "without any restraint or even an attempt at any Equilibrium or Counterpoise, that it must produce confusion and every Evil Work."[6]

In fact, Adams had a fundamental disagreement with Paine on the nature and purpose of government. To Paine's general observation that while society itself was a blessing, "Government even in its best state is but a necessary evil, . . . like dress . . . the badge of lost innocence," Adams replied that "the blessings of society depend entirely on the constitutions of government, which are generally institutions that last for many generations." The "best of governments," he went on, was a republic with "a particular arrangement of the powers of society . . . which is best contrived to secure an impartial and exact execution of the laws." To Adams, then, Paine's simple idea of government was a "Star of Disaster" falling toward tyranny and oppression because it failed to see that a limited government of balanced powers was the only way to assure the just laws that undergirded meaningful personal liberty.

In a short pamphlet entitled *Thoughts on Government*, printed in April 1776 to counteract Paine's ideas and thus provide better guidance for the new states and federation in drafting constitutions, Adams explained his idea of checks and balances. After emphasizing the republican principle wherein equal representation in a legislature chosen in fair and uncorrupt elections would produce a law-making body that would "think, feel, reason, and act" like the people, Adams went on to explain why this, though basic, was a far from complete plan of government. A unicameral legislature would reflect "all the vices, follies, and frailties" of human nature, would "make arbitrary laws for its own interest," and would assure its own self-perpetuation. Thus the legislature should have two houses, the executive should be separate and have a veto over the laws, and the judiciary should be assured independence of each by having fixed, adequate salaries, and tenure during good behavior. Although Adams had in mind in these proposals governments for the individual states, they were applicable as well to the "continental constitution." Adams recommended further that "its authority should sacredly be confined to . . . war, trade, disputes between colony and colony, the post office, and . . . unappropriated lands."[7] In thus urging balance both among branches of government and between national and state authority, Adams foreshadowed much of the Constitution of 1787.

Adhering to these general propositions, Adams took the lead in drafting the Massachusetts Constitution of 1780, which in turn was a model both for other state constitutions and for the federal Constitution of 1787. He stated its fundamental principle in the preamble: "In the government of the Commonwealth of Massachusetts the legislative, executive, and judicial power shall be placed in separate departments, to the end that it might be a government of laws and not of men." His basic argument was that all the vices of government—tyranny, corruption, neglect of the common good, and so on—flowed from the concentration of power, whether in the hands of a monarch or a simple, unicameral legislature. In arranging powers in the Massachusetts Constitution, then, Adams carefully and clearly specified the distinct functions of the two-house legislature, the strongly empowered executive, and the independent judiciary. The constitution also provided explicitly that the people, as members of "a free, sovereign, and independent state," could devolve "to the United States of America" such powers as it might choose to "expressly delegate" to it.[8] Adams, of course, was making the usual revolutionary assumptions that the people were the basic source of sovereignty, that the states were their primary governments, and that they could also, as sovereigns, convey to the union such powers as they saw fit.

Adams's summary of the virtues of separation of powers, set down in his 1787 *Defence of the Constitutions of Government of the United States of America*, referred to the state constitutions, but, as he saw the same principles in the new federal Constitution, he included it in his analysis: "Power is always abused when unlimited and unbalanced. . . . Simple unchecked government is always despotic, whether it be government by a monarch, by Aristocrats, or by the mass of people. All are equally intolerant, cruel, bloody, oppressive, tyrannical. The only sound and lasting government is one so balanced that ambition is made to counteract ambition, power to check power."[9] This understanding, applied by Adams especially to the balance of legislative, executive, and judicial powers soon to be implanted in the federal Constitution of 1787, also included the further dimension of division of power in the federal system of coexisting state and national governments. Both forms of separation of power, moreover, were to Adams essential to liberty in their inherent limitations on tyranny and entirely consistent with the republican principle in so far as the people themselves consented to their inclusion in constitutions they had ratified.

James Madison accepted much of the same emphasis on balance of powers, making it a crucial component of his preparation for helping to draft and ratify the Constitution of 1787. Madison, however, paid less attention to the separation of power among the branches of government, but rather attended especially to the more strictly federal part of the balance, that is, between the national and the state governments. He had begun systematic research in 1786 by compiling a forty-two-page notebook on "Ancient and Modern Confederacies." In it he examined the constitutions of three ancient Greek confederacies, and three modern ones, the Swiss, Dutch, and "Germanic" (the Holy Roman Empire). The major flaw, or "Vice," he saw in each of them was weakness in the general government. Everywhere the parts tended to either overawe or default on the union, causing all the deficiencies attendant on weak and inefficient government: instability, impotence against foreign foes, injustice, corruption, and intrigue. Weakness at the center had left the Greek confederacies easy prey first to Phillip of Macedon and then to Rome, the Swiss union had had to invite in outsiders to settle its internal disputes, and the United Provinces of the Netherlands, though strong in theory, in practice "the Jealousy in each province of its Sovereignty" had caused endless intrigue, inefficiency, and invasion.[10] Thus, though Madison took for granted the separate existence of the states, he saw strengthening the union as the greatest need.

This conviction was confirmed when in the months immediately before the Constitutional Convention Madison pondered "the Vices of the Political System of the United States." In addition to his profound observations about the possibility of good republican government (see chapter 5), it led him again to consider the relation between the states and the general government (the "vices" he enumerated were mainly of the state governments). Madison noticed that in government under the Articles of Confederation, like "in every similar Confederacy," the states "failed to comply with Constitutional requisitions." Furthermore, "in almost every case where any favorite object of a State" opposed federal law, the states simply went their own way. States also often violated treaties with foreign nations, which could cause invasion, "the greatest of public calamities. It ought to be least in the power of any part of the Community to bring on the whole" such a misfortune, Madison thought. Finally, states frequently "trespassed on the rights of each other" and blocked "provision for national seminaries, grants of incorporation for national purposes, and canals and other works of national utility" out of a "perverseness" given effect by the weakness of the Confederation.[11] The fundamental reason for forming a new constitution, then, was to achieve a new balance between the state and national governments that would be more attentive to the needs of the nation as a whole. Only this, Madison believed, would make federation work in the United States where it had so often failed at other times and places.

Madison made his point more generally eighteen months later, after the new Constitution had finally been ratified. "A certain degree of impartiality or the appearance of it, is necessary in the most despotic Governments. In republics, this may be considered as the vital principle of the Administration. And in a *federal* Republic founded on local distinctions involving local jealousies, it ought to be attended to with still more scrupulous exactness." Madison thus began to define with some preciseness the particular and, to him, unique quality needed in the American *federal* republic: though remaining faithful to "local distinctions" for all the valid, liberty-sustaining reasons hallowed in a revolution against a centralized tyranny, the key to preserving them was an adequate national power capable of defending the "local distinctions" from foreign foes, of accomplishing "works of national ability," and of achieving an "impartiality" among the component parts consistent with the common good. As he explained to George Washington on the eve of the Constitutional Convention, he "sought for some middle ground, which may at once support a due supremacy of the national authority, and not exclude the local authorities wherever they can be subordinately useful."[12]

Madison's emphasis on "due supremacy of the national authority" and on the "subordination" of the states, however, left him much more a "nationalist" than many of his convention colleagues. The Virginia Plan, for example, drafted by Madison and the basic working document of the convention, was powerfully nationalist. It gave the national legislature power to "legislate in all cases to which the separate States are incompetent; . . . to negative all laws passed by the several states, contravening in the opinion of the National Legislature the articles of Union; and to call forth the force of the Union against any member of the Union failing to fulfill its duty under the articles thereof."[13] As many of his colleagues realized, and as he himself came eventually to acknowledge, these provisions shifted the balance too far toward national authority. The convention then switched to specified rather than general powers of Congress and to a supreme law clause that gave a national judiciary implicit power to uphold federal law. Instead of Madison's clumsy proposal for a legislative power virtually to declare war on disobeying states, these clauses adjusted the balance by moving closer to a system of divided sovereignty that became the hallmark of American federalism. In fact, the search for this balance was a constant preoccupation of the convention, and its achievement one of its most creative acts. In a way, the long search for a proper relationship between central authority and "local distinctions," which had been crucial to prerevolutionary debates over the respective powers of London on the one hand and the colonial capitals on the other and had remained at issue as the independent states and the Continental Congress had formed constitutions, had reached a culmination. One more try, to be severely tested and redefined in the Civil War and then to be sustained to the present day, was to be made at discovering how to give effect to the idea of *E pluribus unum*.

Madison, speaking as "Publius," explained in *Federalist* Nos. 37 and 39 the basic need to "combine the requisite stability and energy in government with the inviolable attention due to liberty and to the republican form." Combining these elements meant having some power exercised at the national level while preserving some real authority to state and local governments, requiring, as the Constitution provided, that the "national . . . jurisdiction extend to certain enumerated objects only, and . . . [that] the several states [have] a residuary and inviolable sovereignty over all other objects."[14] Although the effective powers of the federal government have, under the pressure of modern conditions, grown enormously in the twentieth century, the continued existence of the states, of a federal system, is unquestioned. Indeed, they remain as cherished repositories of local and regional prerogatives and are thus a vital part of the separation of powers imbedded in American constitutional government.

The root idea of federalism, then, is that the states are to be retained, forever and inviolate, both as governments in their own right and as equal participants in the federal system. The one amendment that is forbidden in the Constitution is that no state "shall be deprived of its equal suffrage in the Senate." There is no way, under the Constitution and in keeping with its intent, that the states can be abolished or even reduced in their basic equality and power in the Senate. The Constitution is thus indelibly *federal*; in fact, that special quality in the Constitution is so prominent, and so uniquely complex, that it has become the new definition of the word itself. Federalism no longer means, at least in the United States, a government consisting of delegates from other governments, but rather now commonly means simply the "mixed" form established in the Constitution of 1787 and explained in *The Federalist Papers*. Just as much as in the indelibility of republicanism, and attention to the public good, the Constitution of 1787 makes no sense without, cannot exist apart from, the idea of federalism. (Despite the misnomer "antifederalist," those who opposed the Constitution were even more attached to federalism than those who in 1787–1788 adroitly called themselves "federalists," knowing it was an idea much favored in the nation. The term "federalist" refers to those, including Madison, who supported the constitution, not to the Federalist political party of the 1790s, to which Madison did not belong.)

In fact, "the most arduous task" at the Constitutional Convention, Publius noted, was "marking the proper line of partition between the authority of the general and that of the state governments." At the convention, the difficulties created by "the interfering pretensions of the larger and smaller States" were added to those of understanding clearly the purpose of the federal system and of finding the right words to describe it. Compromises were necessary, Publius explained, that "sacrificed theoretical propriety to the force of extraneous considerations."[15] The delegates groped for the proper balance between local and national authority that had troubled government for 150 years and that had been at the center of the prerevolutionary debate between London and her

North American dependencies. Was it true, as Tory pamphleteers had claimed before 1776, "that there must be in every state a supreme legislative authority, universal in its extent, over every member" and that once this authority was settled, "its jurisdiction cannot be apportioned; it is transcendent and entire"? Was any effort at "divided sovereignty" thus a contradiction, even a farce?[16] Although Americans after 1776 understood the logical difficulties, they remained determined to achieve a practical division—to enhance republicanism, liberty, and the public good.

The answer, Publius explained, was a constitution that "in strictness, [was] neither national nor federal . . . , but a composition of both." Its mode of adoption had been federal, in that the states as political entities had ratified it and set it in motion. In its legislature, one branch, the House of Representatives, was national in that it was "elected immediately by the great body of the people," while the Senate, which "derived its powers from the States as political and coequal societies," was strictly federal. The fact that in its "ordinary and most essential proceedings," such as collection of taxes and enforcement of its own laws, the general government acted directly on the people "in their individual capacities" made it national. In many other respects, such as the election of the president, the division of legislative powers, and the amendment process, the Constitution was "partly federal and partly national." This federal-national "composite," moreover, was entirely republican in that all of its powers were "derived . . . directly or indirectly from the . . . people." It thus remained faithful, Publius pointed out, to "the fundamental principle of the [American] Revolution . . . to rest all our political experiments on the capacity of mankind for self-government."[17]

The defense of state equality in the Senate revealed especially the powerful sway of the idea in the founding era. It was, Madison writing as Publius conceded, "the result of compromise between the opposite pretensions of the large and small states." Since the alternative to this breach of principle was probably no union at all, prudence required (Madison seemed here to justify his acquiescence in what he and James Wilson in the convention had termed "vicious . . . improper . . . pernicious . . . first principles") "embrace [of] the lesser evil." "Instead of indulging a fruitless anticipation of the possible mischiefs" attendant on this, Madison urged consideration of "the advantageous consequences which may qualify the sacrifice." The equal vote of states in the Senate "allowed to each state . . . at once a constitutional recognition of the portion of sovereignty remaining in the individual states and an instrument for preserving that residuary sovereignty." It would also guard "against an improper consolidation of the States into one simple republic," an objective cherished by the large states as much as by the small ones. Finally, Madison hoped the Senate would be an "additional impediment . . . against improper acts of legislation" and the "excess of law-making" to which republican governments seemed unhappily prone. The "complicated check on legislation," requiring that "no law or resolution can . . . be passed without the concurrence, first, of a majority of the people, and then of a majority of the States," made the federal structure of the Senate a powerful and useful part of the system of checks and balances.[18] Thus, the federal principle embodied in the Senate, though in tension with the idea of majority rule, was seen as sustaining the wisdom and meaningful liberty that went with stability in legislation.

The electoral system for choosing the president, which makes the election, in effect, the sum of separate elections in each of the states, further enshrines the federal principle. Ballots are cast in a way that produces, in the first instance, a *state* result—and that is true whether the electoral college worked as was intended (it never has), or is the meaningless formality it now is. These state tallies often result from campaigns to "carry the state" for a certain candidate, thus emphasizing the integrity and power of a candidate or party in each state. And only when these state contests have been decided (influenced in some degree, of course, as was always intended, by what is said and done elsewhere in the country) are the results added to determine the overall winner. The electoral system for the president simply cannot function unless the states exist as distinct political entities, and it assures that during a presidential campaign there will be a necessary and deliberate focus on the states as such—as a federal, as opposed to a national, system requires.

Yet another way the Constitution recognizes the principle of federalism is in the list of seventeen specific powers of Congress. Rather than adopting such sweeping legislative empowerment as that claimed for Parliament in the Declaratory Act of 1766 ("authority to make laws and statutes . . . in all cases whatsoever"), or even in the Virginia Plan as first presented to the Constitutional Convention ("legislate in all cases to which the separate states are incompetent"), the Constitution grants only specified powers to the Congress. By clear intent, the residual, undefined powers remain with the states. Furthermore, the "necessary and proper" clause, at the end of the specified powers of Congress, has been suspect and controversial since "Brutus" complained about it in the ratification debates (1788) and Jefferson sought to narrow its meaning in arguing the unconstitutionality of the national bank (1791). These reservations reveal the implicit intention in the federal system to secure a meaningful division of powers between state and national governments. The implication was made explicit, moreover, in the uncontroversial Tenth Amendment, revealing the universal acknowledgment in the founding era of the prominence and lasting importance of the states in the full pattern of American government. The Constitution does not suppose, then, that either the pursuit of the public good or the encouragement of citizenship are fully attended to—or even mainly so—at the national level. Rather, the assumption was, and is, that to achieve the manifold benefits that come from good self-government, the United States needs a federal system where, in Madison's words in *Federalist* No. 45, "the powers reserved to the several states will extend to all the objects, which, in the ordinary course of affairs, concern the lives, liberties, and properties of the people, and the internal order, improvement, and prosperity of the state."[19]

The framers also intended, though, that the new general government would indeed, in part, be national. The Constitution and the laws and treaties made under it are "the supreme law of the land," and all executive, legislative, and judicial officers of both the state and federal governments are to be bound by oath to support the Constitution, "anything in the Constitution or laws of any State to the contrary notwithstanding." As the antifederalists complained of emphatically, and as Publius affirmed and celebrated, the new Constitution *did* alter fundamentally the old, confederated nature of the union—it was now to be "more perfect," that is, more responsive to the needs of a national polity with common goals and purposes. Although many people resisted the extent of this change at the time, and though some leaders and theorists (at least until the Civil War) have interpreted "states' rights" to virtually deny the changed character of the union, the portent of the events of 1787–1789 is nonetheless unmistakable: the United States had a government "partly national"; its powers, derived from the people, were extensive and, in the opinion of Madison, Marshall, Jackson, Lincoln, and many others, sufficient to maintain its integrity against the gravest threats of nullification and secession.

But a basic tension, even ambiguity, remained. The division of powers in the Constitution amounted to (though it was never so called) a dividing up of the *sovereign* power—an idea both logically dubious (sovereign means "supreme," or "unlimited" power, so how can it be divided?) and repudiated by the dominant political and legal thought of the day. Traditionally, the sovereign—king or emperor—held full power over his realm and subjects. He made the final decisions in the polity. Even in Great Britain, where the monarchy was a limited one, the functions of government were exercised formally on behalf of the king; he had granted certain powers to Parliament and to his ministers, but the sovereignty still resided in his act and his writ. The "king in Parliament" possessed unlimited legislative power. After independence in the United States "the people" were increasingly thought of as "sovereign," but that did not solve the practical problem of what governments exercised what powers on their behalf. The federal Constitution of 1787, coming as it did *after* the state constitutions were already in effect, was in one sense simply the document wherein the people authorized redivision of their sovereignty (whatever the logical contradictions). It sought throughout to state clearly the federal powers, and those denied respectively to the states and the federal government, as though the people themselves, by ratifying the Constitution, had thus decided which level of government exercised which "parts" of their sovereignty. Even the declaring of the Constitution to be "supreme law," and its authoritative interpretation by the U.S. Supreme Court, does not negate the acknowledged final power of the states in many aspects of government. And it is this complex, ultimately indeterminate system (with sovereignty divided, there is no sovereign power) that is the essence of federalism, the fourth enduring intent and legacy of the framers. It was also a system of government unique at the time, and it is still odd and unusual in a world where great powers—for example, China, France, Japan, and even Great Britain, to say nothing of the former Soviet Union—typically have far more centralized governments, and whose regional or local subgovernments are not separate sovereignties but rather are creatures of the national government.

Federalism is, moreover, related intimately to the vigor of republicanism, liberty, and the public good. By recognizing local units of government, a federal system encourages attention to civic matters at a level most likely to elicit the "public spirit" of citizens vital to good republican government. Furthermore, by dividing the functions of government a federal system protects inherently against the arbitrary and unrestrained exercises of power so dangerous to liberty. As Jefferson explained in 1816 after observing more than twenty-five years of government under the Constitution, the "liberty and rights of man [are] . . . destroyed . . . [by] concentrating all cares and powers into one body [like] . . . the autocrats of Russia and France." To assure human freedom,

the secret will be found to be in the making [of man] himself the depository of the powers respecting himself, . . . and delegating only what is beyond his competence by a synthetical process, to higher and higher orders of functionaries, so as to trust fewer and fewer powers in proportion as the trustees become more and more oligarchical. . . . Let the national government be entrusted with the defence of the nation, and its foreign and federal relations; the state governments with the civil rights, laws, police, and administration of what concerns that state generally; the counties with . . . local concerns, and each ward direct the interests within itself. . . . This would form a gradation of authorities, standing each on the basis of law, holding every one to its delegated share of powers, and constituting truly a system of fundamental balances and checks for the government.[20]

Federalism, that is, encouraged an effective participation by citizens in local affairs that would nourish a public-spiritedness essential to good self-government, provide a means for protecting individual rights, and be an essential part of the system of checks and balances.

In the eyes of the framers federalism was much more than a compromise made necessary by the previous existence of the states. By requiring a dispersal of power hostile to tyranny, the federalists hoped under the Constitution itself to prevent what antifederalists said would be "a hasty stride to Universal Empire," flattering to ambitious men, "but fatal to the liberties of the people."[21] Federalism was a new and creative "composite," as Madison explained in *Federalist* No. 39, that would both allow energetic national government in the public interest and ensure meaningful self-government at the local level.

To sustain four principles, then—republicanism, liberty, the public good, and federalism—is the heart of the philosophy of the Constitution. It is a relatively simple document planting permanently basic propositions, yet providing flexibility for later generations to make their own laws (and even some amendments). Of course a constitution designed to last would have to permit legislatures of later ages to pass laws adapting to circumstances unimaginable in 1787. It is improper, then, either to expect to find a detailed "original intent" on various questions of contemporary policy, or to assert that there is no meaningful way to apply "original intent" to current problems, times and circumstances having changed so much. The very idea of the Constitution insists on a middle way: there *are* enduring principles that, properly understood, provide essential guidelines for contemporary public affairs. These basic principles are as relevant and important to the good of humankind in the 1990s as they were in the 1790s. The whole ethos of the Constitution makes no sense unless we accept the reality of such principles. Yet, at the same time our comparatively short Constitution clearly intends that statute law respond to new and unanticipated circumstances. Although the Constitution must adjust to the times, the times, we might say, must also adjust to the Constitution— because it is a *constitution*.

9
FEDERALISTS AND ANTIFEDERALISTS

The philosophy of the Constitution, and its foundation on the four principles of republicanism, liberty, the public good, and federalism, is revealed in the ratification debate of 1787–1788 and especially in the argument and language of its principal defender, Publius, in *The Federalist Papers*. The crucial starting point is that, like Aristotle, both Publius and his antifederalist critics were conditional democrats. They were for or against the ideas of majority rule, representation, broad suffrage, and so on in so far as those processes seemed likely to result in order, freedom, justice, prosperity, and the other broad purposes of the Constitution. The antifederalists paid particular attention to keeping legislatures in close contact with the people, both to encourage public virtue in the citizenry and to keep legislators mindful of the well-being of those for whom they made laws. The federalists paid more attention to institutional devices for discouraging abuse of power, bringing wise and able leaders into the government, and refining the will of the people. But the objective was the same; somehow to sustain the republican principle. In modern terms, both friends and foes of the Constitution were democrats, believers in government by the people.

The profound question was, and is: who were the wiser democrats? Two hundred years of relatively successful government, steadily enlarging the right to participate as the founders provided, may seem to validate the Constitution and its defenders. On the other hand, a polity closer to the antifederalist ideal of vital local government and intimate understanding between rulers and ruled might have encouraged the evolution of, in Aristotelian terms, an even better society.

The antifederalists had a positive idealism of their own, a republican vision they believed to be far closer to the purpose of the American Revolution than the political and commercial ambitions of the federalists. The antifederalists looked to the classical ideal of the small republic where virtuous, self-reliant citizens managed their own affairs and shunned the power and glory of empire. To them, the victory in the American Revolution meant not so much the chance to become a wealthy world power, but rather the opportunity to achieve a genuinely republican polity, far from the greed, lust for power, and tyranny that had generally characterized human society. Was it possible, they asked themselves, to found society on other bases and with other aspirations that would nourish the virtue and happiness of all the people? Could they break the self-fulfilling cycle where selfish people needed to be controlled by checks and balances that in turn encouraged more and more self-seeking by the people?

To the antifederalists this meant retaining as much as possible the vitality of local government where rulers and ruled could see, know, and understand each other. Thus they cherished the revolutionary emphasis on state and local councils and committees, and the Articles of Confederation where the central government rested entirely on the states. The idea of self-government was tied inextricably to something like a town-meeting directness or at least a state legislature of many annually elected representatives who would really know the people of their districts. Each district, furthermore, would be a town or ward or region conscious of its own particular identity rather than being some amorphous, arbitrary geographic entity. Only with such intimacy could the trust, goodwill, and deliberation essential to wise and virtuous public life be a reality. Anything else, even though resting in some fashion on the consent of the people, would not really be self-government.

The intense antifederalist suspicions of corruption, greed, and lust for power were directed generally at those who ruled from on high and without restraint. Corruption and tyranny would be rampant as they always had been when those who exercised power felt little connection with the people. This corruption would be as true for representatives as for kings and nobles and bishops. The more remote and distantly powerful a government was, the more visions of imperial Rome or Versailles or London came to mind with all their venality, cynicism, corruption, and neglect of the people. Would some future capital of the United States be as filled with courtiers, courtesans, military heroes, and superfluous officeholders as London or Paris or Saint Petersburg? The antifederalists believed it would be so under a constitution that consolidated power in a central government remote from the people.

On the other hand, legends of the Greek and Roman republics, the maturing ideology of natural rights, and the substantial experience of local self-government in the New World seemed to offer a far more alluring prospect. If the basic decency in human nature, most evident among ordinary people at the local level amid family, church, school, and other nourishing institutions, could impinge directly and continuously on government, then perhaps it too might be kept virtuous and worthy of confidence. Then, instead of endless suspicion of and guarding against the evil and corruption of government, it might be possible to trust it and use it for the public benefit. The result might even be a society where honest, hardworking people could enjoy the fruits of their labor, where institutions encouraged and rested on virtue rather than greed, where officials were servants of the people rather than oppressors, and where peace and prosperity came from vigilant self-confidence rather than from conquest and dominion. Antifederalists saw mild, grassroots, small-scale governments in sharp contrast to the splendid edifice and overweening ambition implicit in the new Constitution. The first left citizens free to live their own lives and to cultivate the virtue (private and public) vital to republicanism, while the second soon entailed taxes and drafts and offices and wars damaging to human dignity and thus fatal to self-government.

The antifederalist ideal emerged most clearly and practically in its understanding of what representation and government by consent could really mean. Instead of seeking to insulate officials from popular influence, as, for example, federalists argued should be done with federal judges, antifederalists sought to ensure the public good by requiring close association. If legislators, rather than federal judges appointed for life, had the power to interpret the Constitution, they would do so "at their peril"; if the people disapproved of the interpretation, they "could remove them."[1] The ideal went beyond a close control of officials by the people. In a truly self-governing society, there would be such dialogue, empathy, and even intimacy that the very distinction between ruler and ruled would tend to disappear. Such a close link between officials and the people would embody the idea of liberty as both security of rights and effective voice in public affairs. The antifederalists groped for mechanisms that would give reality to this idea: how could it be achieved, in substance as well as in form, in a large nation?

For antifederalists the bonds between the people and their representatives had to be trustworthy as well as close. Not only, as Melancton Smith put it in the New York ratifying convention (June 1788), should "representatives resemble those they represent," but they should possess especially the virtues most characteristic of ordinary people: they should be temperate, moral, and of restrained ambition. Smith acknowledged that "the same passions and prejudices govern all men," but it was also true that "circumstances . . . give a cast to human character." The wealthy and the powerful, sad to say, were inclined to cheat customers, disdain honest labor, raise armies, put on social airs, and oppress the people. Could they be expected to rule wisely and justly in the interests of all? Rather, it was necessary that people themselves of the "middling sort," average people, perhaps yeoman farmers, take part in government—even be elected to office in large enough numbers to "set the tone" in the capital. Such people, in the daily round of their occupations, Smith observed, had "less temptations, [and] are inclined by habit, and by the company with whom they associate, to set bounds to their passions and appetites."[2] He envisioned, then, a government of popular confidence and respect, vital at the local levels where the virtues of ordinary people could prevail. This idealism was part, of course, of a moral and civic tradition long familiar in the Western world.

The antifederalists had some such positive goal in mind when they hoped the American Revolution might end the ancient equation of power where arrogant, oppressive, and depraved rulers on one side produced subservience and a gradual erosion of the self-respect, capacities, and virtue of the people on the other side. The result was an increasing corruption and degeneracy in both rulers and ruled. Unless this cycle could be broken, independence would mean little more than the exchange of one tyranny for another. The aspirations of the federalists for commercial growth, westward expansion, increased national power, and effective world diplomacy were in some ways attractive and worthy, but they also fitted an ominous, all-too-familiar pattern of "great, splendid, . . . consolidated government" and "Universal Empire" that the American Revolution had been fought to eradicate. Many antifederalists, inchoately perhaps, were unwilling to abandon this ideal and the hope that the New World might be a genuinely different and better place to live.[3]

The ratification contest, then, was at bottom a debate over the future of the nation. Beneath the disputes about detailed clauses were deep differences over what fulfillment of the American Revolution meant. To the federalists, it meant independence, growth in national power, and prosperity, all within a federal system of government retaining the states and deriving its authority from the people, but also responsive to all the needs and exigencies of respectable, energetic nationhood. This purpose was attractive for large numbers of people of all classes and was in their view a legitimate outgrowth of the Revolution.

The antifederalists, on the other hand, sought a society where virtuous, hardworking, honest men and women lived simply in their own communities, enjoyed their families and their neighbors, were devoted to the common welfare, and had such churches, schools, trade associations, and local governments as they needed to sustain their values and purposes. Although this intention was seldom fully or clearly articulated, it permeates antifederalist writing enough to reveal what their positive ideal was. The quick adoption of the Bill of Rights, the ready acceptance of the new Constitution by former antifederalists, and the Jeffersonian triumph of 1801 with its manifold antifederalist overtones all attest to the vigor and influence of antifederalism and its ability to find some fulfillment even under the document opposed so vehemently in 1787–1788. Those ideas, then, as well as the enticing prospects held out by the federalists, are properly viewed as part of the philosophy of the Constitution.

Nonetheless, despite this urgent advocacy of a political outlook emphasizing the vitality of local government attractive to the roughly 50 percent of voting Americans who supported the antifederalists, ideas about government were in the 1780s moving increasingly away from classical republican models derived from Aristotle, Cicero, and others toward the more liberal, individualistic concepts that would dominate American public life in the nineteenth and twentieth centuries. British seventeenth- and eighteenth-century "moderns" such as Francis Bacon, Thomas Hobbes, John Locke, Bernard Mandeville, Daniel Defoe, David Hume, and Adam Smith gave voice to public philosophies emphasizing rational individuals as the basic parts of the body politic, society as a contract among such individuals, and even the subordination of politics to the dynamic of the private, competitive pursuit of wealth (chapter 4). This spirit and ideology, burgeoning as the Constitution came into being, was articulated, many analysts have asserted, in *Federalist* No. 10. The growth of political parties, the increasing pluralism of society, the proliferation of special-interest groups (Madison's "factions"), and the view of Congress as an arena for conflicts of interest, implicit in the Constitution even if unacknowledged by its drafters and defenders, became the liberal dynamic for two hundred years of American political history.

This interpretation, though, goes too far in seeing the Constitution as a modern, liberal document. It is more proper to see it as shaped, uniquely and creatively, by the tension between a still-vigorous classical republican outlook (often stronger among antifederalists than among federalists) and a new, modern, democratic liberalism. Even Madison's famous "countervailing power" thesis in *Federalist* No. 10, always the point of departure for arguments seeking to ground modern conflict-of-interest politics in the Constitution, actually rests in part on civic republican foundations. Madison stood, in a way, both in the classical republican world and in the modern, liberal world. The theory of counteracting factions does elucidate a quintessential dynamic of liberal politics. But this dynamic, at least in its common twentieth-century version, supposes not the neutralization, the reduction to no effect, of the multiplicity of factions, but rather a result or an outcome reflecting the strife of factions that itself defines public policy. There is little or no room in this modern version for an objective "public good," or, in Madison's words, for "the permanent and aggregate interests of the community."

In fact, Madison was arguing, consistent with the classical republican tradition, that human capacity for reason allowed discernment of natural, universal principles or laws of moral and political right. He, and Jefferson, argued further that a "natural aristocracy"—those (of any sex, race, class, religion, wealth, social position, or occupation) who possessed the requisite knowledge, moral sense, conscience, and judgment—would be able to understand those principles. They hoped that eventually, through the spread of education, virtue-sustaining occupations, rational religion, a responsible press, and experience with local government, everyone in society would possess some of this virtue and reason and hence in some degree be part of the natural aristocracy, qualified, in Aristotelian terms, to govern well.

It is precisely at this point that one observes again the chasm between Madison's natural-law outlook, and modern sensibilities that leave little room for universal principles, or for right discerned by reason, or for an objective idea of the public good (see chapter 3). His very words and structure of argument in *Federalist* No. 10 require that such concepts be taken seriously: he sought to neutralize factions so that the "public good" might be discerned and pursued. (The language and argument of the other "Publiuses," Jay and Hamilton, make the same assumptions.)

Insofar as Publius took the public good seriously (as he surely did) he revealed his continued reliance on both an Aristotelian sense of the broad purposes of government and the classical republican tradition. Publius's scorn for the derelictions of the state legislatures, his praise of the wisdom, stability, and continuity he hoped would characterize the Senate, and his aspiration that men of exceptional talent and public spirit would be elected and appointed to office do not so much manifest a class-conscious elitism as reveal his deep commitment to the goal that self-government also be good government—that is, to "the permanent and aggregate interests of the community."

Publius and many other defenders of the Constitution also were nascent modern liberals and friends of a capitalistic economy in that they understood the merits of free trade, accepted a pluralistic society, knew that free politics was likely to result in the growth of political parties, and saw the dangers of a too-large and too-powerful government. They thus moved toward some political axioms and practices that were sharply at odds with their grounding in Aristotelian and classical republican precepts. But the creative novelty of the Constitution arose from the fruitful tension between the two political persuasions. The federalists were not simply elitists bent on limiting popular influence in government, nor were they single-minded harbingers of a new commercial and competitive culture. Some of the lessons learned from the experience with self-government between 1776 and 1787 were sobering and had caused some drawing back from the ideas and practices of those years, more properly seen, perhaps, as wise progress toward a viable democracy, a constitutional polity, and good government—rather than reaction toward an oligarchic and predemocratic past.

The Constitution, then, should not be seen as elitist or antidemocratic but rather as an effort to fulfill both the aspirations for self-government of the American Revolution *and* the classical republican belief in the social benefits of good and energetic government. Publius expressed the dual allegiance in *Federalist* No. 37 when, after acknowledging an "inviolable attention due to liberty, and to the republican form," he set forth further requisites: "Energy in government is essential to that security against external and internal danger, and to that prompt and salutary execution of the laws, which enter into the very definition of good government. Stability in government, is essential to national character, and to the advantages annexed to it, as well as to that repose and confidence in the minds of the people, which are among the chief blessings of civil society."[4]

Publius's language, then, reveals the large, positive conception of the nature of government generally assumed in the eighteenth century. The direct, unabashed arguments on behalf of minimal, laissez-faire government, though perhaps implicit in the thought of Adam Smith and others, reach full expression only in the nineteenth century with Herbert Spencer, William Graham Sumner, and others who spoke of *Man vs. the State*, "The Absurd Effort to Make the World Over," and so on. It is a misreading of the *Federalist Papers*—and almost all the contemporary writings on the Constitution, pro and con—to see in them the arguments for government so prominent in romantic and Social Darwinian thought. Publius knew better than to suppose, as Ralph Waldo Emerson foolishly did, that "with the appearance of the wise man the State expires: the appearance of character makes the State unnecessary" or to suppose as Sumner simplistically did that "a society of free men, co-operating under contract, is by far the strongest society" and that "it is not at all the function of the state to make men happy."[5] To understand this idea helps us recover the real philosophy of the Constitution.

In fact the assumption by Publius that government is an essential, legitimate part of human society, especially for its protection and improvement, was a powerful strand in American political thinking even before 1776 and 1787. On board the *Arbella* in 1630, sailing toward New England, John Winthrop spoke of the broad, providential purposes of their colonization effort and of the large role the government would play in their pursuit. Public interests were always to "oversway" private ones. "Particular estates cannot subsist in the ruin of the public," he insisted. Furthermore, liberty would be a "civic liberty" wherein people were free to do "only that which is good, just, and honest."[6] The purpose of government in the colony was not "for life only, but for the good life." Winthrop's own active, guiding, omnipresent conduct as governor of Massachusetts Bay bore no resemblance at all to the "contract" and "convenience" ideas of government beginning to be articulated in England by the precursors of Hobbes and Locke.

Equally distant from such conceptions were the praises of traditonal British government expressed more than a century later by loyalist Joseph Galloway (see chapter 12). He insisted, in response to rebel appeals for independence to gain natural rights, that meaningful protection of rights could come only from firm and wise government. The good life in the United States would come, Galloway argued, not by following the "miserable sophistry" of revolutionary pamphleteers or the "rash and imprudent conduct" of "designers" for independence, but from the established and guiding power of the British state.[7] Indeed, the British imperial tradition itself furnished yet another rich resource in the theory and practice of active, energetic government.[8] Although the harsh, militaristic, and authoritarian aspects of these traditions were repudiated by the American Revolution and by the constitution makers of 1787, an emphasis on the uses and potential benefits of government remained a part of their political thinking.

These traditions of energetic government continued after the adoption of the Constitution of 1787 in the school of broad construction, expressed first by the unmasked Publius, Alexander Hamilton, written into constitutional law by John Marshall, used by Daniel Webster to resist nullification, and finally woven by Abraham Lincoln into a conception of the nature and uses of the union. In his defense of the constitutionality of the national bank (1791), Hamilton repeated more clearly and explicitly the arguments he had made in *Federalist* No. 23 about the "natural" powers of government to act "in advancement of the public good" and the necessity of its having "great latitude of discretion in the selection and application of the means" for pursuing broad, inherent ends. Marshall's landmark opinions in *McCulloch* v. *Maryland* (1819), *Cohens* v. *Virginia* (1821), and other cases simply elaborated Hamiltonian broad construction into case law under the Constitution. Before Webster perorated "liberty *and* Union, now and forever, one and inseparable" (1830), he had recounted the blessings the country had gained in nearly a half-century of government under the Constitution and the necessity of retaining the full powers of the union to continue those blessings. Lincoln argued in the Gettysburg Address that only by maintaining the national union could the nation "conceived in liberty and dedicated to the proposition that all men are created equal" be true to its origins and fulfill its sweeping destiny. He intended, that is, to *use power* (of the union) to pursue justice. Without the union it was clear to Lincoln that high national purposes would be mere hollow words. Although the tradition of Hamilton, Marshall, Webster, and Lincoln was not the only view of the Constitution before 1865, it was a powerful one that embodied the vigor the founders intended the document to have.

The federalists, then, were not merely Lockean—"radical Whig" advocates of a government of only specified and meager powers—nor was the Constitution understood by its framers or its opponents to be such. Rather, the framers and Publius and the antifederalists stood at an interesting, transitional moment in the understanding of the nature and purpose of government. They believed, as the theory and experience of government in and before their day generally accepted, that its functions and powers were unlimited in the sense that it could do what was necessary to defend its own existence. After all, its dissolution almost always had catastrophic effects on the people.

Yet, both friends and foes of the Constitution also accepted, as post-Lockean theory increasingly argued, that for practical and tactical reasons it was prudent to define clearly the procedures (including limitations) government must follow in pursuit of its broad purposes. The distinction between procedures (means) and ends would not always be clear, and there was a heightening sense of the danger government itself often posed to individual rights. But neither of these circumstances had in 1787–1788 supplanted the ancient connection between energetic government and the good life. This priority was implicit, in fact, in the first printing of the new Constitution, in *The Pennsylvania Packet*, Wednesday, September 19, 1787, where its broad purposes stated in the preamble were set in bold type with capitalized nouns, and the processes of government, in the body of the Constitution, were in small, mostly lowercase type. Justice, Tranquility, Defence, General Welfare, and Liberty were the large, emphatic ends of government, accepted as axiomatic by federalists and antifederalists alike and the necessary preamble to all powers specified in the Constitution.

PART III
THE BILL OF RIGHTS

10
ORIGINS

Liberty, one of the enduring principles of the Constitution, received full, formal definition only with the adoption in 1791 of the amendments known as the Bill of Rights. Indeed, after two hundred years of thinking of the Bill of Rights as the essential bulwark of liberty, Americans are generally surprised that it was not originally part of the Constitution and even more astonished to learn that it was not even considered seriously at the 1787 convention. In fact, only in the last week did the question of a bill of rights reach the floor. On September 12, 1787, the day the committee on style had reported a finished draft of the proposed constitution to the full convention, George Mason, delegate from Virginia, urged that the plan be prefaced with a bill of rights in order to "give great quiet to the people." Expressing a view held by James Madison, James Wilson, and other leading delegates, Roger Sherman of Connecticut objected that though he "was for securing the rights of the people where requisite," he thought that state declarations of rights, still in force, offered sufficient protection. More cryptically, he added that "the legislature may be safely trusted"; he meant that Congress, representing the people, could be trusted not to violate natural rights. With an overwhelming majority in favor of the draft constitution as proposed and hurrying toward adjournment, the convention had patience only for Mason's rejoinder that "the laws of the U.S. [under the new constitution] are to be paramount to state Bills of Rights." It then voted unanimously not to appoint a committee to prepare a bill of rights to be prefaced to the new constitution.[1]

In this brief exchange, so quickly brushing aside Mason's proposal, is the germ of a long and serious debate not over, as Sherman fairly observed, whether the rights themselves should be secured (all agree they should be), but over the most effective means of doing that. One side, long dominant in the United States, sees in the explicit statement and solemn validation of bills of rights, thus sanctified against interference from any source and to be upheld by the courts, the best means for securing basic liberties. The focus is on statement of principle, "higher law," so clearly and categorically that no agency of government, whether intolerant legislatures, heavy-handed bureaucrats, zealous prosecutors, or "hanging judges," will be able to contravene them. The other side, seldom dominant but frequently set forth, sees the protection of liberty in more organic terms. That is, it depends on an attitude—a belief in and support for human liberties by the people of a self-governing society. With such an attitude permeating the citizenry, which is the necessary foundation of any democratic polity, the argument runs, the agencies of government will reflect that spirit and thus not tend to abridge the rights of the people.

To understand these different approaches, we must look at the history of free government the framers had in mind as they considered the need for a bill of rights. They knew, of course, the even then well-rehearsed history of the growth of constitutional limitations on government in England, from Magna Charta (1215) on. But more broadly speaking they saw the progress of free government, of which they meant themselves and the new United States to be the vanguard, as an ebb and flow among nations. Polybius and other classical historians had taught them about the rise and decline of more or less free governments in the ancient world. More immediately, they were poignantly aware of the struggles for freedom (and, closely related, for self-government) among the nation-states in modern Europe. Among the notorious tyrants from Phillip II to Louis XIV and Peter the Great there stood forth two valiant exceptions: the Dutch Republic and the England that emerged from the revolutions of the 1640s and 1688–1689. These were the places where good principles could be discerned, useful institutions modeled, and instructive histories observed. The founders could note in these examples the progress of freedom, self-government, prosperity, and power that they hoped would characterize the United States. The freedoms we associate with the Bill of Rights were part of a much larger configuration of aspirations and practices that amounted to a full-fledged nationhood embodying liberty.

The Pilgrims themselves symbolized the importance of the Dutch Republic in the American typology of freedom. Driven to Holland by Stuart tyranny in England, the Pilgrims practiced their religion as they pleased in Leiden—and saw there the growing power and riches of that comparatively open and tolerant land. Commerce, learning, religion, culture, and good government flourished together. Although the Pilgrims left for the New World with, as William Bradford put it, "a great hope and inward zeal . . . for the propagating and advancing the gospel of the kingdom of Christ in . . . remote parts" and to retain "Englishness" in their children, they had had a lesson in the fruits of freedom that became part of American mythology.[2] In the same century, Holland was a haven for three great philosophers, Descartes from France, Spinoza of a refugee Portuguese Jewish family, and Locke from England, because there they could study, talk, and publish freely.

Fifty years later, another Englishman described more generally how the Netherlands was a beacon to Europeans interested in prosperity and greatness. Sir William Temple, a distinguished philosopher and diplomat who lived in the Netherlands from 1668 to 1670, said its standing resulted, among other things, from the influx "of people out of Flanders, England, France, and Germany, invited by the strength of their towns, and by the Constitutions and credit of their government; by the liberty of conscience, and security of life and goods (subject only to constant laws); from general industry and parsimony; . . . smallness of customs; freedom of ports; order in trade; and interest of persons in the government."[3] Thus, though Temple was impressed by the freedom of religion and other civil liberties more characteristic of the Netherlands than of other countries, he saw those liberties as part of a larger pattern. Freedom of trade, good habits, stable government, and public spirit in the people were also reckoned important. In fact, Temple addressed himself to the broad question, What circumstances in a nation yield the freedom for the people that allows them to prosper, to fulfill themselves, and to be part of a flourishing and creative nationhood? Civil liberties, of course, but Temple saw that these, to mean very much, had to be part of a pervading culture of opportunity, security, industriousness, and responsive government. Furthermore, in a view Temple shared with the American founders, the various parts of this "culture of freedom" each mutually reinforced the other, making a totality necessary to the sustaining of any of the parts. Constitution drafters in the United States both accepted Temple's question as fundamental and agreed that Dutch experience was instructive.

The founders also admired much in the society and politics of their mother country, which Montesquieu and other commentators saw as the successor in the eighteenth century to the Netherlands as the freest and most prosperous nation in the world. The philosopher Voltaire visited England from 1726 to 1728 and noted qualities there similar to those the envious Temple had observed in the Netherlands half a century earlier. "Commerce," Voltaire noted, "which has brought wealth to the citizenry of England, has helped to make them free, and freedom has developed commerce in its turn." He thought the busy English merchant who "sends orders from his office [in London] to Sturat and to Cairo, . . . enriched his country . . . and contributes [more] to the well-being of the world [than the] well-powdered lord who knows precisely what time the king gets up in the morning and what time he goes to bed, and who gives himself airs of grandeur while playing the role of slave in a minister's antechamber." English liberty, born "of the quarrels between tyrants," continued to flourish because of the "happy mixture" of powers among king, lords, and commons. Taxes, levied by the House of Commons, fell on all classes alike according to income. Thus, "the feet of the peasant are not tortured by wooden shoes, he eats white bread, he is well clothed, and he is not afraid to increase the number of his cattle, or to cover his roof with tile, lest his taxes be raised next year." Some combination, then, of the enterprising spirit of commerce, the sensible decline of feudal obsequities, and equitable government sustained Britain's rising freedom.

Voltaire connected the openness and diversity of English society directly to its prosperity when he noted that "Jew, Mahometan, Presbyterian, Anabaptist, Anglican, and Quaker" all did business honestly and profitably in the London Exchange. In an aphorism often quoted by James Madison, Voltaire concluded that "if there were only one religion in England, there would be danger of tyranny; if there were two, they would cut each other's throats; but there are thirty, and they live happily together in peace."[4] Voltaire, like Temple, found meaningful freedom, the sort of freedom that yielded prosperity and creativity and opened opportunity for ordinary people, to result from two interlocking essentials: a diverse and open society encouraging to initiative and enterprise and a responsive and stable government protective of those qualities. Within such a pattern of course explicit statements of freedoms, such as those in the English Petition of Right (1628) and Bill of Rights (1689) and in the Pennsylvania Charter of Privileges (1701) or Stamp Act Congress resolves (1765), were important. So, too, was the development of common and constitutional law on both sides of the Atlantic that limited government and made it less arbitrary. The American founders knew of and valued these statements and this legal history but were also aware that to be really meaningful, they had to be part of an open and self-governing society.

It is this larger sense of the place of freedom in society, and especially in the form of government, that resulted in the apparent neglect by the Convention of 1787 of a bill of rights. Notice that Sherman had thought the trust the people could place in their own elected representatives would be the surest guard against invasions of rights. He knew from histories of the ancient world as well as those of Holland and England that the overall nature of the government—its responsiveness to the people, its inherent limitations on arbitrary power, and its constant regard for "the blessings of liberty"—was the key to genuinely free government. He had in mind, as did most of his colleagues at the convention, the famous Virginia Declaration of Rights, which included not only the usual prohibitions of things rulers were *not* to do, but also many empowering provisions that would establish positive principles of government—and thus how government would impinge on the people (see chapter 5). In the spirit of this Virginia Declaration, largely incorporated into the New York and other state constitutions and as much as anything a statement of the philosophy of the American Revolution, the Federal Convention of 1787 spelled out in detail how the separation of powers in a representative, federal system would ensure both liberty and government for the "common benefit . . . of the people, nation, or community." Broadly speaking, these were the full rights of the people, not only to have certain prohibitions placed on the government, but more fundamentally to provide *for* government that would be able to act for the common benefit and would adhere implicitly to the principles of freedom.

It was this understanding of liberty that Madison, Hamilton, Sherman, Wilson, and other federalists had in mind in 1787–1788 when they defended for a time the absence of a bill of rights in the proposed constitution. Since government could exist legitimately only if it acted for the common benefit, then of course marks of tyranny such as censorship of newspapers or cruel punishments were unconstitutional. The whole idea of a constitution rested on the assumption that only powers clearly granted were to be exercised by the government. Thus, as Hamilton observed, prohibitions necessary against powerful monarchs, as Magna Charta (1215) prescribed against King John, as the Petition of Right (1628) restrained Charles I, and as the English Bill of Rights of 1689 addressed the tyrannies of James II, "have no application to constitutions professedly founded on the power of the people, and executed by their immediate representatives and servants." Foreshadowing the ideal of good self-government to be upheld by Jefferson, Hamilton argued that proper "public opinion, and . . . [the] general spirit of the people," using the processes prescribed in the new constitution, would afford "a better recognition of popular rights than volumes of those aphorisms" that filled bills of rights.[5]

The point the federalists were making was proper, profound, and even filled with republican idealism. If the "general spirit" of the people favored liberty and if the processes of government placed power ultimately in their hands, then was it not superfluous, indeed, even denigrating to the people, to say explicitly, for example, that "Congress [elected by the people] shall make no law . . . abridging the freedom of speech, or of the press"? If the whole motivation and spirit of government, carried into all its processes and branches, was to be reformed, as republican theory made essential, then that, not "volumes of . . . aphorisms," would most securely protect liberty. The opposite argument, that only explicit prohibitions could prevent tyranny, impugned the character and the attachment to liberty of the people who elect the government. In a way, this argument supposed that self-government, just as much as rule by John or Charles or James or George, would tend toward tyranny—and if that was so, how much of a revolution had taken place since 1776? At issue was the crucial question of whether a radically new mode of governing could replace the ancient system of rulers (even a majority) oppressing the ruled. Could the distinction, for example, between rulers and ruled gradually disappear as new ideals of participation and responsible citizenship became realities?

As federalist Thomas McKean of Pennsylvania put the general point, a bill of rights was unnecessary because "in fact the whole plan of government is nothing more than a Bill of Rights—a declaration of the people in what manner they choose to be governed." Benjamin Rush even argued in 1787 that one mark of honor of the proposed constitution was that it had "not been disgraced with a Bill of Rights." Those of the states he regarded as "idle and superfluous instruments [because] men in full possession and enjoyment of all their natural rights, can lose them but in two ways, either of their own consent or from tyranny." The proposed federal constitution, Rush continued, "neither implies the former, nor creates an avenue to the latter. Therefore no cause can operate to this effect—because the *people* are always both able and ready, to resist . . . encroachments."[6] At the deepest level, then, the federalists feared that a bill of rights, or at least a preoccupying emphasis on it in framing a constitution, might weaken the very structure and authority of government upon which the realistic protection of rights depended. It might also distract from the even more vital need, in a republic, to assure full and fair representation of the people and nourish in them, as the Virginia Declaration of 1776 had put it, the "firm adherence to justice, moderation, temperance, frugality, and virtue" foundational to all free governments.

In an interesting way, the antifederalists made the same point about the need for proper character in the people in arguing *for* a bill of rights. An explicit statement of the people's rights articulating their sense of the purpose of their government would keep those propositions clearly in mind and in fact strengthen the government by securing the people's attachment to it. As the "Federal Farmer" pointed out, "we do not by declarations [of rights] change the nature of things, or create new truths, but we give existence, or at least establish in the minds of the people truths and principles which they might never otherwise have thought of, or soon forgot. If a nation means its systems, religious or political, shall have duration, it ought to recognize the leading principles of them in the front page of every family book."[7] The antifederalists saw declarations, or bills, of rights as clarifying and reinforcing understanding of basic principles. They thus contributed powerfully, indispensably, to the same vital purpose emphasized by the federalists: the improvement of the moral and political education of the people that would enable them to elect good representatives and otherwise participate in a public-spirited way in their own government. Madison himself came to emphasize the point in his eventual endorsement of a bill of rights. Both sides, then, were keenly aware of the place a bill of rights might have in a larger understanding of the vitality of republican government—perhaps to diminish it as the federalists at first feared, or to nourish it as the antifederalist hoped. Both sides, of course, favored the substance of a bill of rights.

As this debate over the need for a bill of rights agitated the public in 1787–1788, Madison and Jefferson took it up less polemically and more subtly in their correspondence about the Constitution. In a long letter of October 24, 1787, transmitting the proposed Constitution to Jefferson in Paris, Madison discoursed profoundly and at length on the difficult question of protecting private or minority rights in the face of the power of a potentially tyrannical majority. He did not even mention a bill of rights as a possible agent in such protection. Instead, he was entirely preoccupied with how the structure of the Constitution might or might not result in good government that protected rights at both the state and federal levels.[8] Washington made exactly the same points four months later in a letter to Lafayette:

The general government is not invested with more powers, than are indispensably necessary to perform the functions of a good government; and consequently, that no objection ought to be made against the quantity of power delegated to it. These powers, (as the appointment of all rulers will forever arise from, and at short, stated intervals recur to, the free suffrage of the people,) are so distributed among the legislative, executive, and judicial branches, into which the general government is arranged, that it can never be in danger of degenerating into a monarchy, an oligarchy, an aristocracy, or any other despotic or oppressive form, so long as there shall remain any virtue in the body of the people.[9]

When Madison's letter reached Jefferson in December, he replied at once, finding the Constitution generally to his liking but objecting to two things: the eligibility of the president for unlimited reelection, which Jefferson thought would make him "an officer for life," and the absence of a bill of rights. He urged that "freedom of religion, freedom of the press, protection against standing armies, restriction against monopolies, the eternal and unremitting force of the habeas corpus laws, and trial by jury" be provided for "clearly and without the aid of sophisms." Jefferson thought there were enough clauses in the Constitution granting wide power and unqualified by clear statement of inherent limit to make it necessary to declare the restraints unequivocally in the new Constitution itself. The author of the Virginia Statute for Religious Freedom summarized his contention with a ringing, oft-quoted statement: "A bill of rights is what the people are entitled to against every government on earth, general or particular, and what no just government should refuse or rest on inference."[10]

Madison did not find time to answer this letter for nearly ten months. During that period, when he was heavily engaged in the ratification struggle, he moved slowly and with surprising reluctance toward a willingness to add a bill of rights to the Constitution after its ratification. As late as March 1, 1788, he wrote from New York to a Virginia friend about his still "powerful reasons . . . against the adoption of a Bill of Rights."[11] Hearing of strong opposition to the Constitution even in his own Orange County, especially by the numerous Baptists who feared the absence of a clause ensuring religious liberty, Madison decided to return home. On the way he conferred with an influential Baptist preacher (an old friend, John Leland, who had worked with Madison for fifteen years to oppose religious bigotry in Virginia) and agreed to support a bill of rights for the federal Constitution after its ratification. Leland in return agreed to withdraw his opposition to the Constitution, a trade-off that did much to assure Madison's election to the Virginia Convention, as did similar arrangements for other federalists in many parts of the nation.[12] The federalists, seeing the strong public support for a bill of rights, were quite willing to adjust their position in order to secure ratification since their opposition to a bill of rights had been tactical all along rather than principled.

By the time the Virginia ratifying convention met in June 1788 Madison had agreed to support a bill of rights. His arguments there reveal, however, that his thoughts still turned to other devices to protect essential liberties. When Patrick Henry lamented the absence of a "guard" for religious freedom, Madison asked him, "Is a bill of rights a security for religion in Virginia?" No, said Madison, answering his own question, because if one religion were in an overwhelming majority he was quite sure it would establish itself and legislate public support, despite the prohibitions in the Virginia Declaration of Rights. Rather, Madison declared, echoing Voltaire, freedom of religion "arises from multiplicity of sects, . . . which is the best and only security for religious liberty in any society. For where there is such a variety of sects, there cannot be a majority of any one sect to oppress and persecute all the rest." Extending this reasoning, Madison argued that religious liberty would be especially secure in the United States at large where "such a variety of sects abound . . . that no one sect will ever be able to out-number or depress the rest."[13] As in his more general theory that public liberty would be safe against the designs of a majority's tyranny because of the large number of factions in an "extended republic," Madison thought the diversity spawned by free government a surer protection for natural rights than mere statement of them on a piece of paper.

When Madison finally, in October 1788, answered Jefferson's letter calling for a bill of rights, his comments were still clouded with reluctance. He admitted that some sought "further guards to public liberty and individual rights . . . from the most honorable and patriotic motives," but many others continued to think the addition of a bill of rights "unnecessary . . . and misplaced in such a Constitution." Although Madison asserted that this was no longer his view, he still did not regard "the omission as a material defect." Backhandedly, he said he favored a bill of rights "largely because I supposed it might be of some use, and if properly executed could not be of disservice," but he had not "viewed it in a very important light" for four reasons. First, he accepted some of the argument that "the rights in question are reserved by the [limiting] manner in which the federal powers are granted." Second, he feared some essential rights, especially religious freedom, would somehow be limited by any language used to state them. Third, the "jealousy" and powers of the state governments would afford sufficient protection against infringements by federal authority. Fourth, "experience proves the inefficiency of a bill of rights on those occasions when its control is most needed." Supporting this last argument Madison pointed out that "repeated violation of these parchment barriers [had] been committed by overbearing majorities in every State. In Virginia I have seen the bill of rights violated in every instance where it has been opposed to a popular current."

Generalizing his point, Madison observed that "wherever the real power in a Government lies, there is the danger of oppression. In our Government the real power lies in the majority of the Community, and the invasion of private rights is chiefly to be apprehended, not from acts of Government contrary to the sense of its constituents, but from acts in which the Government is the mere instrument of the major number of the constituents." This was "a truth of great importance," Madison thought, and one "more strongly impressed" on his mind, living among governments resting on consent, than on Jefferson's, living among the despotisms of Europe. There, Madison admitted, "a solemn charter of popular rights" might be useful, even essential, to rouse and unite sentiment against a tyrant. In a republic, on the other hand, Madison argued again that the dispersal of power among the many factions and interests spawned by freedom was the most fundamental guard against oppression and the invasion of rights.

Nonetheless, Madison had come around, he told his friend, to see two important uses for a bill of rights even in a popular government:

1. The political truths declared in that solemn manner acquire by degrees the character of fundamental maxims of free government, and as they become incorporated with the national sentiment, counteract the impulses of interest and passion. 2. Altho' it be generally true . . . that the danger of oppression lies in the [self-] interested majorities of the people rather than in the usurped acts of the Government, yet there may be occasions on which the evil may spring from the latter sources; and on such, a bill of rights will be a good ground for an appeal to the sense of the community.

Even admitting these general grounds of utility, Madison still saw great difficulty in proper phrasing of the rights. He warned against "absolute" statements of the rights because he was sure emergencies would occasionally require that they be overruled. If a rebellion alarmed the people, for example, "no written provisions on earth would prevent . . . suspension of Habeas Corpus." Or, should Spain or Britain station an army near U.S. soil, "declarations on paper would have little effect in preventing a standing [army] for the public safety." Other provisions, such as that against monopolies, might require legitimate exceptions, as in the cases of copyright and patent protection.[14] Altogether, then, though Jefferson and others had persuaded Madison to formulate two practical, critically important grounds for adding a bill of rights to the Constitution, he still thought more important, basic protection of liberty came from the skillful construction of government that would inherently deter invasions of rights.

Replying five months later, Jefferson said he was happy Madison on the whole now favored a bill of rights and sought to bring him around more fully by answering each of his four objections. To the first argument, that in its limited nature the Constitution inherently protected natural rights, Jefferson agreed in part but then pointed out that since it also conferred new powers on the federal government, the people had to be on guard "against [its] abuses of power within the field submitted to them." Second, to Madison's fear that any phraseology of rights might not have "the requisite latitude," Jefferson replied it would nonetheless be useful to be as categorical and as clear as possible in defining basic rights. Third, to the claim that the watchful eye of the states would prevent federal oppression, Jefferson responded that the states needed to "have principles furnished them whereon to found their opposition." Thus a bill of rights "will be the text whereby [the states] will try all the acts of the federal government" and would furnish a standard for judging state actions. Finally, while admitting the occasional inefficacy of a bill of rights in preventing abuses and the possibility that it would sometime "cramp government in its useful exertions," the balance was heavily on the side of the utility of such a bill. The evils attending it, he said, would be "short-lived, moderate, and reparable," while the dangers of not having a bill of rights were "permanent, afflicting, and irreparable, [and] . . . are in constant progression from bad to worse."

Further, Jefferson pointed out that while legislative tyranny might be "the most formidable dread at present," the time might come when the threat would be from the executive department. Then a bill of rights would put a clear "legal check . . . into the hands of the judiciary," which, when rendered independent as it was under the Constitution, "merits great confidence for their learning and integrity." Finally, acknowledging what he knew had been an important consideration in Madison's skepticism about appeals for a bill of rights, Jefferson hoped that it might be added in a way that would not endanger or weaken "the whole frame of government."[15] Jefferson, like Madison, had no sympathy for the kind of antifederalism that used the cry for a bill of rights as a lever either to prevent ratification or to include among proposed amendments restraints on the positive powers of the federal government. At least as much as Madison, Jefferson believed that good self-government depended most fundamentally on a thoughtful and vigilant citizenry able through their representatives to pursue actively the public good.

With this perspective in mind, Madison moved in June 1789 in the First Federal Congress to fulfill the federalist promise to add a bill of rights to the Constitution. He had prepared the way for congressional consideration by advising Washington to include support for a bill of rights in his first inaugural address. The president urged Congress to protect "the characteristic rights of Freemen," but he also warned against "endangering the benefits of an united and effective government" and emphasized the need to have "a regard for the public harmony" as it discerned and pursued "the public good." These words, drafted by Madison at Washington's request, placed the president's enormous prestige behind exactly the public, government-sustaining emphasis Madison thought was crucial in considering amendments. In Congress, using the arguments he had rehearsed with Jefferson, Madison explained why he favored amendments: "It will be proper in itself, and highly politic, for the tranquillity of the public mind, and the stability of the government, that we should [add] . . . a declaration of the rights of the people." He admitted in letters, though, his intense concern that the appetite for amendments, evident in the ratification struggle, be entirely satisfied by "personal liberty" provisions. He thus sought to sidetrack amendments limiting federal powers over direct taxation, the judiciary, regulation of commerce, treaties, and other proposed states' rights measures in order, he wrote Randolph, that "the structure and stamina of the Government are as little touched as possible." Another Virginia friend wrote approvingly that Madison's proposed amendments left "unimpaired the great Powers of the government."[16]

Antifederalists in the Congress (especially in the Senate), though, while favoring the "personal liberty" amendments, were just as intense about not wanting them to exhaust the amending energy. Senator William Grayson of Virginia reported to Patrick Henry, the state's antifederal chieftain, that he feared Congress meant to enact "amendments which shall affect personal liberty alone, leaving the great points of the Judiciary, direct taxation, etc., to stand as they are." Representative Aedanus Burke of South Carolina was so disappointed with Madison's proposals, full of "whip-syllabub, frothy and full of wind, formed only to please the palate," he sputtered, that he thought it best to "drop the subject." He wanted to insist on "solid and substantial amendments" that would shift power from the national to state governments. Harking back to federalist appeals in 1788 to ratify first and then amend, Senator Richard Henry Lee, another Virginia antifederalist, lamented that "the idea of subsequent amendments, was little better than putting oneself to death first, in expectation that the doctor, who wished our destruction, would afterwards restore us to life."[17] In an ironic way, then, what we know as the Bill of Rights resulted from a political victory by those who had thought it unnecessary in 1787–1788 over those who had then been its champions. As Madison's federalist friend Edmund Pendleton put it, he felt "some degree of pleasure, in discovering obviously from the whole progress [of the Bill of Rights], that the public are indebted for the measure to the Friends of Government, whose elections were opposed under pretence of their being adverse to amendments."[18]

Reflecting his conviction that "what may be called a bill of rights" should be seen as part and parcel of a larger pattern of government, Madison had at first proposed that the amendments be inserted at eight different places in the original text, especially in Article I, Section 9, where other restrictions on the federal government already existed. Madison did not object when others proposed adding the amendments as a separate package at the end of the Constitution, but his impulse remained to focus attention as much as possible on a viable frame and structure of government. Furthermore, Madison's support for a bill of rights, though entirely sincere in substance, continued to be phrased in tactical terms: it would fulfill the "campaign promises" of himself and other federalists, it might help persuade North Carolina and Rhode Island to come into the union, and it would "kill the opposition everywhere, and by putting an end to the disaffection to the government itself, enable the administration to venture on measures not otherwise safe."[19] In another irony, Madison's chief concern, even in proposing limitations on government to protect natural rights, was to *strengthen* its support and thus its power to act on behalf of the public good.

Madison's original phrasing of what became the First Amendment further revealed his preoccupation with the public rather than the personal or private character of the five freedoms of religion, speech, press, assembly, and petition. He had at first stated these rights in three separate paragraphs, beginning with one on religion: "the Civil rights of none shall be abridged on account of religious belief or worship, nor shall any national religion be established, nor shall the full and equal rights of conscience be in any manner, or on any pretext, infringed." Two things are notable about this proposal. First, the emphasis on not abridging civil rights, rights related to government, and on not having a national religion has clear reference to the "good health" of the processes of government. These religious rights, that is, are necessary to conduct the public business freely and fairly as well as to protect individual liberty of conscience. Second, the last part of the sentence is Madison's effort to state as fully, clearly, and categorically as possible the rights of conscience, not to limit that right by using inadequate language to protect it, as Madison had worried might happen. Although the final phrasing of the religion clause of the First Amendment is also categorical and perhaps more felicitous, it lacks, but without intending to deny, the explicitness on public aspects in Madison's original proposal.

The second paragraph of Madison's "first amendment proposals" reads "the people shall not be deprived or abridged of their right to speak, to write, or to publish their sentiments; and the freedom of the press, as one of the great bulwarks of liberty, shall be inviolable," while the third reads "the people shall not be restrained from *peaceably assembling and consulting for their common good*, nor from applying to the legislature by petitions, or remonstrances for redress of their grievances [emphasis added]."[20] Throughout, when examined closely, Madison's words (themselves culled from the amendments proposed by state ratifying conventions) have an unmistakable public orientation or purpose beyond their obvious attention to personal rights. The image in the emphasized phrase is that of citizens gathering together to discuss the public business, the very essence of self-government. Furthermore, the petitioning is to address legislators to initiate a dialogue over grievances against the government—a dialogue that eighteenth-century usage required the legislature continue by responding to the petition. (Recall that one of the complaints in the Declaration of Independence was the failure of British authorities to respond to petitions.) Thinking of the press as a "bulwark of liberty" also echoes a contemporary understanding that freedom of the press was vital to ensure true freedom by having the means available for a full discussion of public policy. Even speaking, writing, and publishing "sentiments" has particular reference to deliberations on public affairs.

An early draft of what would become the First Amendment, in the hand of Representative Roger Sherman of Connecticut and probably written before Madison's three paragraphs, both embodied Madison's public emphasis and rested the "the first amendment freedoms" directly on a natural-rights, higher-law foundation:

The people have certain natural rights which are retained by them when they enter into Society. Such are the rights of Conscience in matters of religion; of acquiring property, and of pursuing happiness and Safety; of Speaking, writing, and publishing their Sentiments with decency and freedom; of peaceably assembling to consult their common good, and of applying to Government by petition or remonstrance for redress of grievances. Of these rights therefore they shall not be deprived by the Government of the United States.[21]

Each of the terse, compressed parts of the first amendment, then, derived from more elaborate phrases that had a more explicit orientation toward public expression, a right by the people to have full access to the process of "assembling and consulting for their common good." Since the changes in organization and wording were made largely in committee where no record of discussions survive, we cannot be sure why they were made. The recorded debates in the full House of Representatives and the private correspondence of Madison and others, though, reveal no significant controversies or intentions of substantial change in the altered phraseology. Since Madison's main concern was to gain support for the Constitution from those whose objection was the absence of a bill of rights, he was probably willing to go along with more generally acceptable wording. And doubtless the more forceful eloquence of the single sentence attracted some. In any case, far from the revisions being an attempt to change the substance of Madison's original proposals, it seems apparent that their clearer public meaning simply made explicit what remains implicit in the intent of the First Amendment as adopted. (See chapter 12 for further comment on the public emphasis in the First Amendment.) Justice Louis Brandeis made the same point 140 years later: "Those who won our independence believed that . . . in government the deliberative forces should prevail over the arbitrary, and that the fitting remedy for evil counsels is good ones. Believing in the power of reason as applied through public discussion, they eschewed silence coerced by law."[22]

The preoccupation with the public importance of bill of rights freedoms by its chief draftsman and by most of his legislative colleagues as well probably also clarifies the meaning of the Second Amendment. Its phrasing with a stipulating initial clause controlling the declaration— "a well-regulated Militia being necessary to the security of a free State, the right of the people to keep and bear Arms shall not be infringed"—reveals its necessary connection to a public purpose: the security to a *free* state furnished by having its own militia. Hence, the private, merely personal bearing of arms would seem not to be its point. Madison's explicit attention to public significance in the preceding amendment suggests that in the Second Amendment as well he had in mind the connection of the right with a larger public good itself vital to the constitutional principle of liberty.

In other ways, though, antifederalist sentiment in Congress more signifi- cantly altered Madison's original proposals for a bill of rights. Most crucially, Madison had proposed explicitly that "no state shall violate the equal rights of conscience, or the freedom of the press, or the trial by jury in criminal cases." Reflecting his deep skepticism of state governments, Madison explained that this was "the most valuable amendment on the whole list. If there was any reason to restrain the government of the United States from infringing upon these essential rights, it was equally necessary that they should be secured against the state governments."[23] When a select committee added "freedom of speech" to the restrictions on the state governments, and then the House easily passed the package, the federalists seemed triumphant: under the Constitution the states would be restricted in their powers to interfere with either personal freedoms or with the free process of public deliberation.

In the only recorded opposition in the House to this amendment, Thomas Tucker of South Carolina thought it "better . . . to leave the State Govern- ments to themselves, and not to interfere with them more than we already do."[24] In the more antifederalist Senate, however, the force of Tucker's argu- ment apparently prevailed, because the prohibition on the states was defeated and thus was not forwarded to them for ratification. As both Tucker's argu- ment in the House and the known sentiments of Lee, Grayson, and other Senators indicate, Madison's earnest argument that freedoms of expression needed protection against *all* governments fell before a politically still potent antifederalist conviction: they simply did not want any more words in the Constitution restricting the states. The Senate also eliminated proposals de- claring separation of powers as a principle of the U.S. Constitution, exempting those with religious scruples from military service and forbidding the states from abridging certain rights of Americans—more antifederalist victories.

Debate over the clause on religious freedom also reflected strong sentiment against interference with the states. Members allowed the federal-state issue to overshadow full and clear protection of personal liberties. Instead of Mad- ison's simple and sweeping language that no government, national or state, "shall violate the equal rights of conscience," the House moved to the now famous, also sweeping language, "Congress shall make no law respecting an establishment of religion, or prohibiting the free exercise thereof." Madison's language harked back to his successful effort in 1776 to replace the phrase "full toleration" with the less condescending "free exercise of religion, according to the dictates of conscience" in the Virginia Declaration of Rights. It also reflected the battle in 1785–1786 first to defeat a Virginia bill to pay "teachers of religion" from tax funds and then to enact Jefferson's famous statute of religious freedom proclaiming "that Almighty God hath created the mind free, . . . [and] that all men shall be free to profess, and by argument to maintain their opinions in matters of religion." In these moves Madison and Jefferson supposed they had in Virginia finally separated church and state, secured completely the right to believe or not believe according to conscience, and, as Madison wrote Jefferson, "extinguished forever the ambitious hope of making laws for the human mind."[25] Even in these words about religion, Madison and Jefferson maintained a focus on reasoned discussion: religious opinions were to be maintained by argument in a state where the human mind was to be free. In 1789 Madison meant simply to implant the same categorical language and the same faith in public deliberation in the federal Constitution.

In the First Federal Congress, however, a persistent hostility by states' rights advocates and a powerful, lingering attachment to state support for religion led to critically important revisions to this clause. First, the prohibition against states violating "the equal rights of conscience" was deleted along with the other restraints on the states—the revision doubtless had some support on that grounds alone, regardless of sentiment on religious liberty. Furthermore, the revised language, that "Congress shall make no law respecting an establishment of religion," was favored by some members not only because it would prevent Congress from making national laws establishing religion, but it would also prescribe congressional interference with existing state establishments of religion. Supporters of laws in Connecticut and Massachusetts providing state support for churches saw this phrasing of the First Amendment as prohibiting federal interference with those state laws. Hence, though the freedom of religion clauses of the First Amendment placed sweeping restrictions on national laws about religious establishment and free exercise of conscience, they also were designed deliberately to let states proceed as they wished on such matters—something Madison opposed and had tried his best to prevent. This change protected the established churches of Connecticut and Massachusetts into the 1830s. With all of these revisions in place, Congress, by wide margins in both the House and the Senate, proposed twelve amendments to the states for ratification on September 28, 1789.[26]

The ratification process in the states revealed further the same tensions that had troubled Congress. Two of the proposed amendments, dealing with the size of Congress and forbidding any given Congress from raising its own salary, were not ratified by the states and thus did not become part of the Constitution (though in 1992 three-quarters of the states finally did ratify the congressional salary amendent). Nine states, one short of the required ten, had with little debate approved the ten amendments we know as the Bill of Rights by June 1790. Massachusetts, Connecticut, and Georgia, though, agreed generally with Representative James Jackson of Georgia who told Congress in June 1789 that "our Constitution is . . . like a vessel just launched, and lying at the wharf, she is untried. . . . It is not known how she will answer her helm, or lay her course. . . . In this state will the prudent merchant attempt alterations? . . . He certainly will not. Let us . . . be guided by experience in our alterations. . . . In this way, we may remedy her defects to the satisfaction of all concerned; but if we proceed now to make alterations, we may deface a beauty, or deform a well proportioned piece of workmanship."[27] Strong federalist sentiment in these states, combined with an unwillingness to overuse an amending process that might then be applied for nefarious purposes, prevented ratification—an omission finally repaired in these three states in 1939 as part of the sesquicentennial anniversary of the Constitution.

In Virginia, however, Patrick Henry and his antifederalist allies still controlled the state senate, and they sought to gut and delay the proposals from Congress. They hoped thus to keep the amendment issue alive, compel attention to states' rights measures (especially eliminating federal powers of direct taxation), and perhaps even convene a second constitutional convention to alter the structure fundamentally. Senate defeat of the First, Sixth, Ninth, and Tenth amendments delayed the decision for a year, during which Henry and others hoped to gather public support for their proposals. Instead, though, sentiment, carefully nourished by Madison and Jefferson, swung the other way. In December 1791, opposition to the ten amendments in the Virginia Senate collapsed, and it ratified without a recorded vote.[28] That action made the Bill of Rights part of the Constitution.

The process of adopting the Bill of Rights reveals that except for the New England concerns about their established churches there was little disagreement over the substance of the freedoms guaranteed in the first eight amendments. Federalists and antifederalists alike, as Madison, Wilson, and Hamilton had made clear since 1787, agreed on the virtue and importance of the protected liberties. The disagreement, illuminated in the letters between Madison and Jefferson, was entirely tactical: what language, what assumptions, and what state and federal provisions would provide the most practical security for those liberties?

Perhaps even more revealing, though, is the constant linkage of the "personal liberty issue" with the larger question of the nature and structure of government. The federalists had initially neglected the need for a written federal bill of rights partly because they were skeptical of the effectiveness of any such "parchment barriers" against the mobilized force of public opinion or national emergency in a democracy. More important, Madison and others thought in 1787, were structures of government, especially separation of powers, that would prevent the consolidation of forces hostile to liberty. Governments would respect and protect freedom not because of legal statements saying they should, but because powers were allocated and divided in ways that would inhibit inherently the passage of illiberal legislation and because public opinion cherished it. Conversely, some antifederalists linked the protection of personal liberties not to formal enactment of bills of rights (though they generally favored such enactment), but to reservation of key powers of government to the states, so they would retain a prominence and vitality able to stand up to federal invasions of liberty. Concomitantly, antifederalists believed that only governments at the state and local levels were likely to nourish the virtue and responsible citizenship in the people that was, according to republican theory at the time, the only sure grounds for preserving liberty. Both sides saw an ultimate linkage between effective protection of liberties and the active support of the people for such protection—especially in a self-governing (republican) society.

Inclusion of the Ninth and Tenth amendments in the Bill of Rights arose from the same reservations about the efficacy of declarative statements. The Ninth Amendment, asserting that "the enumeration in the Constitution, of certain rights shall not be construed to deny or disparage others retained by the people," responded to federalist fears that the explicit statement of some rights might by implication seem to deny or diminish some rights not stated. As the Supreme Court would at times recognize, the spirit of freedom might have a wider meaning than could be encased in even the most enlightened language and perspective of any given moment.

The Tenth Amendment, reserving to the states powers not given to the federal government, arose from antifederal conviction that only insistence on the limited nature of the federal Constitution could ensure liberty—a conviction resting, of course, on the more basic proposition that local governments were inherently liberty-protecting, while central governments were inherently tending toward tyranny. Both the nature of language itself and the implicit tendencies of government argued against too much reliance on, in Madison's telling phrase, "parchment barriers." Madison, in fact, even regarded both the Ninth and Tenth amendments as redundant. They simply reiterated propositions that, according to eighteenth-century republican thought, were inherent in the idea of a constitution: that liberty was a concept broader than any time-bound words could encapsulate and that a charter of government accepted (ratified) by the people conferred only the powers stated in the charter. Other powers were of course reserved. Madison's final triumph came in his successful fight to prevent the words "expressly" or "clearly" from being added before the word "delegated" in the Tenth Amendment. As Madison intended (occasionally to his later regret) and as the antifederalists feared, this omission left the door open to broad construction and all the consequences for American government that flow from it.

The answer, then, to the often and suspiciously asked question of why the framers of 1787 omitted a bill of rights from the Constitution is not that they were opposed to or even neglectful of the rights in question. This attitude is evident practically and politically in the agreement by the federalists midway through the ratification debate to add a bill of rights, and in the leadership of Madison and other federalists in carrying the bill through Congress in 1789. In this sense it is proper and only fair to include the Bill of Rights in the original philosophy and intent not only of the antifederalists but also of the eleven states that unanimously proposed the Constitution to the public in September 1787, of the thirty-nine men who signed it, of the eleven states that ratified it in 1787-88, and of the public at large that read the explanations of the Constitution in the newspapers and listened to them at the state conventions. As the exchange of letters between Madison and Jefferson reveals, the agreement on the substance of a bill of rights was so open and so complete that Madison was able to learn from Jefferson good reasons, tactically and procedurally, for adding the explicit bill he had thought unnecessary in 1787.

More fundamental, though, is the idea of republican government itself that surrounded and helps us understand the origins and meaning of the Bill of Rights. The rebellious Britons on the western side of the Atlantic in 1776 saw themselves as taking another step in the "westward course" of free government. Harking back generally to the Greek and Roman republics, but having more particularly in mind first the Netherlands and then Britain as the freest nations in modern Europe, Americans in 1776–1791 sought to be the new vanguard. Most fundamental, following the Dutch model, was independence, breaking the grip of the tyrant. Patrick Henry's ringing words further revealed the historical consciousness: "Caesar had his Brutus, Charles I his Cromwell, and George III may profit by their example."

With independence won, though, Americans were aware that the struggle for free government had only begun. Madison's famous study of "Ancient and Modern Confederacies" (1786) and John Adams's detailed ransacking of history in his *Defence of the Constitutions of Government of the United States* (3 vols., 1787) were but the most systematic of the efforts to learn from the past. More learning came from the experience of British America—colonial charters, the growth of legislative power, and so on—but most insight was presumed to come from what Jefferson saw as 143 years (13 x 11) of experience with constitution writing and self-government in the new American states between 1776 and 1787. As Madison concluded soberly in his "Vices of the Political System of the United States" (1787), much of that experience revealed serious flaws in both conception and practice (see chapter 5). Especially chastening, in his view, were the repeated violations, in Virginia and other states, of bills of rights when "popular passions" were kindled against them. Madison thus believed that the structure of government and ultimately the virtue and responsibility of the citizenry were of the most fundamental importance. Recall that his reasons for coming around to support a bill of rights depended on its ability to sustain the more basic propositions: it would give the judiciary a clearer mandate to assert itself against abuse of liberty in the other branches, and its existence in the Constitution would help educate the citizenry in the meaning of freedom (one thinks, for example, of classroom attention to the Bill of Rights and of the streams of visitors to see the original document in the National Archives).

The founders held this view because they had a larger understanding of the place of government in human life and a larger sense of the positive uses of government in a free society than is often the case when a bill of rights is emphasized in isolation. Madison, for example, would have been appalled at any suggestions that the Constitution was principally a statement of the limits of power, that liberty consisted largely of restraints on the rulers, and that the Bill of Rights was the foundation of the rights of individuals. There is some truth in each of these propositions, of course, but the founders would have seen them as simplistic, incomplete, and pusillanimous in any full understanding of the potential and fulfillment of republicanism, liberty, the public good, and federalism.

In the founders' view at least two ideas about government were more important than bills of rights. First was the structure of the government itself. As Madison outlined in *Federalist* Nos. 10 and 51, in arguments that are still part of every explanation of American government, freedom would be preserved in the United States because the "extended sphere" included so many factions (now usually called special interests) that no one or no combination could tyrannize over the rest, and as checks and balances worked throughout the federal system. With exactly the same reasoning he had used in explaining why religious freedom in the United States rested on "the multiplicity of sects" rather than on parchment statements, Madison insisted that proper institutions and processes of government, carefully arranged to rest ultimately on the people but also to contain internal checks on power, were essential to freedom. Thus, for example, trial by a jury of peers would find better protection in its defense by groups in particular states at one time, and by federal judges defending their powers at another, than as an abstract right. This understanding is why Madison's first explanation to Jefferson in October 1787 of the republican character of the new Constitution dealt entirely with its mechanisms and made no reference to either the absence of a bill of rights or the need for one. More fundamental, though, was the positive idea of what self-government might achieve for the polity as a whole and thus for the individuals in it. Self-government was only partially synonymous with limits on power. It was also synonymous with active government in pursuit of the public good.

Thus, when Jefferson persuaded Madison that "a bill of rights is what the people are entitled to against every government on earth," the two Virginians made a crucial advance in understanding the foundations of freedom. Of course, a citizenry schooled in the meaning of liberty and practiced in the act of self-government as well as a frame of government designed to facilitate action for the public good and deter corruption and tyranny were the prime essentials. But they also accepted and built into the American Constitution a vital role for a bill of rights: it would make legal moves to defend human rights easier, and it would help fix in the public mind the sanctity and meaning of those rights. This is not, then, to reduce from three to two the cheers for the Bill of Rights, but rather to keep in mind its crucial but subordinate place in the larger understanding of self-government that undergirds the Constitution.

11
GOVERNMENT
BY CONSENT

When the Bill of Rights is understood as having a crucial but subordinate place in the larger idea of self-government that undergirds the Constitution, one must understand what this full meaning of self-government, or government by consent, is. The principle of republicanism as understood by the framers of the Constitution (see chapter 5) elaborates this meaning, but the principle receives further illumination from the interpretation of the Bill of Rights itself throughout its history. Those who drafted and adopted the Bill of Rights were well aware of this vital connection (see chapter 10), and subsequent interpretation has struggled repeatedly with it. Two groups of twentieth-century Supreme Court cases, the so-called Flag Salute Cases of the 1940s and two freedom of the press cases of the 1960s and 1970s (*New York Times* v. *Sullivan* and *The Pentagon Papers*) particularly reveal the close connection between First Amendment freedoms and the vitality of government by consent.

Laws in Pennsylvania and West Virginia during World War II requiring school children to salute the American flag provoked a searching examination of the place of First Amendment freedoms in the constitutional system. In 1940 a Pennsylvania law ordered that all teachers and pupils "shall be required to participate in the salute honoring the Nation represented by the flag."[1] Serious questions of free expression and free exercise of religion were raised when religious groups, especially Jehovah's Witnesses, objected that the flag salute pledge required of them an exercise forbidden by their faith—and thus infringed their "free exercise" of religion. When the case, *Minersville School District* v. *Gobitis*, duly found its way to the U.S. Supreme Court, it was regarded as a key test of the standing of personal liberty as the nation faced dire threats from Nazi and Japanese warlords.

The Court itself was in the process of transition from the outlook of the "Nine Old Men" who in the 1930s had invalidated New Deal legislation. As Franklin Roosevelt appointed five new justices in four years (Hugo Black, Stanley Reed, Felix Frankfurter, William O. Douglas, and Frank Murphy), the Court not only changed its so-called liberal-conservative coloration, but took more seriously Justice Frankfurter's doctrine of "judicial restraint." It rejected the judicial activism used by the pre-1937 majority on the Court to void laws passed by Congress because they violated the sanctity of contract, taxation, or other clauses or interpretations of the Constitution. Frankfurter elaborated the argument of Justice Holmes that judges should use restraint in imposing their own views (however couched as constitutional verities) on legislative efforts to deal with social and economic issues. Judges thus should give legislatures (federal and state) maximum flexibility in responding as they (and their constituents) saw fit to the ever-changing problems of a free and self-governing society. Under this idea, and responding to the widespread opinion that the Court in the 1930s had too much imposed its (outmoded?) view on popularly supported New Deal measures, Frankfurter and others slowly turned the Court to a more modest estimate of its surveillance over legislators. In so far as this cleared the path for progressive social legislation, New Dealers and other reformers felt themselves vindicated.

When the Pennsylvania flag salute case came before the Supreme Court, however, Frankfurter led his colleagues to an application of judicial restraint less welcome to his erstwhile liberal supporters. With the same logic he had used to castigate the "Nine Old Men" for imposing their dogmas on New Deal legislation, Frankfurter now urged restraint in judging the Pennsylvania law. If the law was a plausible effort to deal with a matter within the powers of the state, as educational policy always had been, and if it did not clearly and palpably violate the U.S. Constitution, then the Court, whatever the personal opinion of the judges (Frankfurter made clear his own distaste for the law), should not interfere with the legislation. Hence, in an 8–1 decision that upset many civil libertarians, the Court, speaking through Frankfurter, upheld the Pennsylvania law.

As debate raged in the law journals, and as the nation, faced with harassment and persecution of Jehovah's Witnesses in many states, continued to struggle with the protection of civil liberties during wartime,[2] the state of West Virginia passed legislation directing the state board of education to foster and perpetuate in all schools "the ideals, principles, and spirit of Americanism." Under this law, the board resolved that the pledge of allegiance to the flag of the United States become "a regular part of the program of activities in the public schools," that "all teachers . . . and pupils . . . shall be required to participate in the salute," and that "refusal to salute the Flag be regarded as an act of insubordination, and shall be dealt with accordingly." The law and resolves in West Virginia followed closely the Pennsylvania law and even incorporated much language from the Court's Gobitis decision. Thus the state officials felt confident they were in accord with the law of the land and were doing their part to inculcate a patriotism necessary if the nation was to survive and triumph in the war.

When West Virginia schools carried out the board's instructions, children who were Jehovah's Witnesses, instructed by their parents, refused to participate in the flag salute on the grounds that it violated the injunction in the Bible (Exodus 20:4–5) against bowing down to a graven image, which they considered saluting a national flag to be. The Witnesses asserted that according to their religion they could give "unqualified allegiance" only to Jehovah and hence would only pledge "obedience to all the laws of the United States that are consistent with God's law, as set forth in the Bible." Within this doctrine of "higher law," however, the Witnesses were willing to pledge "respect to the flag of the United States and acknowledge it as a symbol of freedom and justice to all." School authorities, nonetheless, obeying the clear language of the state resolves, expelled the refusing Witnesses, denied them readmission unless they complied, declared them "unlawfully absent" and "delinquent" when not in school, and threatened to fine and jail the parents, who were responsible for seeing that their children were in school as the law required. The parents brought suit in U.S. district court claiming that the West Virginia statutes violated their right to freedom of religion as guaranteed by the First and Fourteenth amendments to the Constitution. When a federal circuit court restrained enforcement of the law against Jehovah's Witnesses, the state, citing the 1940 case, appealed to the Supreme Court.[3]

By the time *West Virginia Board of Education* v. *Barnette* reached the Supreme Court in June 1943, civil libertarians had developed strong critiques of the Gobitis decision as a grave infringement of First (and Fourteenth) amendment guarantees of freedom of religion and freedom of expression. The Supreme Court itself in dissents and judgments in 1942 and 1943 had so questioned the Gobitis decision that it appeared a majority might be ready to reverse it. Furthermore President Roosevelt had chosen, as his sixth appointment to the

Court in 1941, Attorney General Robert H. Jackson, a brilliant and eloquent constitutional theorist who had no hesitation in confronting Frankfurter's Gobitis argument or in reversing the 1940 decision.

In delivering the opinion of the Court, Jackson went at length through the earlier decision showing what he thought were its flaws, pointing out the absurdities of enforced ceremonies, and concluding with an eloquent restatement of Jefferson's defense of a bill of rights as "what the people are entitled to against every government on earth." Under the Jefferson doctrine that "Almighty God hath created the mind free," Jackson scorned the required compliance as compelling the "affirmation of a belief and an attitude of mind" without the authorities having any way to determine whether the coerced pupils had "become unwilling converts to the prescribed ceremony" or whether they merely "simulated assent by words without belief and by a gesture barren of meaning." "To sustain the compulsory flag salute," Jackson noted, would require the Court to say "that a Bill of Rights which guards the individual's right to speak his own mind, left it open to public authorities to compel him to utter what is not in his mind." Echoing Milton, Mill, and Holmes, Jackson argued that making patriotic ceremonies compulsory rather than voluntary "is to make an unflattering estimate of the appeal of our institutions to free minds. We can have the intellectual individualism and the rich cultural diversities that we owe to exceptional minds only at the price of occasional eccentricity and abnormal attitudes."

In ringing phrases he went on to enlarge the issue to the full dimensions of freedom of expression. "If there is any fixed star in our Constitutional constellation," he declared, "it is that no official, high or petty, can prescribe what shall be orthodox in politics, nationalism, religion, or other matters of opinion, or force citizens to confess by word or act their faith therein." Thus the action of the West Virginia officials "in compelling the flag salute and pledge transcends constitutional limitations on their power and invades the sphere of intellect and spirit which it is the purpose of the First Amendment to our Constitution to reserve from all official control." The very purpose of a bill of rights, Jackson noted in making explicit his own sense of the limitations of democratic government, "was to withdraw certain subjects from the vicissitudes of political controversy, to place them beyond the reach of majorities and officials and establish them as legal principles to be applied by the Court. One's right to life, liberty, and property, to free speech, a free press, freedom of worship and assembly, and other fundamental rights may not be submitted to a vote; they depend on the outcome of no elections." "The majestic generalities of the Bill of Rights," he asserted, "part of the pattern of liberal government in the eighteenth century, had to be translated . . . into concrete restraints on officials dealing with the problems of the twentieth century."[4] This, of course, is what John Adams, Jefferson, Madison, and others had had in mind in declaring certain principles to be natural rights beyond abridgment, at any time by any government whether monarchy or democracy. (Although Jackson did not speak of "natural rights," his use of "fundamental rights" carries much the same intent and meaning.)

Also hearing *West Virginia* v. *Barnette*, however, was Justice Frankfurter, who gave profound expression to the dilemma imposed on governments resting on consent by bill of rights that "withdrew" certain matters from majority vote. Frankfurter began his dissent by observing that as "one who belongs to the most vilified and persecuted minority in history," especially while the Nazi gas chambers did their deadly work at Auschwitz, he could hardly be "insensible to the freedoms guaranteed by our Constitution." He argued, though, that the Constitution guaranteed simply that "no religion shall either receive the state's support or incur its hostility. . . . It gave religious equality, not civil immunity" and in no sense implied "the subordination of the general civil authority of the state to sectarian scruples." Jefferson had made much the same point in 1788: "The declaration that religious faith shall be unpunished, does not give impunity to criminal acts dictated by religious error." A doctrine of impunity, Frankfurter pointed out, would result not in the separation of church and state, "but the establishment of all churches and of all religious groups." Neither the obvious sincerity of religious convictions nor a claim that such convictions relieved a sectarian of certain civic responsibilities could give religious groups immunity from obeying the law. Frankfurter thus explained his own allegiance to a historically accurate understanding of the religious liberty guaranteed by the Constitution. He also made clear his personal distaste for the law before the Court: "Of course patriotism cannot be enforced by the flag salute." Yet, he was unwilling for the Supreme Court to invalidate a West Virginia law both potentially persecutive and misguided in its means. Why?

To answer this question Frankfurter recurred to a basic premise about the protection of liberty in a self-governing society: it depended most fundamentally on the vitality among the people as a whole (the ultimate rulers) of values and sentiments likely to preserve a free society. Instead of focusing on what he regarded as the ill effect of a foolish and illiberal law, he asked his brethren to consider the source, or cause, of the law. It had been passed by the elected representatives of the people of West Virginia, in whose hands, presumably, rested responsibility both for the preservation of the people's rights and for educational policies that would nourish patriotism and good citizenship in schoolchildren. Yet a law had been passed that even in Frankfurter's opinion was antithetical to those ends. Should he, then, as a judge pledged to uphold the Constitution, strike down the law to defend the people against legislative foolishness and infringement on basic rights? He answered no, because to do so would relieve the legislature of responsibility for its illiberality and, even worse, would teach the people to depend not on their own wisdom and activity in choosing legislators but on the decrees of a distant court for the protection of their liberties. The most profound effect of the Court's decision, then, to Frankfurter, was that it diminished the emphasis on proper values in the citizenry, the need for citizen surveillance and active control of the legislature, and the requirement that legislative bodies themselves be wise and protective of liberty. The effect of the people coming to depend on high courts for defense against their own legislatures would be to weaken both their own responsibility for the quality of their representatives and the bond between the citizens and their elected legislative bodies.

To Frankfurter, more important than the immediate invalidation of a bad law (though not one wholly implausible or clearly unconstitutional) was the long-range vitality in the nation of the very "principles of liberty" that would deter the passage of oppressive legislation in the first place. If the people knew that the protection of their rights depended on the acts of their elected representatives and that they would not be "rescued" from their foolishness or inattention by a high court, would they not be encouraged, indeed spurred, to nourish in their communities the values of a free society, then work to elect legislators with those values, and finally to remove from office those who disregarded them? "The liberal spirit," Frankfurter instructed his colleagues and countrymen, could not be

> enforced by the judicial invalidation of illiberal legislation. Our constant preoccupation with the constitutionality of legislation rather than with its wisdom trends to pre-occupation of the American mind with a false value. The tendency of focussing attention on constitutionality is to make constitutionality synonymous with wisdom, to regard the law as all right if it is constitutional. Such an attitude is a great enemy of liberalism. Particularly in legislation affecting freedom of thought and freedom of speech much which should offend a free-spirited society is constitutional.

Reliance for the most precious interests of civilization, therefore, must be found outside of their vindication in courts of law. Only a persistent positive translation of the faith of a free society into the convictions and habits and actions of a community is the ultimate reliance against unabated temptations to fetter the human spirit.[5]

In sum, Frankfurter believed that the long-range health and vigor of a society both free and self-governing depended on the values, wisdom, and vigilance of its citizenry. Thus he was more than willing in the first place for a democratic government to attend directly and even compulsorily to the training of its young people in the values and habits necessary for its good health. "The ultimate foundation of a free society," Frankfurter had written in the earlier flag salute case, "is the binding tie of cohesive sentiment." Schools that "gather up the traditions of a people, [and] transmit them from generation to generation," he added, created a continuity in words and symbols "of a treasured common life which constitutes a civilization." Legislatures and school boards, chosen by the people, required both basic support and wide latitude, then, in determining the common exercises useful in achieving this vital goal. In a further application of this logic, Frankfurter pointed out that citizens so educated would need to have constant practice in and final responsibility for the conduct of self-government. "Where all the effective means of inducing political changes are left free from interference, education in the abandonment of foolish legislation is itself a training in liberty. To fight out the wise use of legislative authority in the forum of public opinion and before legislative assemblies, rather than transfer such a contest to the judicial arena, serves to vindicate the self-confidence of a free people."[6]

In this view Frankfurter's doctrine of judicial restraint was much more than an admonition of caution and humility to his colleagues on the bench. It was most importantly a necessary part of the constitutional system that had to sustain the liberal spirit and the wise democratic practice of the people without which self-government was, in Madison's words, "a farce or a tragedy." Oppositely, Justice Jackson's eloquent and forthright argument of the Court's authority to uphold freedom of expression was, at the very least, fraught with danger. It cast doubt, of course, on the wisdom of the elective process by enlarging the Court's role as overseer of that process: if the people or their representatives did wrong, the Court would see that they were corrected and perhaps even punished. More critically, though, Jackson's doctrine of the superior insight and wide final authority of the Court would necessarily, in both the short and long run, degrade the values, vigilance, self-confidence, and responsibility of the people. If the courts, not the people themselves in their authority as citizens, were to be the essential guardians of fundamental rights, then would not the whole chain of nourishment for responsible citizenship, from schools and proper occupations to a free press and effective local government, be demeaned?

Jackson and Frankfurter thus raised the key questions about the place of a bill of rights in the overall philosophy of the Constitution: are there some principles—the founders in the Enlightenment era called them natural law—so basic, so absolutely valid, that they were not to be subjected to "the vicissitudes of political controversy"? Or as Jackson put it, explicitly, are there "fundamental rights [which] may not be submitted to a vote, [that] depend on the outcome of no elections"? Jackson took his lead from the opening language of the Bill of Rights itself: "Congress shall make no law . . . ." There were "certain subjects" (Jackson's phrase) that even a duly elected, representative legislature of the people (Congress or state assemblies) could not legally (or morally) make certain laws about. The democratic prerogative of the people themselves was limited by the preexistence of "fundamental rights." Although we do not often phrase these rights as so directly in opposition to the acts of elected legislatures, the whole idea of a bill of rights rests on an assumption of their paramount validity. As the Declaration of Independence itself had stated, certain "truths [were] self-evident" and certain rights were "inalienable" and could not justly be denied or violated by any government, monarchical, aristocratic—or democratic.

In fact, the very concept of a constitution, deliberately and solemnly accepted and ratified by the people of a polity, requires validation of some idea of "higher law." Recall Chief Justice John Marshall's declaration that "all those who have framed written constitutions contemplate them as forming the fundamental and paramount law of the nation. . . . The Constitution is . . . a superior, paramount law, unchangeable by ordinary means."[7] Marshall's reiteration of the words "fundamental," "paramount," and "superior" emphasizes Jackson's point about the nature of the Constitution: it is "higher law," controlling of statute law and "unchangeable by ordinary means," that is not to be made dependent on the outcome of elections or legislative maneuver. Although twentieth-century jurisprudence has leveled broadsides at Marshall's view of the Constitution and modern thought often has little patience with the idea of natural law, Jackson's 1943 opinion (and many subsequent ones endorsing or citing it) makes no sense apart from continued acceptance of some form of higher law. Indeed, contemporary preoccupation with the Bill of Rights as the heart of constitutional protection of personal liberty rests upon this assumption. Furthermore, the mingling in both Marshall's and Jackson's words of a universally valid higher law and of seeing the Constitution itself as the higher law reveals again the conflating of the two concepts in 1787–1791 and a continuing tendency to do that. The Bill of Rights, in fact, explicitly joins the two ideas. Jackson's eloquent words defending the right of schoolchildren on grounds of conscience to dissent from a bureaucratically imposed ritual resonate deeply with American political culture and seem as well to bespeak our most profound moral convictions. Students, for example, hearing the facts of the case, seldom side with the school authorities and state legislators.

Yet, Justice Frankfurter's dissent, hard as it is to take in the particular case at hand (as he himself acknowledged), makes a point at least as profound and at least as basic to American constitutional government. In a quintessentially Jeffersonian way, Frankfurter asks us to consider the whole process of self-government in the state of West Virginia. As the U.S. Constitution requires, West Virginia had a republican constitution prescribing that its laws be passed by a representative legislature. In a further Jeffersonian proposition, the legislature had established a system of public schools whose primary purpose was to train young people in responsible citizenship so they would in turn take part in the enactment of wise and public-spirited laws by electing good legislators and rejecting bad ones. This is what Frankfurter meant, following Jefferson, by saying that only the pervasive existence of a "liberal spirit" in a polity would result in "convictions and habits and actions" (laws) of which a "free-spirited society" could be proud. Although this connection between citizen vitality and the law-making process is not explicit in the Constitution, its importance, expressed so insistently by Jefferson, was assumed by nearly all shades of opinion and is elemental to the philosophy of the Constitution.

So, Frankfurter asked implicitly, what happened to the "liberal spirit," to the nourishment of responsible citizenship, when the Supreme Court attempted to "enforce [it] by the judicial invalidation of illiberal legislation"? Such an act, Frankfurter said, was "a great enemy of liberalism" because it "tends toward pre-occupation . . . with a false value." Making the existence of "a free-spirited society," one whose laws were wise and humane and unfettering, depend on enforcement from outside the community itself undercut the vital responsibility of that community for the good conduct of its own affairs. What, for example, did the Court ruling say implicitly to the people of West

Virginia about its political process? "You and your legislature have been illegal, foolish, and even tyrannical in your flag salute law," the Court seemed to say, "so we, in our better judgment, deny it to you." Other implications followed: (1) The people needed a higher body to protect them from their own foolishness. (2) There was little likelihood that the state would achieve any better legislation.

To Frankfurter, these implicit propositions were demeaning and disastrous for self-government. They repeated the accusations of 2,500-years standing that the people at large (including those in the West Virginia electorate) are so blinded by passions, narrow-minded, ignorant, and subject to demagogic manipulation that they cannot safely be trusted with governing themselves. Hence, the argument went in various guises, someone had to save them from themselves—a philosopher king, a divine-right monarch, a Hobbesian tyrant, a noble aristocracy, a "son of Heaven," an elite party, a fuehrer—or a Supreme Court, protected from political pressures, that knew and could enforce a higher law the people tended to ignore or violate. Although there are vitally important differences among these various substitutes for rule by the people of which Frankfurter was poignantly aware, he was correct in pointing out the difficulty and danger in the common skepticism that impeached the whole idea of self-government. Madison had made the same point in *Federalist* No. 57 in defending popular election of the House of Representatives against those who predicted it would enact foolish and unjust legislation: "What are we to say to the men . . . who pretend to be champions of the right and capacity of the people to choose their own rulers, yet maintain that they will choose those only who will immediately and infallibly betray the trust committed to them?"

Frankfurter's position was purely Jeffersonian. He had described its foundation in upholding the Pennsylvania flag salute law. Public schools in a democracy had as their crucial task to "gather up the traditions" of free government, teach them to future citizens, and thus keep alive and well the "treasured common life" that undergirded the idea and practice of self-government under the Constitution. As Jefferson had put it simply in 1779 in proposing a system of universal primary education, all citizens thus "would be qualified to understand their rights, to maintain them, and to exercise with intelligence their parts in self-government."[8] Only with this nourishment of wisdom, good judgment, and public spirit in the citizenry could self-government be good government. Frankfurter thought it important to encourage states to experiment and take responsibility for this function—hence his willingness, even eagerness, to allow them leeway in their efforts.

Frankfurter was aware, of course, of the potential for abuse by totalitarian regimes indoctrinating young people in their civic duties. But he thought the antidote was not to discard the whole idea of such instruction, but to attend to it steadily and properly in ways faithful to self-governing principles. Societies having such principles, Frankfurter thought, had a particularly high obligation to nourish the political sensibilities of their supposedly ultimately powerful citizens.

Another part of Frankfurter's opinion in the Pennsylvania case reveals his answer to the question, "what can/should be done when the representatives of the people pass as foolish and oppressive a law as one compelling a flag salute?" When democratic processes are in effect (as they were in Pennsylvania and West Virginia), Frankfurter argued, "education in the abandonment of foolish legislation is itself a training in liberty." The people would, through the democratic process, have to exercise their political right to either require the legislators to change the law or remove them from office and elect better representatives. This use of "the forum of public opinion . . . to fight out the wise use of legislative authority" was the indispensable essence of democracy. The short-circuiting of it, the overriding of it by judicial fiat, would contribute to an eventually fatal atrophy of this essence. Instead, Frankfurter sought to make the people responsible for the acts of their representatives, to require use of the processes of open debate, party organization, and free elections to achieve good legislation, and to insist on citizen surveillance of unfaithful legislators and thus the repeal of bad laws. Effective use of this process would, Frankfurter argued, "vindicate the self-confidence of a free people."

At least as problematic, from Frankfurter's point of view, as Jackson's opinion for the Court in the West Virginia case were the concurring opinions of Justices Hugo Black, William O. Douglas, and Frank Murphy. Although they could not accept the "natural law" tendencies in Jackson's argument, they were equally opposed to the West Virginia statute. They argued that

the benefits that may accrue to society from the compulsory flag salute are [not] sufficiently definite and tangible to justify the invasion of freedom and privacy that is entailed, or to compensate for a restraint on the individual to be vocal or silent according to his conscience or personal inclination. . . . Neither our domestic tranquility in peace nor our martial effort in war depend on compelling little children to participate in a ceremony which ends in nothing for them but a fear of spiritual condemnation. If, as we think, their fears are groundless, time and reason are the proper antidotes for their errors.[9]

To Frankfurter this argument compounded the error of second-guessing the state legislature by disagreeing only pragmatically with the intent and effect of the statute. The condescension toward the schoolchildren in the phrase about groundless fears and the lecturing to the legislature were to him the worst sort of judicial demeaning of the democratic process. Selection of means and estimates of the effects of statutes was the very heart of the legislative process, so for the Court to substitute its judgment in these areas was profoundly wrong. The attitude toward the people and the legislature reflected in the Black-Douglas-Murphy opinions, Frankfurter believed, was inconsistent with any constructive faith in democracy.

Frankfurter was aware, as were Jefferson and the framers of the Constitution, that the ideal of wise, active citizenship was a very high one, never more than partially attainable. Observation of American politics since 1776, or even 1943, sustains abundantly this skepticism. The essential proposition, however, remains the same: the quality of government by all the people, like that of any lesser number, depends on how good a job those who govern are doing—how wise and honest and attentive to the common good they are. Frankfurter's point was simply that it behooved the Court to buttress that proposition in every way possible—or at least desist from actions that had the effect, as he thought judicial rescue from on high did, of weakening or undermining it. It is not that Jackson believed he had no responsibility for the vitality of local governments—of course he did—or that Frankfurter had no sense of the Constitution as higher law—of course he did. The issue was one of emphasis. Jackson's emphasis on protecting individual rights is the more obvious and readily understood one in any focus on the Bill of Rights. The plight of children "compelled to participate in a ceremony which ends in nothing for them but a fear of spiritual condemnation," as Justices Douglas and Black put it, is poignant and quickly evokes sympathy. Frankfurter simply asked that in attending to these individual rights the Court not overlook or injure the equally important need to sustain and improve the very processes of government without which the rights themselves would not long survive (Madison had made the same point in at first not emphasizing a bill of rights much). The Constitution requires not only that freedom of conscience and expression be protected but also that the spirit of liberty be embedded in and nourished by all the processes of government, especially in the election and conduct of legislatures. The Constitution insists on faithfulness to *both* propositions.

Another part of the First Amendment, that protecting freedom of speech and the press, needs to be understood with the same emphasis on its place in the larger process of self-government. As Donald Meiklejohn has put it, paraphrasing Justice Hugo Black, the First Amendment is "our charter of self-government, providing the means indispensable to forming that responsible and responsive public opinion by which Americans have agreed to be governed."[10] Jefferson himself acknowledged this public emphasis in his own, to modern minds at least, ambiguous, flawed attitude on freedom of the press. In 1787 he made his famous statement, speaking of democracies, that "were it left to me to decide whether we should have a government without newspapers, or newspapers without a government, I should not hesitate a moment to prefer the latter." While president he made the same point in declaring his trust that for "man to be governed by reason and truth, . . . [we must] leave open to him all the avenues of truth. The most effectual [mode] hitherto found, is the freedom of the press." He thought the good sense of the people during the Alien and Sedition Acts crisis "show[s] that they may be safely trusted to hear everything true and false, and to form a correct judgment between them."[11]

These statements, seemingly categorical enough to suit John Stuart Mill, Justice Holmes, and other heroes of civil libertarian thought, though, were only the bright side of Jefferson's view of the freedom of the press. To many critics there is also "a dark side."[12] Still accepting something of the doctrine of "seditious libel," the idea that words, true or not, could threaten the state (i.e., be seditious) and thus be proscribable in the public interest, Jefferson saw the dissemination of information related to affairs of state as a matter of vital concern to the public at large—and hence at least potentially under governmental control. Even more than in a monarchy where decisions of state were not made by the people, Jefferson thought both the quantity and quality of information related to those decisions in a democracy was of the utmost importance. While president he wrote poignantly of the problem created by poor newspapers: "Nothing can now be believed that is seen in a newspaper, . . . that polluted vehicle." He complained of "the demoralizing practice of feeding the public mind habitually on slander, and the depravity of taste which this nauseous ailment induces." He often despaired, then, of how the public could form good judgment when forced to rely on such inadequate sources. He even supported libel actions in Pennsylvania and Connecticut against a partisan press that "pushed its licentiousness and its lying to such a degree of prostitution as to deprive it of credit." Jefferson proposed to the governor of Pennsylvania "not a general prosecution, for that would look like persecution: but a selected one."[13]

Although most current thinking on freedom of expression would find Jefferson's approach misguided, his concern at least is as important today as it was then. If we find ourselves worried about the format and content of TV news programs or upset at the absence of sustained attention to "issues" in presidential campaigns, we know what was on his mind. There is almost certainly, as Jefferson averred, a direct connection between the completeness and accuracy of available information about public issues and the consequent quality of public decisions (caliber of people elected to office, for example). Consequently in a democracy the nature of public information and public discourse is of great interest to the people and to their government. Education, publishing, and media coverage are not merely matters of the private rights of teachers, authors, or reporters but are also linked closely to the quality of public life—whether decisions of government are constructive or calamitous—and hence are very likely vital to the justice, welfare, and even survival of the polity itself. For Jefferson, Madison, and the other founders, then, the First Amendment of the Bill of Rights had particular reference to the public life of what Washington called "the noblest experiment in self-government."

Two recent cases, *New York Times Co. v. Sullivan* (1964) and the *Pentagon Papers* case (1971), reveal that the Supreme Court continues to take seriously this public emphasis. In the Sullivan case, the Court declared essentially that in matters of legitimate public interest, such as accusations against public officials, the First Amendment protected virtually all speech or press comment. In the so-called "thick skin" doctrine, the Court held that those in public office must expect to endure scathing, perhaps even unfair or libelous attack. In this instance, their "rights" as private citizens could not stand against the wider public need for full inquest into all matters of government. Justice William Brennan declared a "profound national commitment to the principle that debate on public issues should be uninhibited, robust, and wide-open, and that it may well include vehement, caustic, and sometimes unpleasantly sharp attacks on government and public officials." The First and Fourteenth amendments, wrote Justice Arthur Goldberg, concurring, "afford to a citizen and to the press an absolute, unconditional privilege to criticize official conduct despite the harm which may flow from excesses and abuses."[14] Public discussion requires the virtually limitless protection of free expression. Against this fiat, private or balancing needs are secondary.

In the *Pentagon Papers* case, Justice Black led the Court to declare emphatically in favor of the right (one might more properly say "need") of access by the public to all information about public matters—in this case, material compiled by the Johnson administration on Vietnam War decisions. When a Pentagon researcher, Daniel Ellsberg, gave the classified documents to the newspapers, the Nixon administration sought an injunction against publication on national security grounds. The Supreme Court struck down the injunction, citing the public's right to know. In a concurring opinion, Justice Black again made the argument on behalf of unrestrained public speech:

> The government's power to censure the press was abolished so that the press would remain forever free to censure the government. The press was protected so that it could bare the secrets of government and inform the people. Only a free and informed press can effectively expose deception in government and paramount among the responsibilities of a free press is the duty to prevent any part of the government from deceiving the people and sending them off to foreign lands to die of foreign fevers and foreign shot and shell. In my view, far from deserving condemnation for their courageous reporting, *The New York Times* and *The Washington Post* and other newspapers should be commended for serving the purposes that the Founding Fathers saw so clearly.[15]

The argument in both cases emphasizes the orientation of the First Amendment toward protecting full and complete *public* discourse. Only thus could the citizenry fulfill its vital function of understanding and deciding public questions. Although Jefferson's flirtation with restraint on the press in order to protect the quality of discourse rests on assumptions other than Black's, they had the same understanding of the intention of the First Amendment. One suspects, furthermore, that Jefferson and Black, because each agreed with the framers on the public-affairs emphasis of the First Amendment, would have found themselves in practical agreement on nearly all particular cases.

The thrust of emphasis on public discussion is evident if we contrast it with the less direct and more limited protection given, for example, to advertisers and pornographers under the "original intent" of the First Amendment. Such "speakers" deserve some protection to uphold a general atmosphere of free expression, but, lacking as they do direct relevance to the vital discussion of the public's business, advertisers and pornographers might be subject to restraint or regulation in the light of conflicting public needs. Consider, hypothetically, a local ordinance prohibiting the sale or distribution of cigarette advertising, *Hustler* magazine, and publications of the Communist party in supermarkets. The first two regulations might be upheld on public health and public decency grounds (and neither publication makes any pretence of contributing to discourse on public affairs), while the last regulation might be struck down as a violation of the First Amendment because of its palpable restraint on discussion of the public's business. Although the Supreme Court has not been at all clear on this distinction, efforts in that direction would be in accord with perception of the Bill of Rights as a foundation of government by consent.

Justice Frankfurter in the flag salute cases and Justice Black in *The New York Times* case, then, whatever their disputes otherwise, agreed profoundly on the need to keep vital the processes of self-government. Frankfurter would have given hearty endorsement to Black's 1968 statement that only by maintaining free and responsible public decision making could "people develop a sturdy and self-reliant character which is best for them and for their governments."[16] And Black, though he voted with the Court in the West Virginia flag salute case, would certainly have applauded Frankfurter's emphasis on "fighting out the wise use of legislative authority in the forum of public opinion." (In fact Black had voted with Frankfurter in the Pennsylvania flag salute case.) Each was offering a version of the repeated arguments of Publius and Jefferson that self-government is not easy. It requires a willingness both to run risks in order for the public to be fully informed and to compel it to take responsibility for its decisions. All agreed that the basic purpose of the First Amendment was to uphold attitudes and law that would improve the process of government by consent framed in the Constitution.

To see the Bill of Rights (especially the First Amendment) as part of the proper functioning of self-government itself, then, is to see its crucial place in the republican ideology of the founding era. Madison's remark that he had "seen the bill of rights [of Virginia] violated in every instance where it has been opposed to a popular current" and Frankfurter's observation 150 years later that "preoccupation with constitutionality . . . rather than . . . wisdom tends to . . . a false value" make the same point. The foundations of freedom in any society are much broader and deeper than their statement in a bill of rights. Madison insisted that social diversity and the checks and balances of limited government provided implicit protection against the tyranny of "overbearing majorities" and that the "maxims of freedom" needed to be made part of the "sentiment" of the people for them to be securely protected. Frankfurter insisted further that without thoughtful and responsible exercise of legislative power by the people and their representatives freedom was not likely to remain secure. Hence, in an argument to which Jefferson devoted a lifetime, everything depended on "improving the discretion" of the citizenry. The status of liberty, of First Amendment freedoms in any society, then, depends on constructive nurture and practice even more than on explicit prohibitions. Within this understanding, the Bill of Rights is both a consistent (and, Madison soon agreed, necessary) part of the Constitution of 1787 and itself an elaboration on the idea of responsible self-government.

Again, this is not to suppose Justice Frankfurter gave but two cheers for the Bill of Rights or that Madison, Jefferson, and Justice Black were neglectful of private rights. Each was respectful of them and insisted on upholding them, but each was also even more attentive to the role of the Bill of Rights in the larger process of self-government. In denying protection (he hoped temporarily) of a particular private right to faithful children, Frankfurter sought an improvement in the democratic process that in the long run would be the only sure foundation for individual rights of any kind. In forestalling unwarranted reliance on "parchment barriers," Madison sought to focus attention on a structure of government that, again, was the only long-range foundation for individual freedoms. Jefferson complained about the press not because he did not value the liberty of the editors, but because he believed the quality of decisions in a self-governing society depended on the quality of public information. Justice Black was willing to limit the right of public officials to sue for libel not because he depreciated that right in and of itself, but because he held in even higher estimation the improved public discourse that would result from the uninhibited criticism of officers of government. The Bill of Rights, then, is not merely a statement of the rights of individual citizens (though it is that in part), but more fundamentally is part of the vital constitutional process wherein, in Frankfurter's words, the ideals of freedom are "translated . . . into the convictions and habits and actions of a community, . . . the only ultimate reliance against unabated temptations to fetter the human spirit."

The argument thus far can be summarized as follows: Since the very idea of a constitution validates a higher law, it is appropriate that parts of the Constitution, particularly the Bill of Rights, declare "fundamental rights" not to be infringed by legislative majorities or "political vicissitudes." But the First Amendment protections, though valuable as private rights, are themselves even more important as essential contributions to the processes of government by consent. Thus in a full understanding of the philosophy of the Constitution, the Bill of Rights is both part and parcel of the document of 1787, as the federalists insisted, and a necessary, explicit further elaboration of fundamental rights, as the antifederalists insisted. The conventional republican ideology of the founding era, moreover, validated both perspectives, as the quick, largely uncontroversial adoption of the Bill of Rights attests to. Finally, the intention of the Bill of Rights is to make government by consent more likely to result in good government, as that idea has generally been understood in human history.

12

GOOD GOVERNMENT

The complex relation between the ideas of individual rights and of government by consent calls attention to what from an outside perspective is often
seen as a disproportionate emphasis on "rights" in Western culture. This is
especially the case for Anglo-American conceptions of government articulated in the seventeenth century by Sir Edward Coke, John Milton, Roger
Williams, Algernon Sidney, John Locke, William Penn, and many others—a
tradition central, of course, to the formation of the U.S. Constitution and to
government under it ever since. With its manifest value in undergirding individual liberty and resisting tyrannies of all kinds, it has become a central part
of thinking about government—and constitutions—in the Anglo-American
world. Yet, to those of other political traditions, with constitutions (written or
unwritten) resting on very different foundations and patterns of thought, emphasis on the idea of rights has seemed both unsuited to human nature and
antithetical to good government.

In 1922, for example, commenting on what he had been learning of Western
thought and political precepts, the Confucian-trained Chinese philosopher
Liang Chi-Chao condemned "the standard of rights upon which is based all
the political thinking of Europe and America." Chinese philosophy, Liang
wrote, "had none of the religious fervor of the Hebrews or Indians, nor little
interest in mystical or metaphysical thinking in which the Greeks and Ger-
mans excel," nor in the "development of objective science." Rather, the contribution of Chinese thinkers in the 2,500 years since Confucius had centered
"on political philosophy . . . and the ethical conduct of mankind in this life."
Paralleling the inquiries of Aristotle's *Ethics* and *Politics*, Chinese philoso-

phers were mundane, practical, and social in their emphasis. They thus attended particularly to relationships among people, to family and societal habits and values, and to the function and purpose of the most overarching social institution, the state itself.

From this standpoint, Liang took a sophisticated and profoundly critical look at Western political thought and practices. His deep respect for the social emphasis in Confucian thought made him draw back from Western individualism and its attendant emphasis on personal rights—as opposed to the powers of government and to the needs of other people in the society. The deep flaw in rights-based thinking, Liang insisted, was its depreciation of "fellow-feeling among men," or benevolence, regarded as the central precept of Confucian thought. To emphasize the claiming or demanding of one's (personal, selfish) rights damaged eventually "even the relationship between father and son, husband and wife," relationships requiring affection and devotion and mutual support, relationships distorted and poisoned if entered into while preoccupied with protecting the separate rights of each individual. With some rhetorical excess, Liang concluded "it is evident that the expression of rights can only be conflict and murder. That a society built on such foundations will ever be safe is inconceivable."[1]

From Liang's perspective, emphasis should not have been on life as individual rights and fulfillment, but on life as a series of rich relationships that made harmony and benevolence the core of the good society. Insisting on one's personal rights as against both government and other people, and nourishing the competitive, adversarial, and separating attitudes that went with them simply made an acrimonious, self-centered cacophony of human society. Furthermore, it made impossible the idea of a harmonious attention through government to all the unifying and mutually beneficial purposes that a society might seek through wise and public-spirited actions. If citizens were intent on protecting private rights and in maintaining their own particular livelihoods to the deliberate or implicit neglect of the benefits of human accord and social harmony, Liang thought, then contention, social struggle, chaos, and war would be the nation's bitter fruit. Instead, he envisioned a synthesis of Western ideas of a more direct role for the people in government with the Confucian emphasis on goodwill in human relationships and an active, benevolent government in wise pursuit of the general welfare.[2]

What Liang sensed was a serious disproportion in Western culture. The excessive emphasis on individual rights separated and set people against each other in myriad ways, creating what later critics would call an "adversarial

society" whose energies and efficiencies were dangerously drained by quarrel-
ing, separating, sueing, and bargaining. In the public sphere this resulted in a
"conflict-of-interest" politics that ignored or depreciated concepts of harmony,
goodwill, and the public interest. To Liang this simply flew in the face of all
that humankind had learned about morality, a good society, and the uses and
functions of government. In a way more akin to Aristotle than to any other
major Western philosopher, Liang's Confucian tradition emphasized the wise
and harmonious conduct of a nation's public affairs to seek the good life for
all, guided by an active and benevolent government.

Thus, though the foundational Lockean concept of the natural rights of the
people and the limitations this placed on government has been and is a powerful bulwark against tyranny and despotism, two other aspects of our public
life also need emphasis. First, and also central to constitutional government, is
the need to establish justice, promote the general welfare, and so on, through
the creation of a more perfect union: government in its active, positive pos-
ture. Second, the heavy emphasis on the rights of the parts (special interest
groups as well as individuals) in our political system contributes to what Elizabeth Drew in 1989 termed "a paralysis in dealing with the most serious issues
facing the country. . . . The President's reluctance to lead, when coupled with
the fear on the part of most members of Congress of taking any steps that
might make a substantial number of their constituents unhappy," she adds,
"makes for a flight from reality." In American politics, Drew observed, "there
is no reward for being responsible, or for facing the hard questions."

In 1992 Richard J. Barnet offered these as examples of such questions:

What can we do to address the structural economic and political problems
that have produced chronic fiscal difficulties in nearly every major city,
impoverished almost a fifth of the nation's children, threatened the physical, economic, and social security of ever larger numbers of our citizens,
and driven ever widening divisions between the winners and the losers in
our fiercely competitive culture? Why has the quality of life—as it is
measured by job security, educational opportunity, prospects for adequate
and affordable health care, confidence in the banking and insurance systems, habitable and convenient places to live, and breathable air and
drinkable water—declined so precipitously in one generation? What
changes in policy are needed to reverse these processes of deterioration,
to build on the extraordinary resources of the nation, and to renew American society? What kind of foreign policy will permit and encourage the

mobilization of the resources and the energy so urgently needed to repair, restructure, and renew the American capitalist economy? What sort of influence can and should the United States exert on the world economy so that civil society in America can be protected and nourished? What are the core political and economic interests of the United States in a world that is changing faster than our capacity to understand the changes? What are the effective means for promoting and protecting these core interests? And by what political process are they to be defined?[3]

Emphasis on the needs and rights of various parts of the body politic, Drew and Barnet insist, have prevented serious and long-range attention to the general welfare.

John Taylor of Caroline had made much the same point about the dangers of factionalism and emphasis on individual rights as he observed the furious party spirit that raged in the United States in the decade following the ratification of the Constitution. To Jefferson's conjectures that it might be entirely proper to encourage a party opposition to "the Monocrats of our country" and that contending parties might be useful watchdogs on each other, Taylor questioned the whole idea of factions, parties, and even constitutional checks and balances as useful to good government. "What are checks and balances," he asked, "but [encouragement to] party and faction? If a good form of government too often fails in making bad men good, a bad form of government will too often succeed in making good men bad." The difficulty with depending on checks and balances to preserve liberty and define public policy was that to do so assumed and even encouraged a competition of self-interests (factions) that pushed aside any need for disinterested pursuit of the public good. Instead of this "balancing of power against power," which stimulated the growth of factions and parties, Taylor urged a system of government that would give "to liberty an ascendant over power, whether simple or complex." In using "liberty" in this way, of course, Taylor meant the positive act of self-government wherein citizens worked together to produce, as the Declaration of Independence had put it, "laws the most wholesome and necessary for the public good."

Taylor resisted the idea that "party spirit is simply the child of nature" and that free government thus must always rest on the conflict of interest among various factions and parties. Such a view, he thought, exalted "avarice and ambition" and resulted in a government "cold, pitiless and insatiable"—like that, Taylor would have agreed, observed so sadly by the 1989–1992 critics.

Instead, Taylor wished to show that "parties . . . are not naturally the issue of every popular government," but rather that even a democracy might achieve the "union in political principle . . . natural to man under a monarchy." Taylor was not advocating a monarchy but hoped that the harmony and sense of common purpose evident in monarchies at their best might be found as well in a government where the people themselves ruled. He feared instead that the checks and balances written into the Constitution would "make good men bad"; by requiring conflict, manipulation, and compromise to negotiate the complex processes of government, the Constitution required people (both citizens and elected officials) to think and act selfishly and adversarially. The checks and balances, he thought, would force such attitudes and behavior on people in government in order to protect themselves and would, in time, become a self-fulfilling prophecy: people would become "bad," that is factionally oriented and organized, in order to use and be part of their "bad form of government." That form encouraged and validated factionalism, Taylor thought, and thus made "human nature" seem, and be, worse than it really was.[4]

The dialogue between Jefferson and Taylor in fact sheds a bright light on common understandings as government began under the Constitution and the Bill of Rights. Each had hoped and supposed, along with virtually all of the founding generation, that political parties would not flourish or even exist under the new Constitution. Following widely accepted eighteenth-century doctrine, parties (synonymous with faction) were regarded as self-interested (and thus corrupt) intrusions on the political process that were, in Madison's words, "adverse to the rights of other citizens or to the permanent and aggregate interests of the community." Noting the party battles of the 1790s, Washington in his farewell address (1796) condemned "the alternate domination of one faction [party] over another . . . [that] has perpetrated the most horrid enormities, [and] is itself a frightful despotism." His graphic language reveals the intensity of his feelings on "the baneful effects of the spirit of party generally."

Washington had come to these strong words after he had expressed his hopes for how and why the country, under its new Constitution, might be well governed. While admitting that "the spirit of party . . . [was] inseparable from our nature" and might, especially in monarchies, furnish "useful checks upon the administration and serve to keep alive the spirit of liberty, . . . in governments purely elective, [the] spirit [of party is] not to be encouraged." Instead Washington hoped that the country might be governed according to "consistent and wholesome plans, digested by common counsels and modified by mutual interests." The "public administration," he insisted, should not be "the mirror of the ill-concerted and incongruous projects of faction."[5]

Although both Taylor and Washington wrote at a time of bitter partisan debate and intense party effort (indeed, each took part, however reluctantly or indirectly), their words reveal important aspects of the climate of political ideas within which the Constitution was framed and implemented. Taylor sought to "give liberty an ascendant over power," rather than "balance power against power," and to achieve a "union in political principle." Washington also saw benefit in shared political principles and sought government in accord with "consistent and wholesome plans," "common counsels," and "mutual interests," rather than the "ill-concerted and incongruous projects of faction." He also deplored the tendency for divisive, irrational, and self-seeking energies to distract and confound wise and disinterested counsel, while Taylor more profoundly questioned whether the whole system of checks and balances itself, defended so enthusiastically by Publius in 1787–1788, was not pathological in its encouragement of faction and contention. Good government was, then, even under constitutions "purely elective," dependent on public-spirited pursuit of the common good, just as under rule by one or a few.

As the support of the Bill of Rights by Jefferson, Taylor, and even Washington reveals, there are important ways in which a defense of natural, or human, rights is not the same as factionalism and special interest advocacy. Yet both concepts emphasize the parts, whether individuals or groups, rather than the whole. Although defense of one's rights may be self-advocacy at its best and defense of one's interests a less worthy self-advocacy, they are both, as Liang Chi-Chao discerned so poignantly from his more socially oriented perspective, a distraction from *common* counsels. Although Jefferson and the other founders would not have agreed with Liang's denigration of "the expression of rights" and grasped better than he did the use of "rights-thinking" in protecting human freedom, they would have understood the positive side of his concern: care should be taken to preserve attitudes and mechanisms vital to active government in the *public* interest. In fact, that was the conclusion that Madison and Jefferson had shared even as they came to the end of the exchange that had persuaded Madison to support a bill of rights. Neither wanted a bill of rights to weaken, in Jefferson's words, "the whole frame of government" (see chapter 10).

The Constitution, then, even in the midst of the argument that requires inclusion of the Bill of Rights, is seen as subordinating it to a larger understanding of the foundations of good government. There was a certain agreement, moreover, between this subordination of the Bill of Rights, together with the positive condemnation of checks, balances, and factional politics, and Liang's reservations about emphasis on the rights of individuals and the divisions in society. Washington, Taylor, Madison, and many others were registering their conviction both that government was a vital, constructive part of human affairs and that to be good, government had to draw on and mobilize the public-spirited, potentially harmonizing sentiments of citizens and elected public officials. Although Liang was inclined to see individual rights as interfering too much with social harmony and Western civil libertarians tend to see calls for social harmony as too limiting to individual liberties, the political thinking behind the Constitution and the Bill of Rights in fact supposed that individual liberties, properly understood in their public purpose, were essential to a social harmony that was itself the foundation of good government.

Joseph Galloway had made the same point in 1775 when he asked British colonials to consider "whence the rights of America are derived." By this Galloway meant the still largely extant (though increasingly threatened) rights of free press, freedom of religion, trial by jury, taxation only by elected representatives, and so on that were generally referred to by both loyalists and rebels as "the Rights of Englishmen." Having in mind both ancient common law protection and the more specific listing of freedoms in the English Bill of Rights of 1689, Galloway asserted that the foundation of colonial freedoms was "the constitution of the British state." "Protection from all manner of unjust violence, . . . [from] the private injustice of individuals, [and from] the arbitrary and lawless power of the state," Galloway pointed out, came from the existence of effective legislative, police, and court systems that assure to citizens the actual enjoyment of the right. Without this "the right itself [however "inalienable" or morally universal] would be of little estimation. . . . In proportion to the stability of this security," Galloway concluded, "all governments are more or less free, and the subjects happy under them."[6]

If the foundation and reality of bill of rights freedom is seen, then, as imbedded in both a larger framework of constitutional self-government and a political culture pervaded by "the liberal spirit," the many dimensions of a free society, and a richer and less prickly adversarial idea of "rights" than that criticized by Liang Chi-Chao, become visible. He may be in some degree correct that a society that emphasizes personal rights—i.e., encourages each individual to see his or her rights and interests as protected against interference by governments, corporations, groups, and other individuals—is inherently factious and conflict-creating and thus harmful to social accord and a sense of the common good. If so, then it becomes necessary to think of personal rights in a larger context of government and political culture. If, for example, the "natural" way to combat bad medical treatment is to bring a malpractice suit against offending physicians, then the health-care system will be burdened with all the hostility, mistrust, defensiveness, and expense that go with adversarial proceedings. On the other hand, if the education, licensing, and professional practice of physicians were such as to earn the trust and respect of patients and if the culture encouraged compromise and good-natured accommodation in reaching agreements and in resolving differences, then health care might be both less expensive and more effective.

To thus put the matter of health care, of course, raises basic questions about the nature and purpose of government and the consequent place of personal rights in any society. As Galloway's argument about meaningful protection of rights suggests, much depends on how active and constructive a role government is able to play. If it is watchful of the education and licensing of physicians so that the public can generally trust their ability, conscientiousness, and integrity, then people will be more inclined to find their protection against malpractice in such a system of *general* welfare rather than in personal law suits. Furthermore, if the political culture of a society is such that there is a strong habit of community discussion and resolution of public concerns such as health care, then the community might possess skills and human resources that would lead to effective public policy. Similarly, recalling Frankfurter's argument in the flag salute cases (chapter 11), if a community (or state) is in the habit of thoughtful, public-spirited discussion of its educational needs, including the vital encouragement of good citizenship as well as the need for tolerance in a pluralistic society, more constructive solutions—nourishing both democratic processes and personal liberties—are likely to be found than when emphasis is entirely on the rights of particular individuals or groups. And, if Madison, Jefferson, Frankfurter, and others are correct that the long-range survival of both democratic government and personal liberties depends on a liberal spirit pervading society, then Liang Chi-Chao quite sensibly discerns grave liabilities in a "culture of rights" that habitually pits individuals and groups adversarially.

Alexis de Tocqueville also expressed the danger in a too-private orientation when he coined the word "individualism" in 1835 to describe an attitude more prevalent in the United States, he thought, than elsewhere. Individualism was different from the ancient and pervasive "egoism," or selfishness, that had afflicted humankind always and everywhere and had been the bane of countless moral philosophers. Rather, individualism was a "calm and considered feeling" Tocqueville found prominent in the United States, "which disposes each citizen to separate himself from the mass of his fellows—and leaves the greater society to look after itself." Individualism is thus not the common vice of selfish feeling, but rather what Tocqueville calls "a misguided judgment," a "deficiency of the mind" wherein a person supposes his well-being rests on his own habits and abilities and is thus independent of other social forces. This misguided notion, Tocqueville thought, "not only makes every man forget his ancestors but . . . hides his descendants, and separates his contemporaries from him; throws him back forever upon himself alone."[7] The essence of individualism, then, is a choice or judgment that celebrates and extols self-interest and self-achievement and personal rights more or less to the neglect of explicit concern or capacity for benevolence, attention to the common good, or civic virtue.

This individualistic starting point, so common in Western history since the Renaissance and especially in the United States, is particularly important because it has a profound effect on attitudes toward government and personal rights. It carries with it the suppositions that society is no more than the sum of the parts (including groups as well as individuals with special or personal interests) and that the role of government is largely to be the honest broker: to be sure that all interests and groups and individuals are part of the governing process (have "access"), to arrange compromises, and to see that dominant or even disproportionate power that might infringe rights or privileges is, as much as possible, prevented. Definitions of the rights of the governed, of justice, and of the public good all derive essentially from this idea of the nature and purpose of government. The most problematic outcome of the modern preoccupation with interests, rights, and individualism, then, is a vigorous, adversarial factionalism that pits persons and groups and pressures of all kinds against each other in the political arena. Although this approach and the attendant public strife is to some extent legitimated in the philosophy of the Constitution ("sown in the nature of man," Madison said), it is by no means its full purpose—nor is individualism there celebrated as enthusiastically as Tocqueville found it to be fifty years after 1787.

Emphasis on individualism, moreover, becomes profoundly paradoxical in its impact on government under the Constitution. It does provide grounds for resisting encroachments on personal rights, but it also threatens to so atomize, fracture, and antagonize public life that ability to benefit from the good uses of government is weakened. Even the existence of order and law itself, upon which the practical protection of civil liberties depends, might be undermined. It is even more deeply paradoxical that emphasis on individual rights, the "natural rights" so much at the heart of appeals to protect personal liberties of all kinds, is also the essence of a factional, "who-gets-how-much-of-what" understanding of politics that denies any higher law—things about which "Congress shall make no law . . . ." An outlook that sees habitually the rights of individuals and groups as the starting point of government, though in a way inclined to put basic principles above statute law and social conditions, also often has the effect of insisting that the claims, needs, and priorities of individuals and groups must be attended to whatever the public good or long-range perspective might seem to require.

It was this ambivalence and atomizing tendency that so intrigued and at times troubled Tocqueville as he assessed the impact of what he called individualism. Thinking of the high culture of the aristocratic nations of Europe and of the organic sense of wholeness and social cohesiveness in traditional polities, he lamented that American society seemed "devoid of poetry and greatness" and seemed unfavorable "to some of the finer parts of human nature." Yet, observing American government, he felt that "democracy may be reconciled with respect for property, with deference for rights, with safety to freedom, with reverence to religion." He came around to this cautiously more favorable assessment by observing some ways that the individualistic aspects of American society actually had good results. The role Americans had in local government allowed them to see how their individual needs, for example for good roads, required cooperative effort with one's neighbors. This, Tocqueville thought, "leads a great number of citizens to value the affection of their neighbors and kindred, perpetually brings men together, and forces them to help one another, in spite of the propensities which sever them."[8] He even thought, following Jefferson, that the public-spiritedness acquired on the local level might become an instinct or habit and thus be significant at state and national levels of government as well.

American propensity to form private associations, anticipated and nourished implicitly by the federal nature of the Constitution, was even more helpful in combatting the bad effects of individualism. Americans, Tocqueville noted in amazement, formed voluntary associations "to give entertainments, . . . to build inns, to construct churches, to diffuse books, to send missionaries to the antipodes; and in this manner they found hospitals, prisons, and schools." Lacking the noble lords or great families that often sponsored charitable enterprises in aristocratic nations, Americans had to come together, assemblages of relatively equal and powerless individuals, to accomplish such goals as reducing drunkenness, combatting illiteracy, or abolishing slavery. Tocqueville thought that in democratic America, "where men are no longer united among themselves by firm and lasting ties" as was true in traditional societies, it was still possible to achieve communal action by persuading each citizen that "private interest obliges him voluntarily to unite his exertions to the exertions of all the rest."[9] Although he understood that this enlightened self-interest was not a moral substitute for true benevolence or civic virtue, at least it furnished a replacement of sorts. In these reflections Tocqueville revealed a political understanding close to that embodied in the Constitution in that he valued greatly the bonds of accord and public spirit in human society, even as he also valued the vitality of individualism.

Tocqueville made a similar point, more positively and systematically, when discussing the place of religion in American society. Having in mind the time-honored European idea that church and state needed to be connected in order for religion to flourish and for moral precepts to guide the state, Tocqueville was amazed to find that "there is no country in the whole world in which [the Christian] religion retains a greater influence over the souls of men than in America," where church and state were separated, nor any nation where religion more swayed affairs of state. He found this to be true because the absence of government support of churches meant they had to elicit the voluntary, fervent commitment of the faithful. Then, thus armed with genuine zeal for religious and moral principles and aware that no formal connection existed between church and state, the people brought their conscientious convictions to bear on matters of state through elected officeholders who shared or responded to their beliefs. Tocqueville concluded that though "religion in America takes no direct part in the government of society, . . . it must be regarded as the foremost of the political institutions of that country." Tocqueville thought this especially important in the individualistic, anarchic-tending United States because "while the law permits the Americans to do what they please, religion prevents them from conceiving, and forbids them to commit, what is rash or unjust."[10] Like the drafters of the Constitution, Tocqueville cherished the Bill of Rights as much for its contribution to the public good as for its private utility.

Tocqueville had, though, identified a key constitutional dilemma: how could the emphasis on individual rights spawned by freedom and diversity be combined with a positive freedom to pursue good government? In his view, the habits of forming private associations and of utilizing local authorities to deal with social problems were crucial, if informal, parts of good government. The existence of an unofficial but nonetheless powerful moral convergence resting on religious commitment was another key part of the American constitutional polity. Could Liang Chi-Chao be right that the kind of individualistic, rights-oriented political philosophy dominant in the West and especially in the United States in the twentieth century was deeply flawed in its explicit lack of cohesiveness, inattention to relationships, and neglect of the blessings of union? If so, then one must ask as well whether this flaw is fundamental to the Constitution—is it an inevitable projection? Is what Tocqueville saw as a desolate future, where man is "thrown back forever upon himself alone"— what Liang saw as "the collapse of civilization"—the only one possible under the Constitution?

The root constitutional question then becomes whether it is possible to govern well—to form a more perfect union and achieve something of the enormous potential for good that comes from human accord—under political ideas and habits that focus almost entirely on the rights of the parts. The tension or contradiction is apparent: to assume as a starting point that we are at birth autonomous individuals whose path though life requires repeated assertions of our rights and our differentness, especially in the face of a tyranny-tending government, is surely at odds with a conception of life as a matrix of sustaining and fulfilling relationships as well as with the Aristotelian idea that government exists "not for the sake of life only, but for the sake of the good life." The first sees the whole as merely the sum of the parts while the second sees the whole as more than the sum of the parts. Madison's answer to the root question was "no," which was the grounds for his insistence on making the Bill of Rights part of a larger constitutional framework. He and the other founders, we might say, assimilated their fashionable Lockean emphasis on the individual to a bedrock Aristotelian emphasis on good government.

It is this larger pattern of the meaning of good and free government that, as we saw in examining the origin of the Bill of Rights (see chapter 10), the founders understood very well as they drafted and ratified the Constitution. They knew, as the recent histories of the Netherlands and Great Britain had shown, that freedom and self-government depended as much on the general openness of the society, the enterprise and creativity of the people, and the vigor and responsiveness of the government as on abstract statements of principle. But even these abstract statements of principle, called natural rights and set forth in the Declaration of Independence and in constitutions and state bills of rights during the revolutionary era, modern and Lockean as they sounded, were imbedded in an understanding of government still basically Aristotelian. The founders had been taught to think about government in Aristotelian terms: the purpose of all good government was the general well-being and constructive improvement of the polity, whether rule was by one, the few, or the many. There could be good government by one (as Pericles or the Emperor Hadrian proved), by a few (the Dutch aristocracy of the seventeenth century, for example), or by the many (Athens at its best). Or there could be bad government by one (countless tyrants), by a few (English oligarchy under Lord North), or by the many (Athens at its worst).

The key with any number or process of government was the result: was the public good of the polity as a whole (rather than partial, dynastic, class, or factional interest) the guiding idea? How well a society was governed was fundamental: objective standards—the prosperity, creativity, beauty, fairness, etc., of the society—could be used to judge the quality of government, whatever the number of rulers. The founders kept this attention to the importance and quality of government in mind as they absorbed the new Lockean concern for individual rights—thus containing, perhaps with some logical inconsistency, the basic virtues of two different political philosophies. In fact the framers of the Constitution stated the objective ideals, more or less clearly and commonly understood (though of course without agreement on details), in the preamble: justice, common defense, domestic tranquillity, general welfare, and liberty were the purposes for which the processes of government (the rest of the Constitution) were put in place (see chapter 7). To achieve these Aristotelian goals was the essence of the good and just society the founders sought. The Bill of Rights simply made explicit the limitations on the rulers and the rights of the people inherent in such an idea of good government.

This is not to argue, of course, that the society that existed in the United States in 1787–1789 had reached those ideals. The preamble merely set the agenda for later generations. The body of the Constitution, it was hoped, would provide a process of government that would facilitate their gradual achievement. The process, dependent on the wisdom, vigilance, and public spirit of the people (from ordinary citizen to the president), has seemed sometimes to move toward these ideals, sometimes not. American history can be understood, in fact, as some failed and some successful efforts to establish justice, promote the general welfare, and so on. The civic virtues of the leaders and people of each generation—thoughtfulness, patriotism, tolerance, goodwill, fairness, well-informedness—would determine whether it fulfilled or missed its opportunity. This responsibility is implicit in the self-governing, republican principle of the Constitution.

Jefferson and the other most thoughtful founders—Franklin, Washington, Madison, George Mason, and John Adams, for example—as well as every American theorist of public education from Horace Mann to John Dewey and Ernest Boyer have recognized this critical need to train the citizen-officeholders in a self-governing society in these civic virtues. Every public school system in every state in the country, every syllabus for social studies, and almost every college and university in the nation accept some obligation to encourage good citizenship. This is a way of saying that a self-governing nation recognizes that if the common business is to be conducted beneficially, the participants in that governing—potentially everybody—must possess in some degree the qualifications essential to that good conduct. Thus, these civic virtues are as necessary now as they were two hundred years ago if self-government is to be good government.

These qualities, however, acknowledged and nourished explicitly in such functions of state and local government as maintenance of public schools, support of public celebrations, and community organization, also required support from the culture more generally. When John Adams considered why "republican principles" of self-government were more firmly rooted in New England than in some other states, he listed "five particulars": (1) The people had left England in "purer times," attached to liberty and good principles. (2) "Institutions [existed] for the Support of Religion, Morals and Decency." (3) "Institutions [existed] . . . for the Education of Youth, supporting Colleges at the Public Expence and obliging Towns to maintain Grammar schools." (4) Town-meeting government existed, which "makes Knowledge and Dexterity at public business common." (5) "Laws for . . . a frequent Division of landed Property [existed, which] prevents Monopolies of Land."[11] Adams's insight was that self-government worked well only when the society's institutions, habits, and laws nourished the perspective and values always essential to good government—again the same list of civic virtues. This sort of attention to the broader political culture, which Tocqueville would emphasize in 1835, was, as Adams's reflections reveal, already seen as foundational to constitutional government in the founding era.

Although it is possible to think of this political culture in secular terms—as the classical writers did, for example, and as the more secular of the founders such as Jefferson were sometimes inclined to do—in the United States, during most of our national history agreement on the civic virtues has had a strong connection with widely shared religious precepts and values. Sometimes thought of as a kind of "civil religion," these precepts derived from Biblical texts such as the Ten Commandments and the Sermon on the Mount, from centuries of Christian theology and institution building, and from Protestant emphases on individual conscience, hearing and studying the Word, and lay participation in church government. Almost all education in the United States, at least during the eighteenth and nineteenth centuries, was either conducted directly by Christian clergymen or, as with the "McGuffey Reader" emphasis in public schools, was phrased in Christian moral terms. It was widely assumed, moreover, that this Christian worldview was not only generally conducive to the development of the kind of character needed for self-government (John Adams's point about New England) but that Christian precepts should guide the very conduct of government itself. This is not to say, of course, that all Americans paid heed to these precepts, or that they were found *only* in Christianity, or that the precepts translated easily into agreed-upon public policy. It simply suggests that there existed a pervasive like-mindedness on ideas of justice and the public welfare that contributed substantially to the definition of good government under the Constitution—a circumstance that, in a general way, still exists, two centuries later in a much more culturally diverse nation.

Two examples, one from the founding era and one more current, illustrate the informal but important connection between shared values and the substance of good government. James Madison, author of the First Amendment of the Bill of Rights, favored separation of church and state because he believed that religion would then be much more flourishing and influential (see chapter 7). The moral attentiveness and conscientious conviction people brought to their roles as citizens in a self-governing society, thought Madison, would then vastly improve the quality of government. As Tocqueville noted, democratic government in the United States, with its strong centrifugal tendencies of individualism and pluralism, benefited from the widespread agreement in values and principles provided by shared religious convictions. Thus, in a rather ironic way, Tocqueville observed, the officially nonreligious character of the United States resulted in a strengthened commitment to and agreement on important values and habits that undergirded civil society. The Bill of Rights guarantee of religious liberty, then, understood as part of a constitutional polity, was viewed as useful not only in protecting an individual right but also in strengthening the public virtue essential to good government.

A modern version of this same point can be found in a 1970 Supreme Court case (*Walz* v. *Tax Commission*) upholding tax exemption for churches and other charitable institutions. Chief Justice Warren Burger noted in his opinion for the Court that the New York State tax exemption specifically at issue applied to churches and other "entities that exist in a harmonious relationship to the community at large, and that foster its moral or mental improvement." Burger thought the state quite properly undertook to encourage such institutions. Constitutional provisions guaranteeing that religion be neither established nor interfered with could not be construed to prohibit such encouragement. "Few concepts are more deeply imbedded in our national life," Burger added, "beginning with pre-Revolutionary times, than for the government to exercise at the very least benevolent neutrality toward churches and religious exercise generally so long as none was favored over others and none suffered interference." In the same case Justice Brennan upheld the tax exemption both because "churches contribute to the well-being of the community in a variety of non-religious ways" and because they "contributed to the diversity of association, viewpoint and enterprise essential to a vigorous, pluralistic society."[12] Both arguments—the need for institutions to "foster... moral or mental improvement" and to nourish a "vigorous, pluralistic society"—are, of course, entirely in accord with the thinking undergirding the Constitution.

Again, the emphasis is on the vital contribution value-conserving and community-enriching institutions make to the overall well-being of the nation's public (shared) life. Although Burger and Brennan clearly valued the protection of individual religious liberty, they valued as much the contribution churches and other charitable institutions made to the *collective* good. Justice Black made the same point in defending freedom of expression in the 1960s and 1970s (see chapter 11). Thus understood, individual liberties can be relieved of the adversarial, divisive, antisocial connotations Liang Chi-Chao saw in the dominant Western emphasis on rights. Put yet another way, if the civic usefulness of rights such as freedom of expression and freedom of religion is fully understood and appreciated and thus makes its crucial contribution to the openness and good government of the society as a whole, then the more problematic aspects of a preoccupation with individual rights that "disposes each citizen to separate himself from the mass of his fellows... and leaves the greater society to look after itself," are greatly diminished. What is shared, what can be worked out together, and what can be gained from human accord must be emphasized if the "war of all against all," or even a politics of faction and conflict of interest so abhorrent to Taylor and Washington, is to be avoided.

The momentous events in China, Eastern Europe, and the Soviet Union itself in 1989—the two-hundredth anniversary of a similarly momentous year when in 1789 the modern era began with the French Revolution and the start of government under the new Constitution of the United States—dramatize the linkage between a bill of rights and good government. The Soviet constitution of 1936, the Chinese constitution of 1954, and most of the constitutions of the "democratic" republics of Eastern Europe contain lists of the rights of the people, including freedom of expression and protection for the accused. These statements, though, have been classic examples of Madisonian "parchment barriers" because they had no effect when up against the intentions of the all-powerful party or state. The overwhelming fact was that the state and its sole legal instrument, the party, held absolute, irresponsible power. So it did what it pleased, with no allowance or means for resistance, dissidence, protest, or even complaint. This was precisely Madison's point in 1787–1788 when he focused almost entirely on the processes of government, the delimiting and division of powers, checks and balances, and ways for making officials responsible to the people. Only with such mechanisms in place would the rights and liberty of the people be meaningful. Freedom depended not so much on statements of rights as on a vigilant and virtuous citizenry, on an open society, and on "a more perfect Union," that is, on good government.

In every one of the nations of Eastern Europe the key to reform and revolution has been the destruction of the monopoly on power held by the Communist party. Without that destruction, reformers in Warsaw, Prague, and Bucharest were sure they would be neither self-governing nor free. The great enemy of their liberty, they knew all too well after forty years of tyranny, was the unchecked power of the Communist party in each country, kept there by the use or threat of Soviet tanks. With that form of government in place, they were not free, whatever the words about rights in their constitutions. The people of Beijing who lost to the tanks in Tiananmen Square, of course, know exactly the same thing—and so do the people of Moscow who overcame the party and its tanks in August 1991.

The reformers in Berlin and Budapest and Sofia in 1989 knew, too, that their struggle had only begun. Like Americans in 1789–1791, Eastern Europeans may want to have their liberties set forth solemnly in bills of rights. This formality will serve the same important purposes of fixing these rights in the hearts and minds of the people and of providing clear standards for application by the court in case of violations, as Madison foresaw for the United States. But without the processes of honest, effective, yet limited government sustained by freedom-enhancing attitudes and institutions among the people, terror and oppression and empire could easily return. This is what Vaclav Havel has in mind in his repeated insistence that the most critical need in the Czech and Slovak Republic is the growth of a civil society. For the United States this experience suggests the need, as embodied in the Constitution, for a better balance between the assertion of individual rights and other claims of special interests and deliberate, public-spirited attention to the overall conduct of government. It has to do with the ancient idea that rights entail responsibilities and with a clearer understanding that only good government can in the long run sustain personal liberties.

To focus only on the protection of certain individual rights or to denigrate the importance of government and seek dogmatically to diminish it everywhere is to forget the constitutional importance of a wise structure of government, able officials who take public service seriously, and a populace in some degree thoughtful and public-spirited in its exercise of citizenship. Recall again Jefferson's argument in 1779 for universal public education in Virginia: with it citizens "would be qualified to understand their rights [and] to maintain them." So far so good, but he added that citizens would also learn "to exercise with intelligence their parts in self-government."[13] Both of these propositions are essential to the idea of good government implicit in the philosophy of the Constitution.

PART IV

THE CONSTITUTION IN THE TWENTY-FIRST CENTURY

13

THE LIMITS OF CONSTITUTIONAL PRESCRIPTION

Recall again that in 1776 the Declaration of Independence asserted as the first complaint against George III that "he had refused his assent to laws, the most wholesome and necessary for the public good," and that Alexander Hamilton had declared in *Federalist* No. 1 his hope that the new Constitution might establish "good government from reflection and choice." Each statement affirms the importance of the basic republican idea of active self-government to "promote the general welfare." Moreover, each sees self-government as ongoing, the people thinking about and choosing public policy and making laws to achieve the public good. Thus, fundamentally, republicanism is a process wherein a self-governing people identify and deliberate on questions of common concern (laid out generally in the preamble; see chapter 7) and then, through their government(s), decide what to do, or not do, about them. The body of the Constitution sets forth both what the federal portion of this function of government is and what the mechanisms and processes are for making decisions in the allotted areas. The Bill of Rights establishes further guidelines essential if the people are to have the free, fair, and open society necessary for self-governing citizens to make deliberative choices about public policy.

As the two quoted statements and countless other documents of the founding era reveal, this ongoing process was understood to be the leading goal of the American Revolution and the key to achieving true liberty. Implicit was the idea that much of importance would be decided through the process of the polity governing itself over the years. Thus, there was much that the Constitution left unsettled. Since government had as its basic purpose the convenience and well-being of the people (their "general welfare") and since each generation would have its own problems and aspirations, the machinery of government would be in constant, active use (remember Jefferson's famous assertion, in 1789, that "the earth belongs to the living"). The intent of the Constitution, and one of its fundamental axioms, then, is that much is left unsettled in it, in order that the republican principle of ongoing self-government be rendered genuine, central, and vital. There are many matters, therefore, about which the Constitution does not prescribe, about which it intends that the republican mechanisms of federal and state government (themselves guaranteed in the Constitution) should decide as time goes by.

For example, the Constitution deliberately left the question of slavery largely up to the states. In the revolutionary era the states north of the Mason-Dixon line had moved toward either outright or gradual abolition of slavery. In Massachusetts, Connecticut, Rhode Island, Vermont (still a self-proclaimed "independent" nation), and Pennsylvania, slavery was under attack in constitutional provisions, statutes, and court decisions. By the time of the Federal Convention of 1787 it had been substantially eliminated in those states. New York and New Jersey moved more slowly toward abolition, while in the mid-South, slaveholding states of Delaware, Maryland, and Virginia proposals for gradual abolition, eventually defeated, were under consideration.[1] Thus those who framed, ratified, and opposed the Constitution lived in the presence of active, often effective opposition to slavery through republican mechanisms in most of the states of the union.

As the Federal Convention revealed, though, the positive defense of slavery, especially in Georgia and South Carolina, together with a widespread willingness to compromise or at least to acknowledge the existence of slavery in the union, meant that many provisions of the new Constitution not only accepted the presence of slavery but had the clear intent of leaving it alone in the states where it did exist. Thus four provisions more or less explicitly accept slavery: (1) the three-fifths clauses on enumeration for representation and direct taxation (Art. I, Sec. 2 and Sec. 9), (2) the protection of the foreign slave trade until 1808 (Art. I, Sec. 9), (3) the requirement that states return fugitive slaves (Art. IV, Sec. 2); and (4) the prohibition of any amendment of the slave importation or capitation clauses before 1808 (Art. V). According to one accounting, eleven other provisions, such as the protection of states against "Insurrections" and "domestic violence," the requirement that states give "Full Faith and Credit" to the laws and judicial proceedings of other states, and incorporation of the effects of the three-fifths clause into presidential elections, all protected or benefited slaveholding states. Moreover, the insistence on these provisions by the Deep South during the Constitutional Convention, their rather ready acceptance by most other delegates, and the frequent acknowledgment of the "safety" of slavery under the new Constitution in the ratification contest further reveal the widespread condoning of slavery in the founding era.[2] The effect of these clauses, as American history between 1789 and 1861 revealed repeatedly, was to enhance the power of the slave-holding states within the union and to prevent federal action interfering with slavery within the states.

On the other hand, there were vigorous antislavery speeches at the Federal Convention and repeated reference to the close connection between the questions of slavery and of the *federal* nature of the union. Gouverneur Morris declared the slave trade a "defiance of the most sacred laws of humanity" and sought repeatedly to eliminate the benefits the South received from being able to count three-fifths of its slaves in determining congressional representation. George Mason spoke of "the evil of having slaves" and of its "pernicious effect on manners," especially in comparison to the increase of white freemen "who really enrich and strengthen a country." Many delegates spoke of the hope that slavery would soon disappear in the nation, while Luther Martin declared it "inconsistent with the principles of the revolution." James Madison thought it "wrong to admit in the Constitution the idea that there could be property in men" and approved the exclusion of the word "slavery" from the Constitution.[3] Although these antislavery sentiments had little effect on convention decisions (in the face both of insistent Deep South defense of slavery and of a strong tendency among delegates from all sections to compromise and accept its existence), they do reveal a climate of opinion hostile to it in principle.

More significant for the status of slavery under the proposed constitution were comments about its place in the new federal system. Oliver Ellsworth stated the common view that every state should do as it pleased because "the morality or wisdom of slavery are considerations belonging to the States themselves." That was the case under the Articles of Confederation, so he saw no reason "for bringing it within the policy of the new" constitution. John Rutledge and Charles Pinckney of South Carolina claimed jurisdiction for their state and declared, while resisting federal control of the slave trade, that their state might "by degrees" on its own abolish it, as Maryland and Virginia had done. The assumption thus was both that slavery and the slave trade were the legitimate objects of state legislation and that liberalization might be expected even in states presently most committed to slavery. Roger Sherman, while opposing constitutional limitation on the slave trade in Georgia and South Carolina because "the public good did not require it to be taken from them," observed that "the abolition of slavery seemed to be going on in the United States and that the *good sense of the several States* would probably by degrees complete it" (emphasis added). Asserting the federal responsibility regarding slavery, Mason "held it essential . . . that the General Government should have the power to prevent the increase of slavery"—precisely the argument made by Abraham Lincoln and the Republican party in the decade before the Civil War.

Ellsworth then clarified his position by noting that Connecticut and Massachusetts had abolished or were in the process of abolishing slavery. The increase of free but poor laborers, Ellsworth thought, would "render slaves useless. Slavery in time would not be a speck in our Country." After explaining what they took to be the economic benefits of slavery to the whole country and threatening again that the Carolinas and Georgia would never enter a union that interfered with state control of slavery within their borders, the Southerners still held out the option of *state* action against the slave trade: Pinckney said "he would himself . . . vote for it," while Abraham Baldwin thought Georgia "if left to herself, . . . may probably put a stop to the evil." Before the debate concluded, Elbridge Gerry of Massachusetts agreed that though slavery under the federal Constitution could not be interfered with by any state, he hoped the convention "would be careful not to give any [general] sanction to it." John Langdon of New Hampshire urged federal control over the slave trade because he "could not with good conscience leave it with the States who could then go on with the traffic"—again foreshadowing Lincoln's position.[4]

The intent of the framers on the subject of slavery, then, in a climate of opinion where abolitionist sentiment was substantial but an acquiescence in the existence of slavery was dominant, was threefold: First, as the debates at the convention and the clauses of the document there produced show clearly, the Constitution accepted slavery in the states where it existed and afforded explicit protection of that existence under the laws of the union. Second, power over slavery, like many other matters, was divided carefully between the states and the federal government. The existing states were to have sole power within their borders while the federal government would control such general matters as the expansion of slavery to territories under federal jurisdiction—the Northwest Ordinance prohibiting slavery in those vast territories had just been passed by the Continental Congress, for example. Also, on the regulation of the foreign slave trade (except for the specific twenty-year exception), the general government had the power to act—or not act—as the mechanisms of self-government might decide. Third, there was general agreement that the states could themselves abolish slavery, if they pleased, and even a widespread hope and expectation that this state action would "by degrees" lead to the demise of slavery throughout the union.

Thus we can say that under the federal principle slavery was left up to the states within their borders but subjected to national control so far as the territories or international trade were concerned. Furthermore, under the principles of liberty and the public good, slavery was widely understood to be an evil institution incompatible with those principles. But under the principle of republicanism it was also understood that it would be up to the people, in the nation as a whole, but especially within each state where the key power remained, to decide, as Ellsworth had put it, about "the morality or wisdom of slavery." The fact that the delegates, as well as the people generally, were divided, sharply and publicly, on that question, moreover, was precisely what the republican principle supposed would be the case. It required, further, only that open debate continue, that decisions on the subject be taken according to lawful, constitutional processes, and that the gradual enlightenment and liberalizing spirit the framers hoped would accompany free and self-governing institutions, especially within the states, would work their way until slavery "would not be a speck in our Country."

On the issue of slavery as on many other matters, then, the Constitution depended on the sense of justice in the people and in the states for movement toward humaneness and liberalization. The Thirteenth, Fourteenth, and Fifteenth amendments, requiring states to give up slavery and extend the rights of citizenship without regard to race, simply used the federal Constitution to accomplish what some of the states had already done and others were unwilling to do themselves. Thus, the Constitution from the beginning was entirely open to the abolition of slavery *by the states*, as was in 1787 under way in many of them. (In contrast, for example, the Confederate constitution of 1861 gave explicit protection to slavery.) What happened in the 1860s was that the nation first decided, through Lincoln's election, to end the expansion of slavery and then, through the Emancipation Proclamation and Constitutional Amendment, to abolish it entirely. Both of these procedures, following the republican principle, can be seen as within the intent of the framers on the subject of slavery. Furthermore, under the very idea of constitutionalism (see chapters 2 and 3), the fact that the abolition of slavery eventually became part of the Constitution elevated it to "higher law" that can no longer be subject to legislative action. Although the existence of both proslavery and neutral sentiment, and political power in 1787–1788, prevented general acknowledgment of abolition as higher law then, it can, perhaps, be understood to fall in the category of as yet unenumerated rights noted in the Ninth Amendment.

Many questions of social policy are also unmentioned in the Constitution, because, in general, its intention is to leave such matters either to the states or to the Congress. The Constitution neither requires nor prohibits federal highways, social security, medicare, and the like. According to the republican principle, such matters are to be decided by the self-governing people through their elected representatives. Similarly, the Constitution was silent on the question of prohibition of liquor traffic until passage of the Eighteenth Amendment. That amendment, as its quick repeal suggests, was an example of implanting permanently in the Constitution something better left to state or national legislation, as the people might or might not want. One suspects the framers would have opposed the Eighteenth Amendment as not a proper constitutional question, whatever their views on the sale of alcoholic beverages. A similar projection of the republican principle might find problematic the Supreme Court decision that the Constitution proscribes laws forbidding abortion. A policy for or against abortion, as a matter of individual right or social need, is a decision the Constitution probably leaves, under that principle, to legislative bodies. The intent of the framers to leave such matters to the people and their representatives makes clear why they were often so attentive in the rest of their public careers to "informing the discretion" (Jefferson's phrase) of the people, to creating bonds of responsibility between the people and public officials, and to carefully constructing offices, such as the Senate. Only then could wise legislation for the general good be expected.

Foreign policy is similarly left indeterminate in the Constitution. There is no bias in it, for example, on the looming question in 1787 of whether the United States should side with Great Britain or with France in their continuing "great power" rivalry. There are no edicts on any foreign alliances, and even such general questions as isolationism versus internationalism are unmentioned in the Constitution. Rather, the framers intended simply to outline fair and responsive procedures for conducting the nation's foreign affairs in accord with republican and liberty-enhancing principles toward the public good. There is some bias, probably, in clauses in Article I empowering Congress to punish "offenses against the Law of Nations" (Sec. 8) and prohibiting titles of nobility (Sec. 9), in favor of constitutional and republican government in the world, but this does little more than suggest directions for the nation's foreign policy; enactment or non-enactment is left up to later needs and policies of government, which would change with the times.

Perhaps most significantly, even the nation's basic economic system is not dictated by the Constitution. Although clauses about not "impairing the obligation of contract" and about national control of coinage, patents, and copyrights create an environment sympathetic to capitalism, there is no mention of the maxims of *The Wealth of Nations* in the Constitution, nor does it prohibit laws that a later age might label "socialist." As Justice Holmes wrote in protesting the Supreme Court's invalidation of a New York state law regulating hours and working conditions, the Constitution did not "enact Mr. Herbert Spencer's *Social Statics*. . . . A constitution is not intended to embody a particular economic theory, whether of paternalism . . . or of *laissez faire*. It is made for people of fundamentally differing views."[5] Although Justice Holmes overall bespoke a legal philosophy quite different from that of the framers, he nonetheless captured the essentially undogmatic nature of the Constitution on matters of economic and social policy: those questions would be decided by the free citizens of self-governing polities. The framers, hence, would probably not have regarded New Deal legislation as unconstitutional, but rather would have seen it as a plausible response by a self-governing people to new economic conditions and to the changing nature of interstate commerce. Likewise today, there is probably no "intent of the framers" on the question of "regulation" or "deregulation." Such laws contending with changing economic conditions do not, one way or the other, violate basic principles of republicanism, liberty, the public good, or federalism. They are up to the elected representatives of the people to pass or not pass as the times require and/or as they see fit. In sum, the Constitution does not dictate on questions of social policy or economic systems—neither capitalism nor socialism is an enduring, indelible part of the American polity.

Much was to be left, as republican theory requires, to the wisdom, sense of justice, and public spirit of the people. The Constitution provides a framework for self-government and establishes certain enduring principles, but it cannot substitute for, indeed, it absolutely requires the people fulfilling responsibly their "office as citizens" for the nation to be well governed. It also requires active leadership toward the public good. Jefferson explained as he entered the presidency that the people must be led toward "notions of ideal right," while Theodore Roosevelt said his intention as president was to "simply make up my mind what [the people] ought to think, and then do my best to get them to think it."[6] It misreads the thought of the framers to argue that the Constitution so marvelously served as a check and balance on the powers of government and self-interest that no one, neither officials nor people, had to be good or public spirited. As Justice Frankfurter observed in 1943 (see chapter 9), "much that should offend a free-spirited society is constitutional. . . . Only the persistent, positive translation of the faith of a free society into the convictions and habits and actions of a community" (that is of its citizens) could ultimately achieve the purposes set forth in the preamble of the Constitution. Frankfurter, like Jefferson, believed that no frame of government, not even an exalted Supreme Court, could be a surrogate for public-spirited leadership and the active participation of an informed citizenry in protecting and enlarging both the rights of the people and the general welfare of the nation.

Another measure of the undogmatic yet principled nature of the Constitution can be seen in how circumstances obviously unanticipated by the framers can be handled in ways cognizant of their intent. The whole system of modern electric and electronic communications, surveillance, and data collection, for example, was entirely unknown to the founders, so of course the Constitution contains no direct references to wiretapping or other sophisticated invasions of privacy. But does that mean that it is "silent" about the use and effect of such devices? Not if the framers' *clear intent* is kept in mind that the new government in the United States be on the leading edge of efforts to protect private (and public) communications and the concept of one's home as one's castle. In the unequivocal words of the Fourth Amendment, "the right of the people to be secure in their person, houses, papers, and effects, against unreasonable searches and seizures, shall not be violated . . . " That is what it meant, practically, in 1787, to take the idea of human liberty seriously. Hence, it is reasonably certain that Madison, for example, would have agreed with Justice Holmes that wiretapping was, in general, "a dirty business"—a gross invasion of privacy that allowed the government to "play an ignoble part" in the affairs of its citizens.[7]

Following the same principle, laws and court decisions giving full, substantial, and even enlarged meaning to the privileges and protections found in the Bill of Rights would be faithful to the philosophy of the Constitution. (Remember that the framers fully accepted its principle even though for tactical reasons it was not included in the Constitution of 1787—the Bill of Rights, then, is properly thought of as part of the intent of the framers; see chapter 8.) The First Amendment unmistakably intends that the United States be in the forefront of maintaining the liberties of religion and expression so much talked of in the Age of Enlightenment. Although the framers knew nothing of school buses and were generally not cognizant of the more libertarian theories of free expression later articulated by John Stuart Mill and others, it is reasonably certain they would have sanctioned the wider rather than the more restrictive interpretations of Bill of Rights freedoms. Alexander Hamilton, for example, first argued that truth be a proper defense in libel cases, and another framer, James Madison, wrote and acted repeatedly to enlarge religious liberty—surely Hamilton argued in the spirit of *New York Times Co.* v. *Sullivan* (1964) (see chapter 9), and Madison in the spirit of *Wisconsin* v. *Yoder* (1972). Similarly Sixth Amendment insistence on the right of fair trial and access to counsel finds its legitimate twentieth-century fulfillment in *Gideon*, and other "rights of the accused" cases. The Constitution embodies the idea that the United States exert itself on the side of liberty—in the 1990s as well as in the 1790s.

This is not to argue either that the intent of the framers is absolutely clear in every modern instance of interpretation or that they would have been of one mind on modern issues—the debates of the Constitutional Convention and of the ratification contest make that apparent. There was, nonetheless, a general ideology favorable to the enlargement of equitable self-government, the extension of personal liberties, the spread of public-spiritedness, and the protection of the vigor of state and local government—that is to the ideas of republicanism, liberty, the public good, and federalism. Such convictions, and the intention that the nation remain in the vanguard in the growth, maturation, and effective fulfillment of them, are manifest in all of the debates, proclamations, and documents of the founding era and thus form the core of the philosophy of the Constitution.

14

THE CONSTITUTION:
WHAT THE JUDGES
SAY IT IS?

Asked about how the Constitution ought to be interpreted or understood, Chief Justice Charles Evans Hughes once replied, famously, that "the Constitution is what the judges say it is." John Marshall had made the same point in 1803, though he less implied the Constitution's changeability. He declared that deciding how the Constitution should be understood, in order to judge whether legislative acts conformed to it, was "the very essence of judicial duty."[1] This claim for a preeminent judicial role raises not only the question of whether the Supreme Court is in fact the proper body to determine finally the meaning of the Constitution (after two hundred years largely accepted in the United States), but also what guidelines the Court should follow, or set for itself, in interpreting it. Recently this question has been part of the debate over "original intent," that is whether the Constitution should be understood as what the framers (including arguments over who they were and whether they in any sense spoke with one voice) intended, or as it might have evolved in meaning over the years (chapter 1). A closer look at this debate reveals difficulties with many claims made in it but also supports the argument that there are enduring principles embodied in the Constitution and the Bill of Rights.

In 1987, for example, Justice Thurgood Marshall asserted that he did not believe "the meaning of the Constitution was forever fixed at the Philadelphia Convention," nor that "the wisdom, foresight, and sense of justice exhibited by the Framers [was] particularly profound." To him the Constitution in 1987 was "vastly different," in its "respect for individual freedoms and human rights," from the "defective" instrument adopted two hundred years earlier. Marshall emphasized especially the acknowledgment and even support in the

156

Constitution for slavery (see chapter 13), a serious flaw corrected only with the Civil War amendments and then the desegregation decisions of the mid-twentieth century. The framers, Marshall stated, "could not have imagined . . . a woman and a descendent of an African slave" would sit on the Supreme Court. The real "miracle" of American government was not accomplished by those who convened in Philadelphia in 1787, but by those "who refused to acquiesce in outdated notions of liberty, justice, and equality, and who strived to better them." In this process, Marshall thought, "new Constitutional principles have emerged to meet the challenges of a changing society." He hoped this "dramatic progress" would continue.[2]

Marshall, moreover, asserted that these shortcomings were both intentional and based on what the framers thought were enduring principles. He pointed out that Chief Justice Taney had asserted that his decision in the Dred Scott case (1857) simply reflected the framers' belief in African inferiority and exclusion from civil rights. To Marshall, then, the document of 1787 was wrong in intent and principle and, thus, no foundation for "the individual freedoms and human rights, we hold as fundamental today." This imperfection was an indication, moreover, both that the principles in the framers' intent were not themselves worthy of being considered higher law and that the ideas of a later age might better stand as such law. Although Marshall thus acknowledges something as "fundamental," and though he concurred in many Court decisions that held the Constitution paramount to statute law, he also seemed to be saying that the founding ideas were outdated and that the higher law was in fact evolving. Were there really, then, in Justice Jackson's words, "fundamental rights," enduring principles, to be protected by the courts no matter what, in spite of "political vicissitudes" or majoritarian legislation? What happened to the idea of higher law if it was thought of as changing or might be considered outdated? (chapter 11).

This evolutionary view of the fundamental principles embodied in the Constitution and Bill of Rights bears a strong resemblance to Justice William Brennan's argument that "both transformations of social condition and evolution of our concepts of human dignity" required from the Supreme Court "adaptability . . . to cope with current problems and current needs" (chapter 1). The Supreme Court particularly, Brennan notes, had to be aware of these circumstances because it had "to draw meaning from the text in order to resolve public controversies." The Court was thus both a custodian of the meaning of what Brennan calls "the monumental charter of a government and of a people" and a participant in current "public controversies" over "social conditions" and "human dignity." In explaining this role of the Court, Brennan made repeated reference to the Constitution and Bill of Rights as resting on enduring "majestic generalities and ennobling pronouncements." And Brennan's own distinguished career on the Court showed him willing repeatedly to use the Constitution as a higher law to set aside offending statutes and lower court decisions. Like Justice Thurgood Marshall, Brennan adheres to the American idea of constitutionalism and sees his role as a judge accordingly. In this respect they are closer to the idea of "paramount law to be upheld by the courts" articulated by Justices John Marshall and Robert H. Jackson than to the doctrines of judicial restraint and legislative discretion elaborated by Justices O. W. Holmes and Felix Frankfurter.

Yet Brennan's use of phrases such as "social progress," "transformations of social conditions," "the choice to overrule or add to the fundamental principles enunciated by the Framers," "evolution of our concepts of human dignity," "much modified view of the proper relation of individual and state," "the demands of human dignity will never cease to evolve," and "the anachronistic views of long-gone generations" all in some way question the idea of the Constitution as embodying enduring principles.[3] Indeed, like Justice Thurgood Marshall, Brennan seems to be saying that a liberal and humane person in the late twentieth century would not share the concepts of justice and right embedded in a document produced in an age of slavery, sex discrimination, child labor, and cruel punishments. The danger, though, of this interpretation and mode of argument is that it erodes seriously the status of the very document Marshall and Brennan purport to uphold. If the Constitution is an evolving document, responding to new circumstances, on what ground can it be upheld as "higher" law? What gives it standing above state or federal laws, presumably made by elected representatives also responsive to the needs of the times? Indeed, one might argue that such legislators are more likely to be sensitive to current needs than judges more distanced from the real world. The weakness in Brennan's argument is evident at precisely this point: if he emphasizes the *changing* nature of the very document he then applies as a standard for measuring statute law, he has diminished its standing as the higher law that can be used to judge legislative (or executive) acts. The dangerous aspect of Brennan's position, then, is that it comes close to denying the special status of the Constitution. Under his view, is it still a *Constitution* he is expounding, a document, as John Marshall declared in 1803, that is "superior, paramount law, unchangeable by ordinary means, . . . [and embodying] the fundamental principles of our society"?

The Constitution tends to lose its standing as enduring, higher law if it is seen too much as flawed by the shortcomings of its origins and as in need of evolutionary revision. This does not mean that the ideas attending the establishment of the Constitution were not flawed or that there are not many ways in which understanding and application of its basic principles can change as time passes. The alleged "flaws" need rather to be seen in relation to the practical constraints imposed, in the eighteenth century, by the dominant forms of thought and action. And the "evolution" of the basic principles is best thought of as an enlarging understanding, rather than as the discovery of new truths not in any way implicit in, possible within, or derivable from the Constitution. The preamble and the Bill of Rights, for example, express "majestic generalities" that translate and project into repeated, renewed relevance and application as time passes. Thus, though Justices Thurgood Marshall and Brennan accept the Constitution (including the Bill of Rights) as fundamental law and have spoken notably in ways that not only uphold but enlarge it, their reference to the Constitution as "defective" or "anachronistic" and to the need to find "new constitutional principles" and to account for "transformations of social conditions" has a nearly contradictory effect. Can the Constitution really be taken seriously, be used as a powerful bulwark on behalf of higher law and enduring principles, if it is also viewed as transient? Justices Marshall and Brennan may be undermining the very instrument they have used so effectively and eloquently to defend in the twentieth century what had been set forth, perhaps incompletely and unclearly, in the eighteenth. If one emphasizes, rather, that the Constitution embodies enduring principles in need of thoughtful application to changing times, attention is focused on the permanent rather than on the transient, which is itself essential to the very idea of constitutional government.

This understanding, though, has at least as much disagreement with the "original intent" arguments of Robert Bork, Chief Justice William Rehnquist, and others. In Bork's argument, following the words of Justice Joseph Story, "the first and fundamental rule in the interpretation of all instruments is to construe them according to the sense of the terms, and the intention of the parties."[4] Thus, from the text of the Constitution itself, from the debates and resolutions of the Convention of 1787 and of the ratification contest, and from the earliest uses of the Constitution under the new government, the "original understanding" could be gleaned and was then binding on courts interpreting the instrument. Particularly ruled out by Bork are general appeals to "justice" or to a judge's own sense of morality in making decisions. Judges, Bork wrote, "administer justice according to law. Justice in a larger sense, justice according to morality, is for the Congress and the President to administer, if they see fit, through the creation of new law."[5]

In 1985, Attorney General Edwin Meese reviewed a series of Supreme Court decisions where he thought the justices had gone too far in making "policy choices rather than articulation of Constitutional principle." He also criticized the Warren Court for "radical egalitarianism and expansive civil libertarianism." Meese called instead for a *"jurisprudence of original intention."* The Court's recent decisions on prayer in the schools, criminal procedures, and state versus federal power, Meese thought, "all reveal a greater allegiance to what the Court thinks constitutes sound public policy . . . than deference to what the Constitution, its text and intention, may demand. . . . To allow the Court to govern simply by what it views at the time as fair and decent, is a scheme of government no longer popular; the idea of democracy has suffered." Thus, Meese said, he would, as attorney general, "endeavor to resurrect the original meaning of constitutional provisions and statutes as the only reliable guide." Such an approach, entirely faithful to the text of the Constitution and to the words and intentions of those who drafted, ratified, and promulgated it, "would produce defensible principles of government that would not be tainted by ideological predilection."[6] Under this doctrine, Meese and others have insisted that supporting abortion rights, validating a right to privacy, outlawing the death penalty, and prohibiting prayer in the public schools are beyond the scope of the Supreme Court because such powers cannot be found explicitly in the text of the Constitution nor in the intent of its framers. Likewise, statutes to limit political campaign contributions or to prohibit (in most cases) distribution of pornography are struck down because no evidence exists that the framers intended such applications of First Amendment freedoms.

Justice Antonin Scalia makes the case for "originalism" as the lesser of two evils. "Nonoriginalism," he argues, has a "central practical defect [that] is fundamental and irreparable: the impossibility of achieving any consensus on what, precisely, is to replace original meaning, once that is abandoned." Left without the anchor of original intent, the judge confronts two dangerous and omnipresent temptations: either to engage in the dubious business of deciding what "fundamental values of society" are to be the evolving basis for constitutional law, or to simply assert the judges' own moral convictions as the basis for that law. In either case, Scalia observes, "judicial personalization of the law is enormously facilitated."[7] Since such "personalization of the law," or the implanting of current "fundamental values of society" as the standard of judgment, are each deeply at odds with the idea of a higher, lasting law, Scalia regards any form of "nonoriginalism" as corrosive to the existence of constitutional government, which assumes, even requires, such an undergirding idea.

Justice William Rehnquist made what was to him a clear application of original intent when he dissented in *Wallace* v. *Jaffree* (1984). In it, the Supreme Court declared unconstitutional an Alabama statute authorizing meditation (and prayer) at the beginning of the day in public schools. In a careful historical examination of the meaning and intent of the First Amendment ban on laws "respecting an establishment of religion," Rehnquist could find no evidence that the proposers or ratifiers of the amendment in 1789–1791 in any way countenanced the Court's interpretation. Rather he thought they intended two things: to proscribe the establishment of a national religion and to preclude any preference of one religion over another. Citing the Northwest Ordinance (passed in 1787) that allowed (until amended in 1845) federal land grants to sectarian schools, Rehnquist insisted that the First Amendment "establishment clause" did not prohibit evenhanded encouragement to religion in general. The Alabama statute, then, did not violate the intent of the proposers and ratifiers of the First Amendment and thus was constitutional. Rehnquist articulated his general principle of "original intent": "The true meaning of the Establishment Clause can only be seen in its history. As drafters of our Bill of Rights the Framers inscribed the principles that control today. Any deviation from their intentions frustrates the permanence of that charter and will only lead to . . . unprincipled decision-making."[8]

It is true, of course, that the framers could not possibly have intended the Constitution to prohibit prayer in the public schools. Such schools really did not exist at the time. It simply would not have occurred to Madison and others to suppose federal authority either could or needed to extend to school prayer. Hence, literally speaking, Supreme Court decisions forbidding prayer in the public schools are, as Rehnquist argued, outside original intent. Equally clear, at least as far as Madison is concerned, is the intent to free religious convictions as much as possible from any sort of state bias or interference. In his first public act in 1776, he sought successfully to replace in the Virginia Declaration of Rights the conventional assertion that "all men should enjoy the fullest Toleration in the Exercise of Religion" with the more positive, less condescending "all men are equally entitled to the free exercise of religion." Madison thus converted a notion of established privilege granting toleration to others (what conferred the privilege, or power, to tolerate others?) to a positive, substantial right held equally by all. In 1785 he successfully opposed a

Virginia bill to "pay teachers of the Christian religion" (in effect clergymen) from tax-derived funds. Although the bill moved beyond colonial establishment of just the Anglican Church to include other, rapidly growing Christian sects, Madison pointed out that it still subjected people's conscience to the commands of the state. With the same reasoning he opposed the payment of or even the appointment of chaplains for the Congress or for the armed forces. To do so was a form of establishment that infringed conscience.[9] As noted in chapter 10, in drafting the Bill of Rights Madison proposed the most emphatic language possible for protecting religious freedom and sought to apply the guarantee against state as well as federal government.

His intention throughout was to express the most liberal and enlightened principle in the clearest language, so that the United States would be in the vanguard of protecting liberty of conscience. Thus we can say that his intent, and that of most of the founding generation following him, was not only to state an enduring principle but also to keep the nation in a leading position in fulfilling that principle. The import of this for succeeding generations, and for future decisions of the Supreme Court, was to make sure, as unforeseen and unforeseeable situations arose, that in the United States the right of liberty of conscience was fully protected. Madison, then, would have regarded Rehnquist's argument as misguided. In concluding that the founders could not have pronounced about prayer in public schools (true literally), he missed the more important point of the intention to keep the United States in the vanguard in protecting liberty of conscience. Under that dictum, Rehnquist might well have found, with the majority of the Court, that the Alabama statute had indeed been passed in order to lend state support to the religious exercise of prayer—which it was surely Madison's intent to oppose. He had written in 1785: "The opinions of men, depending only upon the evidence contemplated by their own minds, cannot follow the dictates of other men. . . . Religion is wholly exempt from the cognizance of Civil Society," including, of course, state legislatures.[10] (Justice Wiley Rutledge made exactly this point about Madison's view in dissenting in *Everson* v. *Board of Education* [1947], which validated state support for transportation of pupils to religious schools.)

Thus, though the emphasis on original intent in a way seems faithful to the idea of the Constitution as higher law, the effort to find literal, specific "answers" for the issues of other times has the effect of often missing the Constitution's more profound purposes and principles. The more one attempts, as Justice Rehnquist did in *Wallace* v. *Jaffree*, to find specific references in the founding era to modern concerns, the more one is likely to find either no guidance at all or particulars that are confusing or irrelevant. Also, the more one pursues this search for literal guidance in the documents and debates of 1787–1791, the more troublesome becomes the question of who the founders were. When one considers the members of the Constitutional Convention, the delegates to the state ratification conventions, the participants in the printed discussions of the Constitution, the members of the Congress and the state legislatures who proposed and ratified the Bill of Rights, and perhaps others articulating "original intent," the opinions of thousands of disagreeing people are in view. When added to the inaccuracy and incompleteness of the records involved, the picture one looks back on is confusing and chaotic—if the effort is to find specific words that will apply to particular current cases.[11] Word usage and circumstances change too much over time to expect to find detailed guidance. The framers recognized this, of course, and would have regarded attempts at literal interpretation, two hundred years later, as foolish and wrongheaded in the extreme. The point is in some way analogous to disputes over interpretation of the Bible—and the spirit of textual fundamentalism is largely foreign both to the Enlightenment milieu (see chapter 4) of the framing of the Constitution and the Bill of Rights and to the terse yet general, even sweeping language of both documents.

The "jurisprudence of original intent" further argues that since there are no moral principles upon which Americans currently agree, judges are ill-advised to attempt to substitute such principles (theirs or society's) for the Constitution itself. The effect of this argument is to denigrate generally the idea of higher law or fixed principles. If there are none such today, as the original intent theorists insist (see Judge Bork in chapter 1), then one would be inclined, perhaps compelled, to argue that there were none in 1787–1791 either. The Constitution, then, is seen as largely procedural, prescribing ways powers are to be allocated and decisions made as well as prohibiting certain powers to governments. This approach leaves so-called moral decisions and other policy matters, large and small, up to elected officials in the legislative and executive branches. Judges must ensure that agencies of government—Congress, the executive department, state and local courts and legislatures, and so on— conform to these allocations, procedures, and prohibitions. Emphasizing pro- cedural and technical exactness, as this approach does, undermines the idea of a Constitution of enduring principles that need to be understood generally and lastingly. But the framers *were* seeking to promulgate fundamental, higher law, which legislators and judges in later ages would apply to their own, altered circumstances. To understand these more general principles is difficult and not likely to yield certain and unassailable interpretations, but it is more consistent with the paramount nature of a constitution than the supposition that one might find in it literal guidance on every point.

These modern views of original intent, then, all miss the essential character of a constitution itself and overlook the enduring principles of the American documents of 1787–1791. Unless one accepts the idea that "those who have framed written constitutions contemplate them as forming the fundamental and paramount law of the nation" (see chapter 2) and also accepts the abiding vitality of the great principles of republicanism, liberty, the public good, and federalism, then the United States can scarcely regard itself as a constitutional polity. Even more futile, and paralyzing, would be to suppose it currently possible to find good government in the detailed and specific injunctions of two centuries ago. What Justice Jackson called "legal principles and . . . fundamental rights," dependent on no majority votes or transient conditions, must be understood as higher law, to be used as enduring standards, if the United States is to be a constitutional polity. The Constitution makes little sense either as mere rules of thumb used to make decisions in an ever-changing world, or as a two-hundred-year-old repository of specific injunctions to resolve current problems. The proper middle ground is to see its persisting principles—republicanism, liberty, the public good, and federalism—as general guides for the present and the future. That is what the judges, if they are truly faithful to "original intent," should say the Constitution is.

15

PERSONAL LIBERTY AND POLITICAL FREEDOM

In 1783, at the close of the American Revolution, Thomas Pownall, a former royal governor of the Massachusetts Bay Colony, wrote of his admiration for the ideas and forms of government in the newly independent United States. Pownall thought particularly that the many novel concepts of government in the former colonies contrasted sharply with "all the ancient Legislators and Institutors of Republics" in Greece and Rome. In them, Pownall observed, the central effort had always been to form or shape the rulers, whether philosopher-kings or citizens, so that they would rule wisely on behalf of the public good. Since the scope of government was wide ("for the sake of the good life," Aristotle had said) and the responsibilities of the rulers heavy, the Classical Age had felt justified in molding people so they would be able to perform properly their public roles. They thus "forced nature," Pownall said, and left the people "cut off from, and from any use of, many of the essential inalienable rights of the individual which form his happiness as well as freedom."[1]

In summarizing his argument Pownall made a distinction that is crucial to understanding the Constitution and the Bill of Rights. The classical approach to government, he said, "destroyed or perverted all personal Liberty, in order to force into establishment Political Freedom." By "personal liberty" Pownall meant "the inalienable rights of the individual" such as freedom of religion and expression, trial by jury, freedom from unreasonable search and seizure, excessive bail, and cruel and unusual punishment being written into bills of rights throughout the new United States. The protection of these rights, Pownall thought, was the essence of the genuine liberty that suited the human aspirations of the Enlightenment. In this way Pownall endorsed the view of the so-

called "moderns," such formulators of the rising liberal ideology of the autonomous individual and of enlightened self-interest as Francis Bacon, John
Locke, Bernard Mandeville, Voltaire, David Hume, and Adam Smith. Pownall
ignored or rejected the "ancients," British neoclassicists such as Pope, Swift,
and Bolingbroke who admired the Greeks and Romans—Homer, Aristotle,
Livy, Horace, Plutarch, Cicero, and so on—and who believed deeply that
active government in the public interest was essential to a good society.[2]

The "Battle of the Books" between the "ancients" and "moderns" had been
under way for a century or more when Pownall wrote and had been widely
attended to by Americans, many of whom found insight and wisdom on both
sides. Hence, in the minds of the American founding generation the conflict
between "the inalienable rights of the individual," what Pownall called "personal liberty," and the nourishing of human nature to achieve "political freedom" was not nearly so sharp as he presented it. Jefferson mixed "ancients"
and "moderns" in listing "the elementary books of public right" (Aristotle,
Cicero, Sidney, and Locke), and Madison began his study of "politics" in an
Aristotelian frame. In the terms of the twentieth-century scholarly debate over
whether the "liberal tradition" or the "civic republican" tradition was dominant in eighteenth-century America, the founders themselves usually bypassed
that theoretical question as they accepted, perhaps inconsistently, something
of each tradition. Although the intellectual climate was in transition, moving
toward liberalism, and civic republicanism possibly near "repudiation," the
political thinking of the day was shaped by both.[3]

Unlike Pownall, the philosophy of the Constitution upholds both "personal
liberty" and "political freedom." In fact, its very aspiration and genius is to
repudiate the dichotomy and even the tension as much as possible in order that
the virtues of each might be sustained. In many ways, as Pownall's observations reveal, in late eighteenth-century Anglo-America the personal liberty
ideal was the fresher and more explicit one. As articulated by Locke, "the
English Cato," James Burgh, Samuel Adams, Thomas Paine, and a host of
other "Radical Whig" writers on both sides of the Atlantic, the exaltation of
personal liberties was a new and exciting political goal. As such it is a crucial,
indispensable part of the philosophy of the Constitution, and particularly of
the Bill of Rights.

In fact, this personal liberty motif both received most of the explicit attention of political publicists in the founding era and was ascendant in a way that
made it more and more dominant in the nineteenth and twentieth centuries.
But the civic republican tradition that emphasized "political freedom" still had

a powerful hold on the minds of Madison and his colleagues. Also essential were the classical ideas of the importance of the political ("man is a political animal"), and of the need for the wise, active conduct of public affairs and, as John Adams put it in 1776, "a positive Passion for the public good . . . established in the Minds of the People." Without this, Adams declared, "there can be no Republican Government, nor any real Liberty."[4] The focus was entirely on the "political freedom" to take part in a thoughtful and public-spirited way in the affairs of one's political community. Although this "civic republican" outlook would be increasingly overshadowed by the "modern" liberalism of Locke, Adam Smith, and J. S. Mill, in 1787–1791 it was still prevalent enough to make political freedom in the classical sense a crucial objective in the founding documents.

With this in mind, a number of otherwise paradoxical aspects of the drafting and ratification of both the Constitution of 1787 and the Bill of Rights become clearer. The neglect of a bill of rights at the Convention of 1787 (see chapter 10), for example, so puzzling, even shocking to modern sensibilities, is explained both by the assumption that protection of personal liberty was implicit in the Constitution and by the preoccupation of the convention with a frame of government that would embody political freedom. Roger Sherman's remark in opposing addition of an explicit bill of rights that Congress could be "trusted," in other words that effective mechanisms of political freedom would themselves guard personal liberties, reveals the essential sense of linkage between the ideas, rather than tension, that suffused the convention. Madison sustained the same assumption a month later when, in a long letter to Jefferson about the Constitution, he dealt entirely with the structure of government. He failed even to mention a bill of rights. Both events seem quite plausible if one understands the importance of political freedom, as well as personal liberty, in the minds of the founders.

Similarly, the stubborn, even perverse (to modern ears) insistence by James Wilson, Alexander Hamilton, and other federalists in the ratification debates that a bill of rights was redundant, unnecessary, and even dangerous can be understood as part of their concern for political freedom. They insisted that the Constitution as a limited frame of government gave no power to Congress or to the president over religion or the press, for example. Hamilton emphasized instead the "ample and precise" attention given to "the political privileges of the citizens in the structure and administration of government," that is, to political freedom.[5] Again, the linkage in the minds of the framers between personal liberty and political freedom is clear. It is also clear, without denigrating their genuine devotion to personal liberty, that they saw the more urgent and critical task, at least in 1787, to be the "political privileges" (freedom) spelled out "in the structure and administration of government." Indeed, what many historians have seen as a reaction in 1787 against the revolutionary ideals of liberty and self-government was actually an enriched sense of the need, in order to protect personal liberty, to implant more fully and effectively the means of political freedom. The same point was made by Philadelphia newspapers in August 1787 when, implying a natural progression in nation building, they observed that in 1776 there had been a revolution against tyranny (denial of personal liberty), while in 1787 there was under way a revolution in favor of government, or political freedom.[6]

Madison's reluctant words to Jefferson in 1788 about proposals for a bill of rights (see chapter 10)—that its omission was not a "material defect," that it might be of "some use," and that it might "not be of disservice" if properly phrased—become not so much disparagement of a bill of rights as emphasis on the improved mechanisms in the Constitution for self-government. Not only does Madison explain how these alone can ensure protection of personal liberties, but he even sees the improvement of public sentiment (and hence of improved fulfillment of the office of citizen) as the first reason for adding a bill of rights to the Constitution. When Jefferson concurred that adding a bill of rights should not be allowed to weaken "the whole frame of government," the two men revealed their basic agreement on the importance of political freedom.

Finally, the seemingly ironic *opposition* by many antifederalists, especially in Virginia, to the Bill of Rights as proposed by Congress in September 1789 (see chapter 10) can be understood as revealing a primary commitment to *their* idea of political freedom. Of course they favored the substance of the Bill of Rights (personal liberty) as proposed (as did the federalists), but they did not want its enactment to exhaust the impetus for what they regarded as more important: the shifting of powers from the general to the state governments. Although this in part reflected simply a power struggle on behalf of state interests, it also was consistent with the entirely serious antifederal idea that good self-government worked best, perhaps could only be genuine, at the local or state level (see chapter 9). Political freedom, the active participation by members of a society in their own government, could be real, Patrick Henry, Melancton Smith, and many others argued, only if there was intimacy and trust between the governors and the governed. This trust both made the political freedom of thoughtful, public-spirited participation possible and prevented the growth of distant, powerful, and increasingly arbitrary government that would crush personal liberty as well as political freedom. In their own way, then, the antifederalists also accepted the primacy of political freedom.

The antifederalists, just as much as Madison and his colleagues, had most fundamentally in mind the structures and processes that would best assure meaningful self-government. Their enthusiasm for a bill of rights heightened as they saw themselves "losing" on the issue of highly centralized government, which they saw as threatening to personal liberties—recall that George Mason's plea for a bill of rights in the Convention of 1787 rested on his fear of the "paramount" laws of the union under the new Constitution (chapter 10). Likewise Madison thought prohibiting *state* interference with personal liberties would be the "most valuable" part of a bill of rights because it was the poorly constructed *state* governments that lacked the implicit protection of personal liberties he thought was part of the new federal Constitution. In each case, the primary emphasis was on a structure and process of government that would ensure political freedom. On the other hand, concern for a bill of rights (personal liberty) heightened among federalists and antifederalists alike in the presence of forms thought less likely to provide genuine self-government.

In fact, the commitment to both personal liberty and political freedom in the founding era is at the center of the philosophy of the Constitution and the Bill of Rights. The idea of a constitution as higher law, as a statement of the basic principles of the polity, for example, has the effect of sanctifying the importance of public life. The *political* life of the community is seen as having transcending importance and as requiring conduct according to lasting principles and mechanisms. If, as Thomas Paine put it in *Common Sense* (1776), "in America THE LAW IS KING," then the higher law, the Constitution, achieves the paramount position. It is, moreover, a higher law that both protects personal liberty and provides for political freedom. Although *Common Sense* is rightly viewed as a tract extolling personal liberty, Paine insisted at least as much on the achievement of political freedom—the basic reason for the Declaration of Independence.

The four enduring principles of the Constitution also undergird and sustain the balance between these two concepts. Republicanism pays particular attention to the idea of political freedom by addressing the fundamental question of how the nation shall be governed. The ultimate reliance on the people for political power and legitimacy, the mechanisms of representation, and the checks and balances among the branches of government, the basic elements of republicanism, establish the foundation: these are the principles and processes through which the people of the United States are to exercise their political freedom. Their wise and effective embodiment in a constitution, eighteenth-century American political thinking held, was the point and purpose of the Revolution. Everything depended, then, on the formation of "a more perfect union."

Liberty, of course, had particularly to do with the personal rights and privileges that were so central to political discourse in eighteenth-century Anglo-America. When Richard Henry Lee, a signer of the Declaration of Independence, prominent antifederalist, and member of the Congress that proposed the Bill of Rights, was asked what the bases of the American idea of rights were, he mentioned four sources: (1) the philosophy of the natural rights of man emphasized in the Enlightenment (see chapter 4); (2) the rights of Englishmen; (3) the various colonial charters; and (4) what he called "immemorial custom,"[7] perhaps having in mind such things as Biblical precepts, the common law, time honored practices of colonial governments, and what Jefferson often referred to as the free principles of "our Saxon ancestors." The convergence of these influences in the new United States, 1776–1791, led to a widespread and emphatic allegiance to the idea of personal liberty. (Of course women and black slaves, not regarded in the eighteenth century as members of the body politic, were not yet included in the sweeping conceptions.) No government, state or national, that did not pay attention to and guard these liberties and rights would have gained much acceptance at that time. The main debate, then, was not over their substance, but over whether their protection was best understood as implicit, as Madison argued, or as requiring explicit statement, as Jefferson argued and Madison finally agreed to (see chapter 10). Even those most inclined to emphasize explicit statement, though, acknowledged as Jefferson did that political freedom was critical to the meaningful preservation of individual rights.

The idea of the public good both included the protection of personal liberty and required the presence of political freedom. The public good, as a substantive idea of a good or just society conducive to human fulfillment, would of course require the presence of individual liberty. But these personal liberties were also necessary for citizens to be able, in free and reasoned discussion, to take part in that shared pursuit of common objectives that form an essential part of what Aristotle called "the good society." It is precisely at this point that the linkage of the two concepts is again apparent: political freedom required the participation of citizens possessed of personal liberty, while personal liberty would only survive in a society where political freedom also existed. This inextricable combination was the foundation of any effort to pursue the public good. Indeed, the ever-present notion of a public good, always sought if never fully agreed upon or achieved, was the essential end toward which personal liberty and political freedom were means.

Federalism stands as the peculiarly American contribution to the enhancement of both personal liberty and political freedom. Before the American Revolution it was often argued that both logic and British parliamentary theory made divided sovereignty a contradiction in terms: sovereignty meant supreme, final power and thus could be exercised in only one place. In the classic formulation by the British jurist Sir William Blackstone (read and known by lawyers in the colonies), in all forms of government "there is and must be . . . a supreme, irresistible, absolute, uncontrolled authority," which in Great Britain was lodged in Parliament (king, lords, and commons), whose actions "no power on earth can undo."[8] In resisting the implications of this doctrine for self-rule in the colonies, revolutionary writers developed the idea, however inconsistent, of *divided* sovereignty—some powers would be exercised, supremely, by the colonial legislatures, and some by the Parliament in London, supremely. This idea in the 1770s and 1780s became the doctrine of federalism, division of power between the state and national governments, that was gospel to federalists and antifederalists alike. (They disputed merely where and how the dividing line should be drawn.) Federalism, moreover, enlisted support both because it helped protect personal liberties (by dispersing power) and because it provided opportunities for a more genuine exercise of political freedom (by sustaining the vitality of many levels of government). Thus, federalism is at once the most creative idea and the source of the most irresolvable tension in the American frame of government—perhaps in that way providing yet another reflection of the tension in the Declaration of Independence itself between "inalienable rights" (personal liberty) and "the consent of the governed" (political freedom) (see chapter 3).

Seeing the Bill of Rights as part of the *public* life of the nation, in its origins, in its nourishment of government by consent, and in its connection with good government, likewise acknowledges the importance of both personal liberty and political freedom. This view deliberately rejects understanding the Bill of Rights as a charter largely separate from the Constitution that by explicit statement, compared with the 1787 document, provides protection for personal liberty. Rather, the Bill of Rights is properly understood as an explicit statement of what was already implicit in the 1787 Constitution and (especially the First Amendment) as undergirding the capacity of the citizenry "to speak, to write, or to publish their sentiments . . . and to peaceably assemble and consult for the common good" (see chapter 10). The Bill of Rights thus keeps in view the vitality of the mechanisms of government by consent in the nation (see chapter 11) and has as its final goal not merely upholding the personal liberty of the people but also sustaining their vast stake in the kind of political freedom that can make self-government also be good government (see chapter 12).

Perhaps the most revealing, deeply insightful, and profoundly sobering of all the documents related to the drafting and ratification of the Constitution and the Bill of Rights is James Madison's analysis, written on the eve of the 1787 Convention, of "The Vices of the Political System of the United States" (chapter 5). Madison attempted in it to be entirely realistic about the problems faced in republican government: elected representatives might be unfaithful to their trusts, election campaigns might "prevail on the unwary to misplace their confidence," demagogues might "varnish . . . sophistical arguments . . . with the glowing colours of popular eloquence," and the people themselves might be motivated by "base designs." These dangers, he thought, brought into question "the fundamental principle of republican government" that the majority should rule. It seemed entirely possible that the majority might not be "the safest Guardians both of public Good and of private rights."[9]

Madison thus acknowledged personal liberty ("private rights") and political freedom ("public good") as the twin goals of the American Revolution, which he hoped the Constitution about to be drafted might fulfill. An improperly structured government, unmindful of the sobering realities of politics and of human nature, would surely propel the United States into the endless cycle of history where societies lurched back and forth between tyranny and chaos. A proper structure, a wise arrangement of powers and limitations, is what Madison had always in mind in drafting both the Constitution and the Bill of Rights. He did not agree with Pownall's argument that the establishment of political freedom, with all its obligation to seek government for the public good, would "destroy or pervert" personal liberty. In fact, as his linking of "public Good and . . . private rights" in 1787 reveals, Madison saw them as the twin foundations of the documents he was about to "father"—and his colleagues, whether federalist or antifederalists, largely agreed. A proper understanding of the Constitution and the Bill of Rights, then, requires an awareness of this dual commitment, an acknowledgment of the unbreakable linkages between them, and a grasp of how, taken together, they amount to a higher law that can provide lasting guidance in the pursuit of good government.

NOTES

CHAPTER 1. THE QUESTION OF ORIGINAL INTENT

1. William Brennan, *The Constitution of the United States: Contemporary Ratification* (Washington, D.C.: Georgetown University, October 12, 1985); pp. 5, 6, 10, 15.

2. Robert H. Bork, *The Tempting of America* (New York, 1990), pp. 252, 257.

3. Alastair MacIntyre, *After Virtue* (New York, 1984), p. 232.

CHAPTER 2. THE CONSTITUTION AS HIGHER LAW

1. John Adams, "Novanglus," January 23, 1775, in Robert Taylor et al., eds., *The Papers of John Adams* (Cambridge, Mass., 1977), 2: 230; Alexander Hamilton, *A Full Vindication of the Measures of Congress . . .* , December 15, 1774, in H. C. Syrett et al., eds., *The Papers of Alexander Hamilton* (New York, 1961), 1: 47; Thomas Jefferson, *Notes on Virginia* (1782), Query VIII, in A. Koch and W. Peden, eds., *The Life and Selected Writings of Thomas Jefferson* (New York, 1944), p. 217.

2. Elisha Williams, *. . . A Seasonable Plea for the Liberty of Conscience* (Boston, 1744), reprinted in E. S. Morgan, ed., *Puritan Political Ideas* (Indianapolis, Ind., 1965), pp. 276–277.

3. Thomas Paine, *Common Sense* (Philadelphia, 1776), reprinted in Merrill Jensen, ed., *Tracts of the American Revolution* (Indianapolis, Ind., 1967), pp. 426, 434.

4. OED, quoting "Dissertation on Parties," in *The Works of Lord Bolingbroke* (London, 1754), 2: 130.

5. "Mayflower Compact," November 11, 1620, in D. J. Boorstin, ed., *An American Primer* (New York, 1966), p. 21.

6. Donald Lutz, *The Origins of American Constitutionalism* (Baton Rouge, La., 1988), explains these and other instances of early American constitutions.

173

7. John Dickinson, *An Address . . . to Barbados* (Philadelphia, 1766), and John Adams, 1765, quoted in Bernard Bailyn, *The Ideological Origins of the American Revolution* (Cambridge, Mass., 1967), pp. 68, 77.

8. John Locke, *Second Treatise on Civil Government* (1690), Book 8, "of the Beginning of Political Societies," in Ernest Barker, ed., *Social Contract* (New York, 1960), p. 56.

Chapter 3. Constitutionalism in the United States

1. *McCulloch* v. *Maryland* (1819), 4 Wheaton 316; *Marbury* v. *Madison* (1803), 1 Cranch 137.

2. *Martin* v. *Hunter's Lessee* (1816), 14 U.S. 1 Wheaton 304, 326; *McCulloch* v. *Maryland*; *Cohens* v. *Virginia* (1821), 17 U.S. 6 Wheaton 264.

3. Cited in Gerald Stourzh, *Alexander Hamilton and the Idea of Republican Government* (Stanford, Calif., 1970), p. 70.

4. Allan Bloom, *The Closing of the American Mind* (New York, 1787), p. 26

5. Quoted by John Wise, *A Vindication of the Government of New England Churches* (1717), reprinted in Morgan, ed., *Puritan Political Ideas*, p. 255.

6. *Weems* v. *United States* (1910), 217 U.S. 349; *Olmstead* v. *United States* (1928), 277 U.S. 438; *West Virginia State Board of Education* v. *Barnette* (1943), 319 U.S. 624.

7. Generalizations from teaching many hundreds of students modern American political thought, 1965–1992.

8. Jefferson to the citizens of Albemarle County, February 12, 1790, quoted in Noble Cunningham, *In Pursuit of Reason: The Life of Thomas Jefferson* (New York, 1988), p. 133.

Chapter 4. The Enlightenment

1. Antoine-Nicolas de Condorcet, *Sketch for a Historical Picture of the Progress of the Human Mind* (1794), trans. June Barraclough, in Peter Gay, ed., *The Enlightenment* (New York, 1973), pp. 800–805.

2. Samuel Adams, "A State of the Rights of the Colonists," 1772, in Jensen, ed., *Tracts of the American Revolution*, pp. 235–237.

3. Thomas Paine, *The Rights of Man* (1791).

4. All quoted in Robert R. Palmer, *The Age of Democratic Revolution* (Princeton, N.J., 1959), 1: 238, 258.

5. Diderot, *Le Philosophe* (1743), quoted in H. S. Commager, *The Empire of Reason* (Garden City, N.Y., 1978), p. 259.

6. Palmer, *Age of Democratic Revolution*, 1: 240.

7. Quoted in Saxe Commins, ed., *Basic Writings of George Washington* (New York, 1948), p. 489.

8. Adams to Jefferson, November 13, 1815, and Jefferson to Adams, January 16, 1816, in Lester Cappon, ed., *The Adams–Jefferson Letters* (Chapel Hill, N.C., 1959), 2: 456, 458.

CHAPTER 5. REPUBLICANISM

1. Locke, *Second Treatise*, Book 8, in Barker, ed., *Social Contract*, p. 57.
2. John to Abigail Adams, May 17, 1776, in L. H. Butterfield et al., eds., *Adams Family Correspondence* (Cambridge, Mass., 1963), 1: 410–411.
3. "Demophilus," quoted in Gordon S. Wood, *The Creation of the American Republic, 1776–1787* (Chapel Hill, N.C., 1969), p. 229; and Merrill Jensen, "The American People and the American Revolution," *Journal of American History*, 57 (1970):29.
4. F. N. Thorpe, ed., *The Federal and State Constitutions* (Washington, D.C., 1909), 5: 3084–3092.
5. "Centinel," No. 1, Philadelphia *Freeman's Journal*, October 5, 1787, reprinted in Ralph Ketcham, ed., *The Antifederalist Papers* (New York, 1986), p. 231.
6. Jensen, "American People and American Revolution," *JAH* 57 (1970):29.
7. All quotes from Madison, "Vices of the Political System of the United States," April 1787, in R. A. Rutland et al., eds., *The Papers of James Madison* (Chicago, 1975), 9: 345–358.
8. Nos. 51 and 10, Clinton Rossiter, ed., *The Federalist Papers* (New York, 1961), pp. 84, 322.
9. Pendleton to Madison, April 7, 1787 in *Papers of Madison*, 17: 517.
10. Debate of May 31, 1787, in Ketcham, ed., *Antifederalist Papers*, pp. 40–41.
11. Debate of August 7, 1787, in ibid., pp. 145–150.
12. Debates of July 13–14, 1787, in ibid., pp. 109–113.
13. Pendleton to Madison, January 29, 1788, in *Papers of Madison*, 17: 526–527.
14. James Otis, "The Rights of the British Colonies Asserted and Proved," 1764, in Jensen, ed., *Tracts of the American Revolution*, p. 26.
15. J. Q. Adams, "Address on July 4, 1821," reprinted in W. Lafeber, ed., *John Quincy Adams and American Continental Empire* (Chicago, 1965), pp. 44–45.
16. Quoted in Julian P. Boyd, "Thomas Jefferson's Empire of Liberty," *Virginia Quarterly Review* 24 (1948):550.

CHAPTER 6. LIBERTY

1. Bailyn, *Ideological Origins of the American Revolution*, pp. 230–319.
2. Jefferson to Madison, December 20, 1787, in *Papers of Madison*, 10: 337.
3. Virginia Declaration of Rights, June 12, 1776, in F. N. Thorpe, ed., *Federal and State Constitutions, Colonial Charters, and Other Laws* (Washington, D.C., 1909), 7: 3012–3014.

4. Debate of July 17, 1787, in Ketcham, *Antifederalist Papers*, p. 116.
5. Debate of August 10, 1789 in ibid., p. 150.
6. Rossiter, ed., *Federalist Papers*, No. 10, p. 78.
7. Rossiter, ed., *Federalist Papers*, Nos. 1, 37, and 70, pp. 35, 226–227, 423.

CHAPTER 7. THE PUBLIC GOOD

1. Jefferson to Henry Lee, May 8, 1825, in Koch and Peden, eds., *Writings of Jefferson*, p. 719.
2. Aristotle, *Politics*, Book III, chapter 9, Jowett trans., Modern Library Edition (New York, 1943), pp. 142, 144.
3. Thorpe, *Federal and State Constitutions*, 3: 1888–1911.
4. Madison to Robert Walsh, March 2, 1819, in Gaillard Hunt, ed., *The Writings of James Madison* (New York, 1910), 8: 430–432.
5. Debates of May 31, July 17, and August 9, 1987, in Ketcham, *Antifederalist Papers*, pp. 39, 116, 158.
6. Jefferson, "Autobiography," 1821, in Koch and Peden, eds., *Writings of Jefferson*, p. 52.
7. Benjamin Rush, "Thoughts upon the Mode of Education Proper in a Republic" (1786), and Washington to Robert Brooke, March 16, 1795, both in S. A. Rippa, ed., *Educational Ideas in America* (New York, 1969), pp. 119, 127.
8. Madison to W. T. Barry, August 4, 1822, in Hunt, ed., *Writings of Madison*, 9: 103–109.
9. *Walz* v. *Tax Commission*, (1970), 397 U.S. 664, 1237–1242.
10. Jonathan Edwards, *Visible Union of God's People* (1747), in A. Heimert and P. Miller, eds., *The Great Awakening* (Indianapolis, Ind., 1967), p. 566.
11. Hamilton to Washington, February 23, 1791, in S. McKee, Jr., ed., *Alexander Hamilton's Papers on Public Credit, Commerce, and Finance* (New York, 1957), p. 108.
12. Hamilton to J. A. Bayard, January 16, 1801, in Syrett, ed., *Papers of Hamilton*, 25: 319–324.
13. Jefferson, Sixth Annual Message, December 2, 1806, in M. D. Peterson, ed., *The Portable Thomas Jefferson* (New York, 1975), p. 326.
14. Jefferson to E. Gerry, January 26, 1799, and First Inaugural Address, March 4, 1801, in Koch and Peden, *Writings of Jefferson*, pp. 323, 545.
15. Jefferson to Henry Lee, May 8, 1825, in Koch and Peden, eds., *Writings of Jefferson*, p. 719.
16. "Reflections on the State of the Nation" (1749), in *The Works of Lord Bolingbroke* (Philadelphia, 1841), 2: 458–459.
17. "Lectures on Law" (1790), in R. G. McCloskey, ed., *The Works of James Wilson* (Cambridge, Mass., 1967), 2: 577.
18. Bolingbroke, "The Idea of a Patriot King" (1749), in J. Hart, ed., *Political Writings of Eighteenth Century England* (New York, 1964), pp. 232–240.

CHAPTER 8. FEDERALISM

1. First Inaugural Address, March 4, 1801, in Koch and Peden, eds., *Writings of Jefferson*, p. 324.

2. Voltaire, *Philosophical Letters*, 1733 (Indianapolis, Ind., 1961), p. 36.

3. Otis, "The Rights of the British Colonies" (1764), in Jensen, ed., *Tracts of the American Revolution*, pp. 21, 33.

4. "Cato's Letters," No. 73 (1722), in D. L. Jacobson, ed., *The English Libertarian Heritage* (Indianapolis, Ind., 1965), pp. 193–200. These "Letters" were reprinted often in the British colonies in the years before independence.

5. Paine, "Common Sense" (1776), in Jensen, ed., *Tracts of the American Revolution*, pp. 405–406, 432–433.

6. John to Abigail Adams, March 19, 1776, in Butterfield, ed., *Adams Family Correspondence*, 1: 363; and *Diary and Autobiography of John Adams* (Cambridge, Mass., 1961), February–April 1776, 3: 330–333.

7. "Thoughts on Government" (1776), in G. A. Peek, ed., *The Political Writings of John Adams* (Indianapolis, Ind., 1954), pp. 84–92.

8. Ibid., pp. 95–103.

9. Quoted in ibid., p. 106.

10. "Ancient and Modern Confederacies," April–June 1786, in *Papers of Madison*, 9: 3–22.

11. April 1787, in ibid., pp. 348–350.

12. Madison to Edmund Pendleton, October 20, 1788, and to Washington, April 16, 1787; in ibid., 11: 306–307; 9: 383.

13. "The Virginia Plan," May 29, 1787, in Ketcham, ed., *Antifederalist Papers*, pp. 37–38.

14. Rossiter, ed., *Federalist Papers*, pp. 226, 245.

15. *Federalist* No. 37, in ibid., p. 227.

16. Joseph Galloway, "The Mutual Claims of Great Britain and the Colonies" (1775), and Martin Howard, Jr., "A Letter from a Gentleman at Halifax" (1765), in Jensen, eds., *Tracts of the American Revolution*, pp. 71, 353.

17. *Federalist* No. 39, in Rossiter, ed., *Federalist Papers*, pp. 377–378.

18. *Federalist* No. 62, ibid., pp. 377–378.

19. *Federalist* No. 45, ibid., pp. 292–293.

20. Jefferson to J. C. Cabell, February 2, 1816, in Koch and Peden, eds., *Writings of Jefferson*, pp. 660–661.

21. "John DeWitt," November 5, 1787, in Cecelia Kenyon, ed., *The Antifederalists* (Indianapolis, Ind., 1966), p. 105.

CHAPTER 9. FEDERALISTS AND ANTIFEDERALISTS

1. "Brutus," No. 15, *New York Journal*, March 20, 1788, in Ketcham, ed., *Antifederalist Papers*, p. 309.

2. Melancton Smith, speech at the New York Convention, June 21, 1788, in ibid., pp. 342–344.

3. Patrick Henry, speech at the Virginia Convention, June 5, 1788, in ibid., pp. 207–208. Ralph Ketcham, *From Colony to Country: The Revolution in American Thought, 1750–1820* (New York, 1974), pp. 127–135; and Herbert J. Storing, *What the Anti-Federalists Were For* (Chicago, 1980), provide fuller accounts of antifederalist political thought.

4. *Federalist* No. 37, in Rossiter, ed., *Federalist Papers*, pp. 226–227.

5. Emerson, "Politics" (1844), in W. H. Giliman, ed., *The Selected Writings of Ralph Waldo Emerson* (New York, 1965), p. 357; W. G. Sumner, "What Social Classes Owe Each Other" (1883), in Louis Hacker, ed., *The American Tradition* (New York, 1947), pp. 715–717.

6. Winthrop, "A Model of Christian Charity" (1630), and *Journal*, May 1645, in Edmund S. Morgan, ed., *Puritan Political Ideas* (Indianapolis, Ind., 1965), pp. 90, 139.

7. Galloway, "Mutual claims of Great Britain and the Colonies" (1775), in Jensen, ed., *Tracts of the American Revolution*, pp. 377, 399.

8. Stephen S. Webb, "Army and Empire: English Garrison Government in Britain and America, 1569–1763," *William and Mary Quarterly* 34 (1977):1–32.

CHAPTER 10. ORIGINS

1. Adrienne Koch, ed., *Notes of Debates of the Federal Convention of 1787* (Athens, Ohio, 1966), p. 630.

2. Harvey Wish, ed., *William Bradford: Of Plymouth Plantation* (New York, 1962), p. 40.

3. Sir William Temple, *Observations upon the United Provinces of the Netherlands* (1673) (New York, 1972), p. 118.

4. Voltaire, *Philosophical Letters* (1733) (Indianapolis, Ind., 1961), pp. 39–40, 34–38, 26.

5. *Federalist* No. 84, Rossiter, ed., *Federalist Papers*, pp. 513–515.

6. Thomas McKean, Pennsylvania Convention, November 1788, and Benjamin Rush, "Remarker," *Boston Independent Chronicle*, December 27, 1787, both in Storing, *What the Anti-Federalists Were For*, p. 68.

7. "The Federal Farmer" (1787), in ibid., p. 70. In that work Storing elaborates the arguments of this and the preceding paragraph.

8. Madison to Jefferson, October 24, 1787, in *Papers of Madison*, 10: 206–219.

9. Washington to Lafayette, February 7, 1788, in Saul Padover, ed., *The Washington Papers* (New York, 1955), p. 244.

10. Jefferson to Madison, December 20, 1787, in *Papers of Madison*, 10, 336–337.

11. Madison to G. L. Tuberville, March 1, 1788, in ibid., 10: 550.

12. R. Ketcham, *James Madison, A Biography* (New York, 1971), p. 251.

13. Madison, speech, June 12, 1788, in *Papers of Madison*, 11: 130–131.

14. Madison to Jefferson, October 17, 1788, in ibid., 11: 297–300.

15. Jefferson to Madison, March 15, 1789, in ibid., 12: 13–15.

16. Washington, First Inaugural Address, April 30, 1789, in W. B. Allen, ed., *George Washington: A Collection* (Indianapolis, Ind., 1988), p. 462; Madison, speech, June 8, 1789, Madison to E. Randolph, June 15, 1789, and Joseph Jones to Madison, June 24, 1789, in *Papers of Madison*, 12: 207, 219, 258–259.

17. Grayson to Henry, June 12, 1789, and Lee to Henry, September 14, 1789; W. W. Henry, *Patrick Henry, Life, Correspondence, and Speeches* (New York, 1891), 3: 391, 399; Burke, *Annals of Congress*, 1: 774, all quoted in Leonard W. Levy, *Freedom of Speech and Press in Early American History* (New York, 1960, 1963), pp. 228–229.

18. Pendleton to Madison, September 2, 1789, in *Papers of Madison*, 17: 544.

19. Madison to Richard Peters, August 19, 1789; ibid., 12: 347; quoted in Paul Finkelman, "James Madison and the Bill of Rights, A Reluctant Paternity," *Supreme Court Review*, 1990, p. 345.

20. Amendments to the Constitution, June 8, 1789, *Papers of Madison*, 12: 201.

21. Roger Sherman, quoted in Eugene Gressman, "Bicentennializing Freedom of Expression," *Seton Hall Law Review* 20: 378 (1990), p. 402.

22. *Whitney* v. *California* (1927), 274 U.S. 375. William Lee Miller, *The Business of May Next: James Madison and the Founding* (Charlottesville, Va., 1992), pp. 269–273, interprets the First Amendment in a manner similar to the discussion here.

23. Debate of August 17, 1789; *Papers of Madison*, 12: 344.

24. Debate of August 17, 1789, *Annals of Congress*, 1: 783–784.

25. Madison to Jefferson, January 22, 1786, in *Papers of Madison*, 8: 474.

26. Irving Brant, *James Madison* (Indianapolis, Ind., 1950), 3: 269–272.

27. James Jackson, speech, June 8, 1789, *Congressional Register*, 1: 416.

28. Levy, *Freedom of Speech and Press*, pp. 230–233.

CHAPTER 11. GOVERNMENT BY CONSENT

1. *Minersville School District* v. *Gobitis*, 310 U.S. 586 (1940).

2. Paul Finkelman, "The Flag Salute Cases," in *The Encyclopedia of Supreme Court Cases* (forthcoming), describes the heated atmosphere in the nation surrounding the Jehovah's Witnesses during wartime and is highly critical of Frankfurter's opinions.

3. *West Virginia State Board of Education* v. *Barnette*, 319 U.S. 624 (1943).

4. Opinion of the Supreme Court, Justice Robert Jackson, *West Virginia* v. *Barnette*.

5. Dissenting Opinion, Justice Felix Frankfurter, ibid.

6. Opinion of the Supreme Court, Justice Frankfurter, *Minersville School District* v. *Gobitis*.

7. *Marbury* v. *Madison*, 1 Cranch 137 (1803).

8. Jefferson's "Autobiography," 1821, in Koch and Peden, eds., *Writings of Jefferson*, p. 52.

9. Concurring opinions of Justices Hugo Black, William O. Douglas, and Frank Murphy, *West Virginia* v. *Barnette*.

10. Donald Meiklejohn, "Public Speech in the Burger Court: The Influence of Mr. Justice Black," *University of Toledo Law Review* 8, 7 (Winter 1977): 301.

11. Jefferson to E. Carrington, January 16, 1787, and to John Tyler, June 24, 1804; in Koch and Peden, eds., *Writings of Jefferson*, pp. 411–412, 576.

12. Leonard Levy, *Thomas Jefferson and Civil Liberties: The Darker Side* (Cambridge, Mass., 1963).

13. Jefferson to John Norwell, June 11, 1807, in Koch and Peden, eds., *Writings of Jefferson*, pp. 581–582; Jefferson to Thomas McKean, February 19, 1803, in P. L. Ford, ed., *The Writings of Thomas Jefferson* (New York, 1892–1899), 8: 218–219.

14. *New York Times Co.* v. *Sullivan*, 376 U.S. 270, 276 (1964). Donald Meiklejohn, "Public Speech and Libel Litigation: Are They Compatible?" *Hofstra Law Review* 14, 3, (Spring 1986): 547–569, analyzes the case cogently.

15. *New York Times Co.* v. *United States*, 403 U.S. 713 (1971).

16. Hugo Black, *A Constitutional Faith* (New York, 1968), p. 63.

Chapter 12. Good Government

1. Liang Chi-Chao, *History of Chinese Political Thought* (New York, 1930, 1969), trans. L. T. Chen, esp. pp. 7–10, 56–57, 150–152, 196–199.

2. Philip C. Huang, *Liang Chi-Chao and Modern Chinese Liberalism* (Seattle, Wash., 1972), pp. 147–157.

3. Elizabeth Drew, "Letter from Washington," and Richard J. Barnet, "The Disorders of Peace," *New Yorker*, October 30, 1989, pp. 104–106, and January 20, 1992, pp. 62–63.

4. Jefferson to John Taylor of Caroline, June 4, 1798, and Taylor to Jefferson, June 25, 1798, in *John P. Branch Historical Papers of Randolph-Macon College*, 2 (1908), pp. 271–276.

5. Washington, Farewell Address, September 17, 1796, in James D. Richardson, ed., *Messages and Papers of the Presidents 1789–1897* (Washington, D.C., 1897), 1: 205–216.

6. Joseph Galloway, *A Candid Examination of the Mutual Claims of Great Britain and the Colonies* (New York, 1775), reprinted in Jensen, ed., *Tracts of the American Revolution*, pp. 350–399, esp. p. 377.

7. Alexis de Tocqueville, *Democracy in America* (1835–1840), vol. 2, part 2, chapter 24 (Reeves trans.), H. S. Commager, ed. (New York, 1946), pp. 310–311.

8. Ibid., p. 316.

9. Ibid., pp. 319–322.

10. Ibid., pp. 200–203.

11. John Adams to Abigail Adams, October 29, 1775, in L. H. Butterfield et al., eds., *The Book of Abigail and John* (Cambridge, Mass., 1975), pp. 111–112.

12. *Walz v. Tax Commission*, 397 U.S. 664 (1970).

13. Thomas Jefferson, "Autobiography," 1821, in Koch and Peden, eds., *Writings of Jefferson*, p. 52.

CHAPTER 13. THE LIMITS OF CONSTITUTIONAL PRESCRIPTION

1. William M. Wiecek, *The Sources of Antislavery Constitutionalism in America, 1760–1848* (Ithaca, N.Y., 1977), pp. 43–61.

2. Paul Finkelman, "Slavery and the Constitutional Convention: Making a Covenant with Death," in Richard Beeman et al., eds., *Beyond Confederation* (Chapel Hill, N.C., 1987), pp. 188–225.

3. Debates of August 7, 21–22, 25, 1787, in Max Farrand, ed., *The Records of the Federal Convention*, 3 vols. (New Haven, Conn.: 1937), 2: 220–223, 360–370, 417.

4. Ibid., 2: 220–223, 360–370.

5. *Lockner v. New York* (1905), 198 U.S. 74.

6. Jefferson to Walter Jones, March 31, 1801, in H. A. Washington, ed., *The Works of Thomas Jefferson* (New York, 1884), 4: 392–393; T. Roosevelt, quoted in E. J. Hughes, *The Living Presidency* (New York, 1973), p. 166.

7. *Olmstead v. U.S.* (1928), 277 U.S. 469.

CHAPTER 14. THE CONSTITUTION: WHAT THE JUDGES SAY IT IS?

1. *Marbury v. Madison* (1803); 1 Cranch 137.

2. Thurgood Marshall, "The Constitution's Bicentennial: Commemorating the Wrong Document?" *Vanderbilt Law Review* 40 (1987): 1338–1341.

3. Brennan, *The Constitution . . . Contemporary Ratification*, pp. 6, 10, 15.

4. Joseph Story, *Commentaries on the Constitution of the United States* (Boston, 1833), 6: 135.

5. Bork, *The Tempting of America*, p. 6.

6. Edwin Meese, "The Supreme Court of the United States: Bulwark of a Limited Constitution," *South Texas Law Review* 26 (1986): 458–466, reprint of a speech to the American Bar Association, July 9, 1985.

7. Antonin Scalia, "Originalism: The Lesser Evil," *Cincinnati Law Review* 73 (1989): 449–465.

8. Rehnquist, dissenting, *Wallace v. Jaffree* (1984), 472 U.S. 91–114.

9. Ketcham, *Madison*, pp. 165–166.

10. Madison, "Memorial and Remonstrance against Religious Assessments," June 20, 1785, in *Papers of Madison*, 8: 299.

11. Paul Finkelman, "The Constitution and the Intentions of the Framers: The Limits of Historical Analysis," *University of Pittsburgh Law Review* 50 (1989): 351–358, explores the problem and provides bibliographical information on the "original intent" controversy.

Chapter 15. Personal Liberty and Political Freedom

1. Thomas Pownall, *A Memorial Addressed to the Sovereigns of America* (London, 1783), quoted in Paul Rahe, *Republics Ancient and Modern: Classical Republicanism and the American Revolution* (Chapel Hill, N.C., 1992), p. 49.

2. Joseph Levine, *The Battle of the Books: History and Literature in the Augustan Age* (Ithaca, N.Y., 1991).

3. Rahe, *Republics Ancient and Modern,* pp. 543–572.

4. John Adams to Mercy Warren, January 8 and April 16, 1776, *Papers of John Adams,* 3: 398; 4: 124–125.

5. Hamilton, *Federalist* No. 84, in Rossiter, ed., *Federalist Papers,* p. 515.

6. *Pennsylvania Packet* and *Pennsylvania Herald,* August 1787.

7. R. H. Lee to George Mason, May 15, 1787, in J. C. Ballagh, ed., *The Letters of Richard Henry Lee,* 2 vols. (New York, 1911) 2: 419.

8. Sir William Blackstone, *Commentaries on the Laws of England,* 4 vols. (Oxford, 1765–1769), quoted in Bailyn, *Ideological Origins of the American Revolution,* pp. 201–202.

9. *Papers of Madison,* 9: 354.

BIBLIOGRAPHICAL ESSAY

Especially under the stimulus of the "bicentennial season" of the last half-dozen years, the literature on the Constitution and the Bill of Rights has become enormous. I suggest here only the small portion of that literature which bears on the context of political ideas that nourished the Constitution and the Bill of Rights and on the consequent understanding of those documents that might be inferred. Particularly, I do not deal with most of the huge literatures on the general history of the founding era, on the clause-by-clause explication of the Constitution in case law, on the history of constitutional law, and on the myriad contemporary efforts to enlist the Constitution on behalf of various causes. Even in the limited field remaining, I mention only those works I have found most useful and insightful. The source notes indicate the specific sources, mostly primary, for particular portions of the text.

Primary Sources

The basic reliance, of course, must throughout be on now-abundant primary sources. The most important general collections are the following: Max Farrand, ed., *The Records of the Federal Convention*, 4 vols., (New Haven, Conn., 1937), and James Hutson, ed., *Supplement to Max Farrand's The Records of the Federal Convention of 1787* (New Haven, Conn., 1987); Merrill Jensen et al., eds., *Documentary History of the Ratification of the Constitution of the United States* (Madison, Wis., 1976–); Herbert Storing, ed., *The Complete Anti-Federalist*, 7 vols. (Chicago, 1981); F. N. Thorpe, ed., *The Federal and State Constitutions, Colonial Charters, and Other Laws*, 7 vols. (Washington, D.C., 1909); Charles S. Hyneman and Donald S. Lutz, eds., *American Political Writing during the Founding Era, 1760–1805*, 2 vols. (Indianapolis, Ind., 1983); Bernard Schwartz, ed., *The Bill of Rights: A Documentary History*, 2 vols. (New York, 1971); Ellis Sandoz, ed., *Political Sermons of the American Founding Era, 1730–1805* (Indianapolis, Ind., 1991); Paul L. Ford, ed., *Essays on the Constitution of the United States* (Brooklyn, N.Y., 1892); Philip Kurland and Ralph Lerner, eds., *The Founders' Constitution*, 5 vols. (Chicago, 1987); and Jonathan Elliot, ed., *The Debates of the Several State Conventions . . .* , 5 vols. (Philadelphia, 1866).

The papers of some of the leading founders are also important sources: William T. Hutchinson et al., eds., *The Papers of James Madison* (Chicago and Charlottesville, Va., 1962–); Harold C. Syrett et al., eds., *The Papers of Alexander Hamilton*, 26 vols. (New York, 1961–1979); Leonard Labaree et al., eds., *The Papers of Benjamin Franklin* (New Haven, Conn., 1956–); Lyman Butterfield et al., eds., *The Adams Papers* (Cambridge, Mass., 1961–); Julian P. Boyd et al., eds., *The Papers of Thomas Jefferson* (Princeton, N.J., 1950–); Robert Rutland, ed., *The Papers of George Mason*, 3 vols. (Chapel Hill, N.C., 1970); and Robert McCloskey, ed., *The Works of James Wilson*, 2 vols. (Cambridge, Mass., 1967).

Convenient one-volume source materials are Clinton Rossiter, ed., *The Federalist Papers* (New York, 1962); Ralph Ketcham, ed., *The Anti-Federalist Papers and the Constitutional Convention Debates* (New York, 1986); Helen Veit et al., eds., *Creating the Bill of Rights: The Documentary Record from the First Federal Congress* (Baltimore, Md., 1991); Ralph Ketcham, ed., *The Political Thought of Benjamin Franklin* (Indianapolis, Ind., 1965); Adrienne Koch and William Peden, eds., *The Life and Selected Writings of Thomas Jefferson* (New York, 1944); Marvin Meyers, ed., *The Mind of the Founder: The Political Thought of James Madison* (Indianapolis, Ind., 1973); and Morton J. Frisch, ed., *Selected Writings and Speeches of Alexander Hamilton* (Washington, D.C., 1985).

SECONDARY SOURCES

The most searching studies of the political thought of the founding era have arisen from the debate, now thirty years or more old, between the so-called liberal and civic republican interpretations of that era. The works of Louis Hartz, *The Liberal Tradition in America* (New York, 1955); Caroline Robbins, *The Eighteenth Century Commonwealth Man* (Cambridge, Mass., 1959); and J. G. A. Pocock, *The Machiavellian Moment* (Princeton, N.J., 1975), set the basic terms of the debate. Lance Banning, *The Jeffersonian Persuasion* (Ithaca, N.Y., 1978); Drew McCoy, *The Elusive Republic: Political Economy in Jeffersonian America* (Chapel Hill, N.C., 1980); Isaac Kramnick, *Republicanism and Bourgeois Radicalism: Political Ideology in Late Eighteenth Century England and America* (Ithaca, N.Y., 1990); John Diggins, *The Lost Soul of American Politics: Virtue, Self-Interest, and the Foundations of Liberalism* (New York, 1984); and Joyce Appleby, *Capitalism and a New Social Order* (New York, 1984), extend the argument, while Garrett Sheldon, *The Political Philosophy of Thomas Jefferson* (Baltimore, 1991); and, especially, Paul Rahe, *Republics Ancient and Modern: Classical Republicanism and the American Revolution* (Chapel Hill, N.C., 1992) offer recent, rich interpretations.

Study of the intellectual foundations of the Constitution can best begin with the seminal writings of Douglass Adair, *Fame and the Founding Fathers*, ed. Trevor Colbourn (New York, 1974), and of Martin Diamond, especially "Democracy and *The*

Federalist, A Reconsideration of the Framers' Intent," *American Political Science Review* 53 (1959). The most important interpretations are those of Bernard Bailyn, *The Ideological Origins of the American Revolution*, enlarged ed. (Cambridge, Mass., 1992), and Gordon Wood, *The Creation of the American Republic, 1776–1787* (Chapel Hill, N.C., 1969). Other works that survey important patterns of thought are Willi P. Adams, *The First American Constitutions: . . . the State Constitutions in the Revolutionary Era* (Chapel Hill, N.C., 1980); Jack Rakove, *The Beginning of National Politics: An Interpretive History of the Continental Congress* (Baltimore, 1979); Donald Lutz, *The Origins of American Constitutionalism* (Baton Rouge, La., 1988); Forrest McDonald, *Novus Ordo Seclorum: The Intellectual Origins of the Constitution* (Lawrence, Kans., 1985); Ralph Ketcham, *From Colony to Country: The Revolution in American Thought, 1750–1820* (New York, 1974); and Richard B. Davis, *The Problem of Slavery in the Age of Revolution 1770–1823* (Ithaca, N.Y., 1975); Peter Onuf, *The Origins of the Federal Republic: Jurisdictional Controversies in the United States, 1775–1787* (Philadelphia, 1983); Peter Onuf and Cathy Matson, *A Union of Interests: Political and Economic Thought in Revolutionary America* (Lawrence, Kans., 1990); Robert Shalhope, *The Roots of Democracy: American Thought and Culture, 1760–1800* (Boston, 1990); Thomas Pangle, *The Spirit of Modern Republicanism: The Moral Vision of the American Founders and John Locke* (Chicago, 1988); Garry Wills, *Inventing America* (Garden City, N.Y., 1978); Henry S. Commager, *The Empire of Reason* (Garden City, N.Y., 1978); and John P. Reid, *The Concept of Liberty in the Age of the American Revolution* (Chicago, 1988).

More specifically on the Constitutional Convention and the Constitution itself, Carl Van Doren, *The Great Rehearsal* (New York, 1948), and Clinton Rossiter, *1787: The Grand Convention* (New York, 1966), provide lively and insightful accounts of the Convention. William Lee Miller, *The Business of May Next: James Madison and the Founding* (Charlottesville, Va., 1992), is a more recent, especially engaging view of the framing and ratifying process, while E. S. Corwin, *The "Higher Law" Background of American Constitutional Law* (New York, 1955) is an authoritative older account. Leonard Levy, ed., *Essays on the Making of the Constitution*, 2d ed. (New York, 1987), reprints classic writings by Charles Beard, Andrew C. McLaughlin, and others about the Constitution, while Morton White, *Philosophy, the Federalist, and the Constitution* (New York, 1987) is a recent interpretation of the documents. Among the many good recent collections of essays about the Constitution are Terence Ball and J. G. A. Pocock, eds., *Conceptual Change and the Constitution* (Lawrence, Kans., 1988); Neil L. York, ed., *Toward a More Perfect Union* (Brigham Young University, 1988); Richard Beeman et al., eds., *Beyond Confederation* (Chapel Hill, N.C., 1987); R. Horwitz, ed., *The Moral Foundations of the American Republic* (Charlottesville, Va., 1986); the July 1987 issue of the *William and Mary Quarterly*, vol. 44, no. 3; and the December 1987 issue of the *Journal of American History*, vol. 74, no. 3.

Robert Rutland, *The Ordeal of the Constitution: The Antifederalists and the Ratification Struggle of 1787–1788* (New York, 1966); Steven Boyd, *The Politics of Opposition: Antifederalists and the Acceptance of the Constitution* (Millwood, N.Y., 1979); and Jackson Turner Main, *The Antifederalists: Critics of the Constitution* (Chapel Hill, N.C., 1961) provide good accounts of the ratification process, emphasizing the antifederalist perspective. Forrest McDonald, *We the People: The Economic Origins of the Constitution* (Chicago, 1958), is the most detailed explanation of the subject, while Herbert Storing, *What the Anti-Federalists Were For* (Chicago, 1981), is a stimulating and scholarly account of antifederalist political thought. George W. Carey, *The Federalist: Design for a Constitutional Republic* (Urbana, Ill., 1989); David Epstein, *The Political Theory of the Federalist* (Chicago, 1984); Albert Furtwangler, *The Authority of Publius: A Reading of the Federalist Papers* (Ithaca, N.Y., 1984); and Garry Wills, *Explaining America: The Federalist* (New York, 1981), interpret federalist thought. Kermit Hall, ed., *The Formation and Ratification of the Constitution* (New York, 1987), is a useful collection of essays.

Robert Rutland, *The Birth of the Bill of Rights, 1776–1791* (Chapel Hill, N.C., 1955); Irving Brant, *The Bill of Rights: Its Original Meaning* (Indianapolis, Ind., 1965); and Bernard Schwartz, *The Great Rights of Mankind: A History of the American Bill of Rights* (New York, 1977) survey the history of the Bill of Rights. Leonard Levy, *Freedom of Speech and Press in Early American History* (New York, 1963); Alexander Meiklejohn, *Free Speech and Its Relation to Self-Government* (New York, 1948); William Lee Miller, *The First Liberty: Religion and the American Republic* (New York, 1985); Robert Morgan, *James Madison on the Constitution and the Bill of Rights* (New York, 1988); Walter Berns, *Freedom, Virtue, and the First Amendment* (Baton Rouge, La., 1957); and Paul Finkelman, *An Imperfect Union: Slavery, Federalism and Comity* (Chapel Hill, N.C., 1980), offer important interpretations of issues surrounding the Bill of Rights. Dozens of law reviews throughout the country, especially during the bicentennial season, published hundreds of articles on various Bill of Rights provisions. U.S. Supreme Court cases, in addition to interpreting the clauses of the Bill of Rights, often make lengthy historical expositions of their origins and meaning.

The following biographies offer not only commentary on the roles of their subjects during the founding era, but also often contain important interpretations of the Constitution and the Bill of Rights: George Billias, *Elbridge Gerry, Founding Father and Republican Statesman* (New York, 1976); Noble E. Cunningham, *In Pursuit of Reason: The Life of Thomas Jefferson* (New York, 1987); Ralph Ketcham, *James Madison, A Biography* (New York, 1971); Edward Handler, *America and Europe in the Political Thought of John Adams* (Cambridge, Mass., 1964); John Kaminski, *George Clinton: Yeoman Politician in the New Republic* (Madison, Wis., 1990); Dumas Malone, *Jefferson and His Time*, 6 vols. (Boston, 1948–1981); Drew McCoy, *The Last of the Fathers: James Madison and the Republican Legacy* (Cambridge, Eng., 1989); Robert D. Meade, *Patrick Henry, Practical Revolutionary* (Philadelphia, 1969); John Reardon, *Edmund Randolph: A Biography* (New York, 1975); Clinton Rossiter, *Alexander Hamilton and the Constitution* (New York, 1964); Geoffrey Seed, *James Wilson* (Millwood, N.Y., 1978); Gerald Stourzh, *Alexander Hamilton and the Idea of Republican Government* (Stanford, Calif., 1970); and Carl van Doren, *Benjamin Franklin* (New York, 1937).

Of the huge literature on the "original intent" controversy, mostly in the law reviews, the following offer some of the most searching interpretations: Robert H. Bork, *The Tempting of America* (New York, 1990); Raoul Berger, *Federalism: The Founder's Design* (Norman, Okla., 1987); Paul Finkelman, "The Constitution and the Intentions of the Framers: The Limits of Historical Analysis," *University of Pittsburgh Law Review* 50, no. 5 (1989); Leonard Levy, *Original Intent and the Framers' Constitution* (New York, 1988); and Laurence Tribe, *On Reading the Constitution* (Cambridge, Mass., 1991). Leonard Levy et al., eds., *Encyclopedia of the American Constitution*, 5 vols. (New York, 1986), is a useful reference work on its subject.

INDEX

Printed in the United States
61694LVS00002B/69